Protecting Canada's Endangered Spaces
AN OWNER'S MANUAL

To Jean Fusners,
Thanks for your
help on all this!

[signature]

April/96.

MONTE HUMMEL, GENERAL EDITOR

Protecting Canada's Endangered Spaces

AN OWNER'S MANUAL

KEY PORTER BOOKS

Canadian Cataloguing in Publication Data

Protecting Canada's endangered spaces

Includes bibliographical references and index.

ISBN 1-55013-710-7 (pbk.)

1. Wilderness areas - Canada. 2. National parks and reserves - Canada. 3. Nature conservation - Canada. I. Hummel, Monte, 1946 - .

QH77.C2E54 1995   333.78'2'0971   C95-931619-1

The publisher gratefully acknowledges the assistance of the Canada Council, the Ontario Arts Council and the Ontario Publishing Centre.

Key Porter Books Limited
70 The Esplanade
Toronto, Ontario
Canada M5E 1R2

Front cover photo: George Smith
Illustrations: Michael Dumas
Design: Peter Maher
Typesetting: Heidy Lawrance Associates

The World Wildlife Fund wishes to acknowledge the following people who generously donated services to the production of this book:

Colour Separations: John Fisher and Jean-Pierre Paquette,
    Les Industries Tri-Graphique Inc., Saint Laurent, Québec
Michael Innes, N.S. Digital Technologies, Halifax, Nova Scotia
Earl Hadwen, Mutual-Hadwen Imaging Technologies, Ottawa, Ontario
Richard McCallum, Quality Color Press Inc./Screaming Colour Inc., Edmonton, Alberta
Printing Services: David G. Friesen, Friesens, Altona, Manitoba

Henderson Book Series No. 27

The Henderson Book Series honours the kind and generous donation of Mrs. Arthur T. Henderson, who made this series possible. The Canadian Parks and Wilderness Society (CPAWS) gratefully acknowledges Mrs. Henderson's support of our efforts to build public support for protecting Canada's wilderness areas.

Printed and bound in Canada

95 96 97 98 99 6 5 4 3 2 1

Dedicated to Guy Coté (1925 to 1994) who fought so hard for Mont Pinnacle in Québec, and to Bob Graham (1941 to 1993) who committed his career to marine conservation in Canada and beyond.

Contents

SECTION THREE — Lessons Learned

Acknowledgements

It's certainly gratifying when a general editor's dream roster of authors, all busy people, agree to contribute to a book. Thank you all.

The diversity of the contributors and their writing styles, like diversity in nature, is something I've tried to respect and preserve. Furthermore, I thought readers should hear from some of our critics. After all, if criticism is well-taken, our case will only be made stronger by taking it into account.

Thank you to Laurie Coulter, our editor, who does nothing but improve everything she reads; to John McCutcheon who helped us find donors for the colour separations, among other things; to Michael Dumas who kindly donated his excellent drawings to begin each chapter; and to all the nature photographers who made their work available to help protect what they capture on film. Thanks and recognition are also due to World Wildlife Fund's Pegi Dover who oversaw the maps, charts, drawings, photo selection, and many other aspects associated with the physical production of this book; to Kim Bilous who pulled together testimonials from people across the country; and to Jan Marsh who calmly typed, circulated, and tracked draft manuscripts and references under real time pressures.

I must thank a good friend, Glen Davis, who talked us into this project against my instincts which were to spend 100 per cent of our time lobbying for wilderness protection rather than writing about it. Glen obviously believes the writing can greatly assist the protecting, and he has been proven right before.

Finally, a heartfelt thanks to those family members, including my own, whose childhoods and personal lives have been put on hold while those of us who do this for a living travel and burn the midnight oil. For you especially, I hope it all proves worthwhile.

Foreword

■✹■ Department of Foreign Affairs   Ministère des Affaires étrangères
and International Trade   et du Commerce international

Ambassador for the Environment   Ambassadeur à l'environnement

F o r e w o r d   t o

Protecting Canada's Endangered Spaces

This book is all about going into action, individually
and collectively, in a campaign of personal responsibility to
save and protect Canada's endangered spaces. It sets out what is
at stake and how we can do what must be done, now and in the long
term. It tells why we must assert our stewardship over this
wonderful land that belongs to all of us and which will be the
home of generations yet to come.

This book speaks to us of beauty and splendour, of the
infinite variety of wild places and of all living creatures that
dwell therein. It reminds us of our values - material and
spiritual - and the extent to which some of what is best about us
as Canadians comes from our magnificent natural heritage.

And it does something else: it awakens within us a
recognition of our duty and a sense of urgency. Duty, because it
is clear that each one of us must be, however modestly, part of
the action. And a sense of urgency, because the pressures, some
well intentioned, and some less so, of population, urbanization
and industrialization, threaten the very existence of these
precious places.

Much has been accomplished. There is much more to be
done. Within these covers is a guide to action, now and
tomorrow, and the clear warning that, as the lawyers say, time is
of the essence.

Sincerely,

[signature]

John A. Fraser, P.C., Q.C.

125 promenade Sussex Drive
Ottawa, Canada
K1A 0G2

Tel: (613) 944-0886   (604) 666-5423
Fax:(613) 944-0892   (604) 666-5471

Preface

I am writing this preface in an isolated cabin by a frozen northern lake. Inside, my wood fire crackles out warmth. Outside, the lake ice creaks and grumbles under an arctic cold front, breaking the spell of silence cast by winter constellations. At times like this, I ask myself: "Am I one of the last?"

One of the last to enjoy a star-filled night sky unspoiled by light pollution? One of the last to dip a paddle into a river and drink cold water as it streams down the blade? One of the last to see a wild bald eagle, or grizzly bear, or small white lady's-slipper orchid? One of the last to have the choice to experience these things, or to at least know they are out there, or to pass that choice on to my children?

It strikes me that many other people have been "one of the last" without realizing it at the time. They lived their lives while crucial options were being lost and they did nothing about it, not because they didn't care, but because they simply didn't know what was at stake.

I believe you and I live at precisely such a time in Canada. Unlike previous generations, however, we cannot offer ignorance as an excuse for inaction. We have a once-only opportunity to ensure that significant parts of our country remain in a wild, natural state, changing only at the hands of nature, and serving as benchmarks for measuring the changes we are making to so much of the rest of our lands and waters. But it's truly a time-limited offer.

I don't want to be one of the last. Do you?

Monte Hummel
Loon Lake, December 1994

Introduction

MONTE HUMMEL AND ARLIN HACKMAN

The underlying premise of this book is that those of us who live in Canada have a right to insist that sizeable, representative parts of it survive in a wild state. The crucial question is whether we, its owners, will exercise that right before it's too late.

When World Wildlife Fund (WWF) Canada launched the Endangered Spaces campaign in September 1989, we ran a full-page newspaper ad reproducing two documents: the Canadian Charter of Rights and Freedoms, with the caption, "This Charter protects Canadians," and the Canadian Wilderness Charter with the caption, "This one protects Canada." The ad's attached coupon invited people to sign the Wilderness Charter and read, "It's my country, my future, my right."

Since 1989, more than 600,000 citizens from every part of the country have signed the Canadian Wilderness Charter, making it one of the largest petitions in Canadian history. In addition, nearly 300 organizations have endorsed the charter, and thereby the Endangered Spaces campaign goal. Organizations as diverse as the Canadian Chamber of Commerce, the Canadian Labour Congress, the Girl Guides of Canada, Greenpeace, Indigenous Survival International, and the United Church of Canada, as well as high-level councils in the forestry, mining, and petroleum industries, have signalled their support for our conservation goal.

Our original book, *Endangered Spaces*, which was published in 1989, has become a Canadian best-seller many times over. We were supported in 1991 by a unanimous motion from the House of Commons, and in 1992 by a signed Statement of Commitment from the unprecedented Tri-Council Meeting of all the federal and provincial environment, parks and wildlife ministers. Perhaps most important, every jurisdiction (every province and territory, and the federal government) has said, in writing, that it will achieve the Endangered Spaces goal of completing a network of representative protected areas by the year 2000.

So we have, without a doubt, managed to establish the Endangered Spaces goal as mutually agreed-upon public policy for Canada. Few, if any, environmental goals have garnered this kind of backing. Armed with such support, it's difficult to imagine not succeeding!

But having a good idea, even with widespread support and measurable commitments, is one thing. Actually pulling it off is quite another. And the latter is proving difficult. In fact, at the current rate of progress, we will never make it.

This book, therefore, concentrates on *how* we should protect Canada's endangered spaces, rather than why. The first section details the practical lessons learned by those of us involved in the Endangered Spaces campaign over the first five years of a ten-year effort; the second lays out, province-by-province, what we think needs to be done to reach the goal by the year 2000; the third section concludes

THIS CHARTER PROTECTS CANADIANS.

THIS ONE PROTECTS CANADA.

Although your human rights are assured, did you know that your country's rights aren't? Today, only about 5% of Canada is protected as true wilderness. And every 15 seconds, another acre of Canada's wilderness heritage is lost to you and your family forever – mined, ploughed, cut down, contaminated, developed or dammed.

Help win the race for Canada's Endangered Spaces by supporting the efforts of the Endangered Spaces Campaign, with more than 260 endorsing organizations across Canada. The goal of the Campaign is simple: to represent Canada's natural regions with protected areas by the year 2000. Add your signature to the *Canadian Wilderness Charter* now and ask your friends and family to do the same.

THE CANADIAN WILDERNESS CHARTER

1 Whereas humankind is but one of millions of species sharing planet Earth and whereas the future of the Earth is severely threatened by the activities of this single species,

2 Whereas our planet has already lost much of its former wilderness character, thereby endangering many species and ecosystems,

3 Whereas Canadians still have the opportunity to complete a network of protected areas representing the biological diversity of our country,

4 Whereas Canada's remaining wild places, be they land or water, merit protection for their inherent value,

5 Whereas the protection of wilderness also meets an intrinsic human need for spiritual rekindling and artistic inspiration,

6 Whereas Canada's once vast wilderness has deeply shaped the national identity and continues to profoundly influence how we view ourselves as Canadians,

7 Whereas Canada's aboriginal peoples hold deep and direct ties to wilderness areas throughout Canada and seek to maintain options for traditional wilderness use,

8 Whereas protected areas can serve a variety of purposes including:

a) preserving a genetic reservoir of wild plants and animals for future use and appreciation by citizens of Canada and the world,

b) producing economic benefits from environmentally sensitive tourism,

c) offering opportunities for research and environmental education,

9 Whereas the opportunity to complete a national network of protected areas must be grasped and acted upon during the next ten years, or be lost,

1 **We agree and urge:** That governments, industries environmental groups and individual Canadians commit themselves to a national effort to establish at least one representative protected area in each of the natural regions of Canada by the year 2000,

2 That the total area thereby protected comprise at least 12% of the lands and waters of Canada as recommended in the World Commission on Environment and Development's report, *Our Common Future,*

3 That public and private agencies at international, national, provincial, territorial and local levels rigorously monitor progress toward meeting these goals in Canada and ensure that they are fully achieved, and

4 That federal, provincial and territorial government conservation agencies on behalf of all Canadians develop action plans by 1990 for achieving these goals by the year 2000.

☐ IT'S MY COUNTRY, MY FUTURE, MY RIGHT.

Please add my signature to the *Canadian Wilderness Charter.* SIGNATURE _____

NAME _____

ADDRESS _____

CITY _____ PROVINCE _____ POSTAL CODE _____

Please return to:
Endangered Spaces Campaign
c/o World Wildlife Fund
90 Eglinton Avenue E., Suite 504
Toronto, Ontario M4P 2Z7
Get your friends, family and neighbours to sign as well (further space on back).

WWF

with perspectives from key players whose support is essential if we are to achieve our goal. In this way, we have tried to produce a handbook for success. *Protecting Canada's Endangered Spaces* is a practical manual for all Canadians as the owners of something magnificent that can be protected, kept, and saved — or neglected, taken from us, and lost.

THE 12 PER CENT FIXATION

Before exploring strategies and actions, we should clarify exactly what we are trying to achieve. In the case of the Endangered Spaces campaign goal, this is particularly important, because there have been some serious misunderstandings — sometimes quite innocent and genuine, and at other times deliberate and rather self-serving. The children of the great American conservationist Aldo Leopold said of *A Sand County Almanac* that, although their father's essays were "widely read and quoted, their basic tenets have been all but forgotten in the glare of national publicity." We know the feeling.

The goal of the Endangered Spaces campaign is "to establish a network of protected areas representing all the natural regions of Canada by the year 2000." We added in the goal statement, as a guideline only, that such a network should add up to "at least 12 per cent of the lands and waters of Canada."

From the beginning, we were well aware that referring to a percentage would immediately attract attention. On the one hand, if we didn't give any kind of quantitative guideline, we were vulnerable to being accused of having a vague, "unfinishable agenda" that constituted a conservation land-grab. On the other hand, if we did refer to a percentage, we ran the risk of it being considered a rote target, not to be departed from, regardless of what good science and conservation biology indicated was necessary. There would be objections from one side, claiming that 12 per cent was arbitrary, and therefore exorbitant, and from the other side, claiming it was arbitrary, and therefore inadequate. Sure enough, all of this has happened.

To set the record straight, Endangered Spaces is not a campaign to protect 12 per cent of Canada. The 12 per cent guideline was derived from *Our Common Future*, the 1987 report of the World Commission on Environment and Development, chaired by Prime Minister Gro Brundtland of Norway. It suggested (on page 147) that "nearly 4 per cent of the Earth's land area is managed explicitly to conserve species and ecosystems," and (on page 166) "that the total expanse of protected areas needs to be at least tripled if it is to constitute a representative sample of Earth's ecosystems."

We deliberately cited the Brundtland Report because so many governments and businesses (and some conservationists) were busy agreeing with it. Mentioning 12 per cent was strictly a tactical move on our part to associate the Endangered Spaces concept with a document that had already received widespread support, particularly from potential critics of protected areas. And that's all it was.

We never said that 12 per cent was a specific target or ceiling. In fact, it has been carefully used from the start, as it was in the Brundtland Report, as a bare minimum. We never suggested that 12 per cent was a science-based figure, although the more important goal of adequately representing all our natural regions certainly is. Furthermore, we never stated that our goal was to protect 12 per cent of Canada,

NOVEMBER 25, 1992 - AYLMER, QUEBEC

Endangered Spaces goal becomes public policy. Ministers sign Tri-Council Statement of Commitment

The Canadian Council of Ministers of the Environment, The Canadian Parks Ministers Council, and the Wildlife Ministers Council of Canada

A Statement of Commitment
To Complete Canada's Networks of Protected Areas

Preamble

This Statement is intended as a public statement of consolidated political will to complete Canada's networks of protected natural areas by the year 2000. Realization of this commitment will build upon more than a century of conservation efforts in Canada. The Statement's endorsement by three separate federal-provincial councils is a recognition of the need for both inter-jurisdictional and inter-disciplinary cooperation. This Statement is the beneficiary of many international commissions, resolutions and declarations – the World Conservation Strategy, the World Charter for Nature, the World Commission on Environment and Development, Caring for the Earth: A Strategy for Sustainable Living; and most recently, in February 1992, the Caracas Declaration from the Fourth World Congress on Parks and Protected Areas – all of which have signalled the urgency to complete the world's networks of protected areas. The World Commission on Environment and Development has recommended that at least 12% of the planet be set aside in protected areas.

It is understood that nothing in this Statement shall in any way prejudice Aboriginal or treaty rights, the land claims process or self-government negotiations.

Premises

On the occasion of Canada's 125th anniversary, the Canadian Council of Ministers of the Environment, the Canadian Parks Ministers' Council, and the Wildlife Ministers' Council of Canada have come together to recognize that:

• Canada's natural heritage – its wildlands, waters and wildlife – unites and defines us all as Canadians

• Canada has a special global responsibility to protect its natural heritage given that:

  • Canada is steward of almost 20% of the planet's wilderness (excluding Antarctica), 20% of its fresh water, and 24% of its remaining wetlands

  • Canada is one of the few nations that still has an opportunity to represent its natural regions and features, and to conserve its critical wildlife habitat

• Protected areas have scientific, educational, inspirational and recreational values for humankind and contribute to sustainable development

• Protected areas are essential to Canada's environmental health, biological diversity, and ecological processes

• The ecological health of protected areas is affected by the quality of the surrounding environment

• The opportunities to protect Canada's natural regions and wildlife habitat are quickly being foreclosed

• Canada's natural heritage should be safeguarded through a variety of protected areas, including national and provincial parks, ecological reserves, wildlife management areas and migratory bird sanctuaries

• Protected areas must be complemented by sound public and private stewardship of all of Canada's lands

• Aboriginal peoples have a significant and unique role in the protection of Canada's natural heritage

• The protection of Canada's natural heritage cannot be achieved by any one government or agency

• Canadians want to be involved in decisions affecting protected areas

Commitments

And therefore, in the interest of present and future generations of Canadians, Council members will make every effort to:

• **Complete Canada's networks of protected areas representative of Canada's land-based natural regions by the year 2000 and accelerate the protection of areas representative of Canada's marine natural regions**

• **Accelerate the identification and protection of Canada's critical wildlife habitat**

• **Adopt frameworks, strategies, and time-frames for the completion of the protected areas networks**

• **Continue to cooperate in the protection of ecosystems, landscapes and wildlife habitat**

• **Ensure that protected areas are integral components of all sustainable development strategies**

The Honourable Pauline Browes
Minister of State (Environment)
Government of Canada
Canadian Council of Ministers of the Environment

The Honourable Harry J. Enns
Minister of Natural Resources
Government of Manitoba
Canadian Parks Ministers' Council

The Honourable Titus Allooloo
Minister of Renewable Resources and Municipal and Community Affairs
Government of the Northwest Territories
Wildlife Ministers' Council of Canada

Aylmer, Quebec, November 25, 1992

25 NOVEMBRE, 1992 - AYLMER, QUÉBEC

**Les objectifs de la campagne Espaces en danger sont désormais une politique officielle du Canada.
Les ministres des trois conseils signent l'engagement formel.**

Le Conseil canadien des ministres de l'environnement, le Conseil canadien des ministres des parcs canadiens, le Conseil des ministres de la faune du Canada

Engagement formel
de compléter le réseau canadien des aires protégées

Préambule

Il s'agit ici d'une déclaration publique par laquelle les autorités politiques du Canada s'engagent, d'un commun accord, à terminer, d'ici l'an 2000, le réseau canadien des aires naturelles à protéger. La réalisation de ce réseau sera le fruit de plus d'un siècle d'efforts pour conserver notre milieu naturel. Le fait que trois conseils fédéraux-provinciaux distincts soient parties à cet engagement constitue un signe de l'importance d'une coopération non seulement inter-gouvernementale mais aussi interdisciplinaire. Cet engagement fait suite à bien des commissions, résolutions et déclarations internationales – la Stratégie mondiale pour la conservation, la Charte mondiale de la nature, la Commission mondiale sur l'environnement et le développement, Sauvez la planète : stratégie pour la durabilité de la vie et, plus récemment, en février 1992, la déclaration du quatrième Congrès international sur les parcs et les aires protégées (Caracas); toutes soulignent l'importance qu'il y a à terminer, en toute urgence, partout dans le monde, les réseaux des aires protégées. La Commission mondiale sur l'environnement et le développement a recommandé qu'au moins 12 p. 100 de la superficie de la planète soit réservée à titre d'aires protégées.

Il est entendu que rien dans cet engagement ne doit nuire aux négociations relatives aux droits ancestraux ou issus de traités, aux revendications territoriales ou à l'autonomie gouvernementale des autochtones.

Motifs

À l'occasion du 125e anniversaire du Canada, le Conseil canadien des ministres de l'environnement, le Conseil canadien des ministres des parcs et le Conseil canadien des ministres de la faune du Canada ont d'un commun accord convenu que :

- Le patrimoine naturel du Canada – ses terres vierges, ses eaux et sa faune – nous unit et nous définit tous comme Canadiens et Canadiennes
- Le Canada a tout particulièrement, vis-à-vis de la planète, la responsabilité de protéger son patrimoine naturel, étant donné
  - qu'il a la garde de presque 20 p. 100 des aires de nature sauvage de la planète (à l'exception de l'Antarctique), de 20 p. 100 de son étendue d'eau douce et de 24 p. 100 de ses terres encore humides
  - qu'il est l'un des rares pays qui puissent encore représenter ses régions et ses caractéristiques naturelles et conserver ses habitats fauniques très importants
- Les aires protégées ont une valeur scientifique, éducative, esthétique et récréative pour l'humanité et elles contribuent au développement durable
- Les aires protégées sont essentielles à la santé de l'environnement canadien, à sa diversité biologique et à ses processus écologiques
- La qualité du milieu ambiant influe sur la santé écologique des aires protégées
- Les occasions dont dispose le Canada pour protéger ses régions naturelles et les habitats de sa faune diminuent rapidement
- La meilleure façon pour le Canada de sauvegarder son patrimoine naturel serait de protéger certaines de ses aires naturelles qui se présentent sous diverses formes : parcs nationaux et provinciaux, réserves écologiques, aires de gestion de la faune, refuges d'oiseaux migrateurs
- Outre la protection des aires désignées, il faut assurer une saine gestion, publique et privée, de toutes les terres du Canada
- Les peuples autochtones du Canada ont un rôle important et unique à jouer dans la protection du patrimoine naturel du Canada
- Nul gouvernement ou organisme ne pourrait, seul, réussir à protéger le patrimoine naturel du Canada
- Les Canadiens et Canadiennes veulent participer aux décisions relatives aux aires protégées

Engagements

Par conséquent, au nom des générations actuelles et futures, les membres des conseils mettront tout en oeuvre :

- **Pour compléter, d'ici l'an 2000, les réseaux d'aires protégées du Canada qui sont représentatifs des régions terrestres naturelles du Canada et accélérer la protection des aires représentatives des régions marines naturelles du Canada**
- **Pour hâter l'identification et la protection des principaux habitats fauniques du Canada**
- **Pour adopter des structures, des stratégies et des échéanciers pour le parachèvement des réseaux d'aires protégées**
- **Pour continuer à coopérer avec les autres pour la protection des écosystèmes, des sites naturels et des habitats fauniques**
- **Pour veiller à ce que les aires protégées fassent partie intégrante de toutes les stratégies de développement durable**

Pauline Browes

L'honorable Pauline Browes
Ministre d'État (Environnement)
Gouvernement du Canada
Le Conseil canadien des ministres de l'environnement

Harry J. Enns

L'honorable Harry J. Enns
Ministre des Ressources naturelles
Gouvernement du Manitoba
Le Conseil canadien des ministres des parcs

Titus Allooloo

L'honorable Titus Allooloo
Ministre des Ressources renouvelables et des Affaires municipales et communautaires
Gouvernement des Territoires du Nord-Ouest
Le Conseil des ministres de la faune du Canada

Aylmer (Québec), le 25 novembre 1992

and therefore 12 per cent of every province, and therefore 12 per cent of every natural region — the interpretation adopted by some jurisdictions and expressed as their official policy!

The goal, we repeat, is to establish a network of protected areas representing all the natural regions of Canada. Since stating that goal, WWF, in cooperation with leading experts in the field, has done considerable technical homework to determine precisely what requirements must be met to "adequately represent a natural region with protected areas." We have also worked on a necessary companion concept — namely, "ecological integrity." This work is summarized in the early chapters of this book. We strongly urge those who have become fixated on percentages to read these carefully. Based on our technical standards, WWF has now mapped the geographic requirements for new protected areas across the country to meet the Endangered Spaces goal. These maps serve as the basis for WWF's advocacy and progress evaluation in each jurisdiction.

Finally, 12 per cent has been used as a hook to criticize the campaign for disregarding "the other 88 per cent" of the landscape. It's true that the focus of Endangered Spaces is the establishment of core wildland reserves, because that's an ambitious task in itself and we won't get another chance to do it. But that doesn't mean our conservation vision stops at the park gate. Clearly, if the effect of designating protected areas is to merely intensify resource exploitation on surrounding lands and waters, there is little overall gain for conservation. The fact is, we need *both* protected areas and sustainable use elsewhere to achieve our conservation mission. "Sustainable use" here means using natural resources such as forests, fishes, and agricultural land in a manner that ensures they will be healthy and available to future generations, indefinitely.

In the end, ecological sustainability depends on achieving economic stability by carefully extracting more and more value from a fixed amount of raw material — in other words, doing more with less. Protected areas alone won't get us there, but they are a necessary first step in disciplining our demands on the land so that it remains a healthy and beautiful homeplace.

HOW ARE WE DOING?

At the midpoint of the Endangered Spaces campaign, of the 453 natural regions in Canada, only 18, or 4 per cent, are judged to be "represented" by protected areas; 46, or 10 per cent, are "moderately represented"; 134 or 30 per cent, are "partially represented"; and 255, or 56 per cent, have little or no representation. A natural region is judged by WWF to:

- be *represented* when all of the enduring features (relatively stable landforms and seaforms and their accompanying plant and animal communities) are considered to be adequately captured in protected areas;
- be *moderately represented* when at least 50 per cent of the major enduring features are adequately captured, and at least 80 per cent of the remaining features are either moderately or partially captured in protected areas;
- be *partially represented* when up to 50 per cent of the major enduring features are moderately or adequately captured and at least 50 per cent of the

remaining features are at least partially captured; and at least 80 per cent of all features are partially captured in protected areas;

- have *little or no representation* when none of the major enduring features are moderately or adequately captured and less than 80 per cent of features are partially captured in protected areas.

Our goal will not be accomplished until 100 per cent of our natural regions are in the "represented" category. Only 4 per cent are in that category now. This stark figure reveals the true magnitude of the task ahead. Nevertheless, 40 per cent of our natural regions have either moderate or partial representation, so a significant portion is part way there. Most challenging, of course, is the 56 per cent of natural regions which have little or no representation at all, including virtually all the marine regions. WWF's research also indicates that we have already lost the opportunity to establish a protected area 50,000 hectares or larger in more than 100 of Canada's natural regions. These are located primarily in the south of nearly every province, where the most habitat has been lost to human development. Ecological restoration will be needed in many of these regions, a costly, long-term venture which reinforces the urgency of designating large wildland reserves in the remaining natural regions where we still have that option.

A few additional comments are needed at this point. First, when we launched the Endangered Spaces campaign, New Brunswick, Newfoundland, and the Northwest Territories hadn't even finished a classification of their natural regions. As a result, they didn't have the basic frame of reference with which to judge representation, let alone measure progress. This first task has now been completed in every province and territory, although, because the land-classification systems differ from jurisdiction to jurisdiction, the natural-region lines don't meet at the political borders. From a practical standpoint, the Endangered Spaces campaign deliberately chose not to require that all natural regions be determined using the same classification system, because waiting for that would have meant never getting out of the starting gate!

Second, these natural-region determinations have become something of a "moving target" because some have changed since the campaign was launched. For example, Nova Scotia went from 9 to 77 natural regions, Alberta from 17 to 20, Yukon from 13 to 23, and British Columbia from 57 to 110. Our response to this has been: "Fine, determine as many natural regions on whatever basis you wish, but your commitment to represent all of them with protected areas by the year 2000 still stands." In effect, a network of protected areas to represent Nova Scotia is likely to do the job whether the province has been subdivided into 9 or 77 natural regions.

Third, the provincial natural-region totals don't necessarily take into account marine natural regions. Chapter 2 explores this problem in more detail. Here, we simply want to signal that the federal government, and those provinces and territories with ocean coasts or Great Lakes, are far behind in determining the basis for an effective network of marine protected areas. We have recognized the distinct challenges of marine protection through a revised goal of completing the marine spaces system by 2010.

Fourth, although the Endangered Spaces campaign is not intended to protect a predefined percentage of Canada's area, it is fair to ask how much of our country, so far, actually enjoys legal protection up to the Endangered Spaces standard, which means "no logging, mining, or hydro-electric development." The answer, at the mid-point of the campaign, is about 5.2 per cent, up from 2.6 per cent in 1989. Although national parks make up approximately half the *area* protected so far, and do help with representation in a few natural regions, the overwhelming majority of natural regions will be adequately represented only as a result of protected areas established by the provinces and territories, and they are far behind in this task. First Nations are, in effect, forming a third level of government, which is proving increasingly crucial to our goal with respect to lands and waters formerly controlled by federal or provincial jurisdictions.

So, what bottom-line response can we give to the question "How are we doing?" The fair answer must be twofold. On the one hand, in the first five years we have received outstanding public support and clear political commitments to the Endangered Spaces goal, along with some measurable progress on the ground. After all, we have almost doubled the amount of land legally protected up to our standard. On the other hand, the majority of the work lies ahead of us, and at the current rate of progress we won't even come close to completing the job on time. The cold fact is we are currently losing wilderness at the rate of 100 hectares per hour in this country, so the pace at which we are making conservation gains is still far outdistanced by the pace at which we are experiencing losses.

In order to accomplish the Endangered Spaces goal, we believe we must not just muddle along and hope we succeed, but deliberately plan for success, using a well-known planning technique called "backcasting." This simply means defining where we want to be in the year 2000 (call that Point B), comparing this with where we're at in every jurisdiction right now (call that Point A), then laying out a critical path or action plan to get us from A to B. This is the approach taken in Section Two of this book, which provides a backcasted blueprint for every province and territory, and the federal government.

In turning his eye to the possibility of establishing "a representative series of wilderness areas" in Canada, Aldo Leopold correctly surmised in 1949: "It will be contended, of course, that no deliberate planning to this end is necessary; and that adequate areas will survive anyhow." However, Leopold went on to warn that "all recent history belies so comforting an assumption."

Leopold was right. Certainly recent history in Canada confirms that to sit back and be complacent or fatalistic about the future of wilderness will mean failure. Yet, the momentum and tantalizing accomplishments of the Endangered Spaces campaign to date lead us to believe we have also glimpsed the possibility of success.

THE BIGGER PICTURE

In recent years, there has been growing recognition that conservationists traditionally associated with the movement to "save *species*" cannot succeed unless we "save *spaces*." In other words, if we don't conserve the underlying ecological processes and larger natural systems upon which species depend, we will simply be fiddling while Rome burns — hence, the torrent of interest in conserving "biological diversity" (or biodiversity). Simply defined as "the variety of life," biodiversity includes the full range of genes, species, communities, ecosystems, functions, and evolution-ary processes.

The importance of conserving biodiversity is undeniable and has been argued from virtually every standpoint, including aesthetics, economics, ethics, and survival. In June 1992, at the Earth Summit in Rio de Janeiro, Canada was the first industrialized country to sign a new International Convention on Biological Diversity. Now this country, along with many others, has prepared a National Biodiversity Plan, as required by the Convention.

The common-sense thinking behind the Convention and national biodiversity plans is this: If we are to conserve the world's biodiversity, then each political jigsaw piece of the world — each country — is going to have to conserve its particular piece of the bigger puzzle. As the largest part of the North American continent, Canada forms a major jigsaw piece of that world puzzle. Indeed, many of us are now embarked on conservation planning which includes a network of protected areas that help conserve biodiversity on a continental basis.

However, Canada itself resembles a jigsaw puzzle — a biological tapestry of unique natural regions. If we are to have any hope of conserving the biological diversity of this country, one key accomplishment must be a network of protected areas left in a natural condition, representing our national and natural mosaic of ecosystems.

It is no exaggeration to say that accomplishing the Endangered Spaces goal would be one of the most important contributions Canada could make to conserving biodiversity in North America, and therefore to doing our part on the world scale. In fact, there are now Endangered Spaces–style campaigns under way elsewhere in the world, recognizing that this is a responsibility all nations have to themselves and to others.

But here's the difference: Most other countries have long since lost options which we still have in Canada. They must, of necessity, embark on very long-term, expensive restoration efforts to regain their natural heritage. They have pushed through a loss threshold which we have not yet reached, but which looms on the horizon.

Will we Canadians acknowledge what's on that horizon, and beyond? Will we grasp an opportunity so regrettably lost by others? Will Canada be the first country in the world to have deliberately saved the most fundamental pieces of its natural fabric? For now, for a few more moments in terms of our natural history, it still can be done. And it must be done.

Tool Kit for Success

1 / Building the Ark: The Science Behind the Selection of Protected Areas

KEVIN KAVANAGH, REED NOSS, AND TONY IACOBELLI

As Canadians, we hold a deep fondness for the magnificent, varied landscape of our country. Classic Canadian postcards depict familiar scenes: snow-capped Rocky Mountains, expansive prairie plains, autumn-coloured forests draped over rolling Québec hills, and ocean waves crashing along rugged Nova Scotia coastlines. Even though many of us may not be familiar with the scientific term for it, these postcards of landforms, vegetation, and wildlife vividly portray some of the "ecological diversity" of Canada. But these are not the only elements of our natural world that vary across the country. Ask Canadians to describe the climate where they live, and they may well boast that "their region" doesn't experience southern Ontario's humid summers, or British Columbia's damp winters, or the blizzards and ice storms of the Maritime provinces, or the extreme windchill felt across the prairies.

So, provincial rivalries aside, Canadians recognize their country as a collection of "regions," defined largely by a combination of natural elements such as physical landscape, vegetation, and climate. Zoom in a little closer, and people will continue to identify different landscapes within their province, county, township, or municipality, and even within their own "homeplace" — the "back forty" or backyard.

World Wildlife Fund (WWF) Canada believes that in order to maintain the biological diversity — the rich variety of life and its associated natural processes — of our various homeplaces we must establish a network of carefully selected protected areas (nature reserves, national parks, wilderness areas, etc.), together with sound stewardship over the remaining landscape. These protected areas must be in the right place, and of the right size and the right configuration. That is, they must "represent" viable examples of each natural region. Representative protected areas, then, contain or "adequately capture" the typical natural features of a particular region of Canada.

WWF is not alone in calling for a network of representative protected areas. For example, the Canadian Council on Ecological Areas (CCEA), a national body with members from all Canadian jurisdictions, has recommended the establishment of such a network, and in 1991 the Canadian Environmental Advisory Council advised the federal Minister of the Environment that "a network of protected areas . . . is an integral part of the global sustainable development agenda."

The importance of completing a network of representative protected areas has also won international acceptance. In 1993, the principal recommendation of the Caracas Declaration emanating from the Fourth World Congress on National Parks and Protected Areas read: "We strongly urge all governments and appropriate national and international bodies: To take urgent action to consolidate and enlarge national systems of well-managed protected areas with buffer zones and corridors, so that by the year 2000 they safeguard the full representative range of land, freshwater, coastal and marine ecosystems of each country. . . ."

Consistent with this approach, the Endangered Spaces campaign emphasizes the importance of preserving ecological diversity across the country through completion of a system of protected areas that collectively represent all of Canada's natural regions. The challenge has been to make this goal practical and achievable, while adhering to principles of conservation biology. In this chapter, we outline a set of science-based criteria that can be applied across the nation in order to achieve ecological representation through protected areas. In this way, the Endangered Spaces campaign is based on the same scientific principles that guide conservation actions required to maintain biological diversity.

SETTING UP THE PLANNING FRAMEWORK

An appropriate planning framework in the form of ecological or natural regions encompassing different landscapes is required to guide the establishment of protected areas. Without such a framework, choosing where to designate protected areas becomes little more than a random exercise driven more by political opportunity than by conservation biology. In order to represent Canada's biological diversity, the planning framework must have ecological boundaries. But in choosing where to draw such boundaries, one must consider the scale at which planning will be conducted. If the scale is too fine, the information needed to map natural regions on a land base the size of Canada would become excessively laborious, and it would not account for some of the large-scale natural processes, such as wildfire, needed to renew some ecosystems. On the other hand, if the scale is too coarse, important pieces of our biological diversity could be missed. Since natural-habitat loss in Canada continues at a rapid rate (100 hectares per hour), there is a need to balance time-consuming, fine-scale information-gathering exercises with quicker coarse-scale planning that can still deliver protection to Canada's biological diversity.

Stan Rowe, one of Canada's leading landscape ecologists, suggests that, "because organisms cannot long survive without their equally creative matrix of air-water-soil-sediments, the preservation of ecosystems 'at the landscape level' is the necessary practical approach for all those in land management concerned with biodiversity. This is the 'filter' that, if made sufficiently large, catches everything, whether we know it on sight or not." In this sense, drawing natural-region boundaries at scales that encompass landscape features such as major valley systems or watersheds provides a suitable framework to plan for individual protected areas. For the purposes of the Endangered Spaces campaign, a natural region is defined as a geographic area characterized by broad similarities in landform, geology, climate, and vegetation-cover, mapped at scales generally ranging from 1:5,000,000 to 1:7,500,000. At this scale, boundaries most often reflect fuzzy transitions on the landscape such as gradations between level, hilly, and undulating terrain. Sharp, well-defined delineations such as the treeline between alpine and sub-alpine zones typical of mountainous areas are exceptions.

SETTING ECOLOGICAL STANDARDS

Canada's federal, provincial, and territorial governments have developed frameworks of natural regions for protected-areas planning. In monitoring the progress of each jurisdiction towards the Endangered Spaces campaign goal, WWF assesses the extent to which protected areas represent or capture appropriate ecological units within each natural region.

Based on a landscape approach to meeting conservation goals, we have decided that protected areas should represent "enduring features" of the landscape as the primary elements of ecological diversity. Stan Rowe provides the reasons for this decision:

> Scientists have a very rudimentary knowledge of biodiversity, said ecologist Otto Solbrig in 1991, a statement whose accuracy will stand unchallenged for many years. Worldwide, only about 1.4 million species of organisms have been described, out of a probable 30 or 40 million. In Canada, researchers place the number of identified species — the big ones — at around 70,000, which means that a few hundred thousand little ones are lurking incognito in the northern mountains, forests, grasslands, and tundra. Because we know that organisms are inseparable from their landscape/waterscape systems, and because (compared with organisms) the identification of different kinds of land/water units is relatively easy, a preservation program for terrain in its inclusive sense can go a long way towards compensating for taxonomic ignorance.

WWF defines an enduring feature as a part of the landscape that has relatively uniform types of mineral soil deposits or bedrock outcrops. In addition, these materials, within an enduring feature, have similar origins; they may be the result of deposits from flooding or layers left from retreating glaciers. Each enduring feature can also be characterized by consistent changes in elevation, for example, hilly or flat. Specific examples of enduring features are "a low-elevation flood plain that has sandy soils in its surface layers" or "the middle elevation of a steeply sloped mountainous area with bedrock at the surface." WWF identifies and maps enduring features at scales of approximately 1:500,000 to 1:1,000,000.

To represent adequately the biological diversity of each natural region, examples of every region's enduring features will need to be included in protected areas. This approach, at a coarse scale, may also apply to landforms beneath our oceans and Great Lakes. (WWF is currently evaluating criteria for assessing ecological representation of marine natural regions for marine protected areas.) The identification and mapping of enduring features is the primary basis upon which WWF assesses progress towards the Endangered Spaces campaign goal. By comparing mapped enduring features with existing protected-area boundaries, on a natural-region–by–natural-region basis, WWF can determine those enduring features which are not yet captured by the protected-areas system. These unrepresented enduring features are the "gaps" in the system. A "gap analysis," therefore, shows where there is insufficient protection of enduring features and ecological communities in existing protected-areas systems. WWF's gap analysis is conducted using the natural-region framework, within which enduring features are mapped, of provincial and territorial governments. An overlay of existing protected areas is placed over these mapped units to reveal gaps in the protected-areas system.

The results obtained from a gap analysis not only help define the job that existing protected areas do in protecting a natural region's biological diversity, but also provide guidance for the selection of new candidate sites to achieve better representation of a region's ecological diversity. The specific gap-analysis methodology undertaken by WWF, under the direction of the CCEA, draws heavily from projects undertaken by specialists in ecological land classification. Discussion papers are now available through WWF Canada which detail how this work has been adapted to the Endangered Spaces campaign for the purpose of assessing progress in protected-areas planning.

ECOLOGICAL INTEGRITY IN A PROTECTED-AREAS NETWORK

Simply *representing* the enduring features of a natural region in a protected-areas network will not guarantee that all species native to the region will survive, or be able to migrate elsewhere when conditions change. Nor does representation by itself ensure the maintenance of natural processes such as wildfire which are necessary to keep ecosystems and their wildlife populations healthy. Conserving biodiversity over the long term requires that another important criterion be met — namely, "ecological integrity." The CCEA generally defines ecological integrity as the capability of a protected area to support and maintain assemblages of wildlife and natural communities in a manner which ensures that their composition, structure, and functional organization are comparable to those of similar ecosystems of the region.

Designing protected areas in Canada must take stock of human impact on the region as well as the natural character of the region itself. In a region with intact wilderness, for example, a protected area that adequately samples the physical habitats and biological communities is likely to maintain the integrity of wildlife populations as long as the surrounding area remains wild. Species will follow their normal shifts in abundance and distribution, but will not suffer regional extinction any faster than they would naturally.

By contrast, in natural regions that are undergoing human development, such as logging or urbanization, the ecological integrity of a protected area becomes more difficult to maintain as the surrounding area becomes less natural. For instance, local extinctions of wildlife species within isolated reserves cannot be easily reversed through recolonization from neighbouring wildlife populations, because the human-altered landscapes (clear-cuts, ploughed fields, etc.) create barriers to wildlife movement. Just as important, roads and other forms of access within or between protected areas can lead to losses of large carnivores (bears, wolves, etc.) and other species sensitive to human exploitation or persecution, including increased hunting, noise, and road-kills. Whatever the cause, as species disappear from a reserve or network of reserves, ecological integrity declines.

Selecting sites for protected areas which maintain ecological integrity is part of the larger process of "land management" (considered broadly to include options ranging from intensive exploitation to strict protection). Proper land management includes:

- completing biodiversity inventories (documenting wildlife species, natural communities, and landforms);
- identifying areas with high species richness, unrepresented habitats, and other key sites needing protection;

No nation worldwide has a conservation strategy that can match Canada's in terms of vision, breadth, scientific defensibility, public acceptance, and probability of ultimate success. While the United States flounders about in endless debates over whether biodiversity is worth protecting and what is ecosystem management, Canada has an official policy to protect its natural heritage. All of Canada's senior governments have endorsed the primary goal of the Endangered Spaces campaign.

REED NOSS, *Maintaining Ecological Integrity in Representative Networks*, 1995

- zoning reserves and the surrounding landscape to protect sensitive areas, while allowing compatible human uses in appropriate zones;
- monitoring and assessing biodiversity under a range of experimental management techniques; and
- changing or adapting land management to new information as it becomes available.

These principles have led WWF to recommend that the following objectives be used to guide the design of protected areas within and across the natural regions of Canada:

1. *Sustain key geological, hydrological, ecological, biological, and evolutionary processes within normal ranges of variation, while building a conservation network that is adaptable to a changing environment.* Simply keeping natural processes operating in some fashion is not difficult — we could not stop them if we tried! However, we have to consider their rates and magnitudes. Too much or too little of any of them, too rapidly or too slowly, or in the wrong place or time, could lead to a dramatic decline in ecological integrity within a particular protected area. Therefore, maintaining natural processes within the limits or ranges of variation that are considered "natural," "historic," "acceptable," or "desirable" for ecological systems is crucial.

In many cases, where ecological integrity has been compromised, the resulting loss of biodiversity can be traced to human activities that altered some aspects of natural-disturbance regimes or other processes. For example, putting fires out and stopping floods have had severe impacts on biological communities that were, in fact, shaped by such natural disturbances. In Canada, most forest communities and prairie grasslands require periodic fire for their continued health. Suppression of fires has led to unnatural accumulations of dead wood and other changes in vegetation in parts of the Canadian boreal forest region, while woody shrub and aspen invasion has occurred in prairie grassland habitats. Occasional natural flooding along river valleys is also necessary in our prairie regions to maintain stands of cottonwood trees. It is critical, however, to distinguish desirable from undesirable changes in natural communities, as stated by Dan Botkin in *Discordant Harmonies*: "To accept certain kinds of change is not to accept all kinds of change. Moreover, we must focus our attention on the rates at which change occurs, understanding that certain rates of change are natural, desirable, and acceptable, while others are not."

2. *Maintain or restore viable populations of all native species in natural patterns of abundance and distribution.* Planning should consider the viability of species populations over a period of centuries. Over such long periods of time, species will be added to and deleted from regions as a consequence of natural extinctions and range changes in response to climate and other factors. Our recommendation is to keep, wherever possible, rates of extinction and shifts

in abundance and distribution within the range of variation expected in landscapes unaltered by human activities.

To do this, it is important to identify those species most sensitive to human activities in each natural region. These include extinction-prone species, such as spotted owls in old-growth forests, plus others that play "keystone" or "umbrella" roles in their ecosystems, such as grizzly bears in the foothills and mountains. When one is designing reserve networks, and monitoring the effects of various management approaches, these wildlife species are among the most important indicators of ecological integrity. Providing enough secure habitat for such species is a necessity.

3. *Encourage human uses that are compatible with the maintenance of ecological integrity.* A philosophy that considers humans to be separate from nature is inconsistent with all we know about humans evolving in the natural world and being interdependent with it. Human psychology suggests that conservationists will be most successful when they encourage some kinds of human use rather than simply restricting uses in reserve networks.

SELECTING PROTECTED AREAS

With the above objectives in mind, WWF gives priority to the following kinds of sites:

1. Roadless, undeveloped, or otherwise essentially wild areas of significant size. Undeveloped areas, especially when they are less accessible to humans, or when they offer refuge to species sensitive to human activities.

2. Concentrations of rare species. These are obvious "hot spots" of biodiversity that should be included within reserves.

3. Areas of unusually high species richness. These are areas where many different species can be protected efficiently.

4. Unusual plant or animal communities, forest succession stages (such as old-growth), or animal concentration areas such as bird or seal breeding sites; waterfowl staging areas; winter-range or calving grounds for caribou, moose, or elk; bear denning areas; and snake "hibernacula" (areas where large congregations of snakes survive the winter).

5. Sites with unusual habitat conditions, such as artesian springs, ice-free bays, outcrops of unusual rocks or surface material, and mineral licks.

6. Watersheds of high value for fish or other aquatic life.

7. Sites that are sensitive to development, such as watersheds with steep slopes or unstable soils.

8. Sites recognized as important or sacred by aboriginal peoples. The value of traditional knowledge should not be underestimated. People who have inhabited a region for a long time often have a profound knowledge of local natural features and areas rich in wildlife. Other areas may be important for cultural or spiritual reasons.

9. Sites that could be added to existing protected areas to form larger areas with greater ecological integrity.

In planning for the ecological integrity of protected areas, it is important to recognize that such sites can become little more than "islands of green" unless some form of corridors or linkages are available for wildlife movement across the land-

Preservation of wild and semi-wild areas is increasingly important and I urge the involvement of everyone in this task: setting aside rivalries and pooling efforts among agencies, directing energy and time to the practical task of getting new areas established as quickly as possible.
STAN ROWE, *Ecodiversity, The Key to Biodiversity,* 1993

scape. These need not be officially designated as protected areas, but they should be specially managed in a manner that meets both human and non-human needs. In keeping with the goals of the Endangered Spaces campaign, the selection and design of core protected areas is considered the most urgent and important first step; buffer zones and corridors can, in most cases, be factored in later.

Once the selection and design of core reserves is complete, a management strategy must be developed based on research and monitoring. And, since any conservation plan is an experiment with an uncertain outcome, flexibility is required in implementing the management strategy over the years so that changes can be made. As Egler said, "Ecosystems are not only more complex than we think, but more complex than we *can* think."

These are the scientific principles driving the Endangered Spaces campaign. If they are followed, we believe these underlying technical ideas could go a long way to protecting the natural landscapes which touch the heart and shape the psyche of Canadians. In the face of uncertainty over details, the prudent course is to risk erring on the side of protecting too much. Options for land and water conservation, once lost, cannot easily be regained. As many ecologists have concluded, what we can accomplish through protected-areas planning in the next decade or two may well determine how much biodiversity persists over the next hundreds, thousands, or even millions of years.

2 / Marine Protected Areas

CHERI RECCHIA AND JOHN BROADHEAD

From space, an astronaut gazing down at the Earth can't help but marvel at the abundance of water. Oceans and seas cover almost three-quarters of its surface. Twelve billion cubic metres of water, vaporized by the Sun's energy, swirl and stream within planetary weather systems that envelop whole hemispheres. Molecules of water, lifted from the surface of the South Pacific, fall as snow on Canada, and melt into rivers draining vast landscapes of forest, tundra, prairie, and mountain.

With three large oceanic shorelines, Canada has the longest coastline and second-largest continental shelf of any country in the world. We are also blessed with some of the largest freshwater lakes and rivers. Ironically, the sheer size of our marine environments may have contributed greatly to their degradation. We have thought of our oceans, lakes, and rivers as endless in their ability to provide us with food and other resources, and in their capacity to absorb our wastes.

Canada is certainly not the sole or worst offender in this regard; but neither have we a record of which to be proud. Some fish stocks in the Northeast Atlantic are among the most depleted in the world, in part a result of overfishing by Canadians. The northern cod have been fished to the brink of extinction, when once they were so numerous they impeded the passage of sailing ships. But despite increasing evidence of degradation — polluted fish and shellfish, garbage-strewn shores, and plummeting fish populations — we still resist the idea that we have truly damaged our marine and aquatic environments. On the Pacific coast, the blame for millions of "missing" salmon is laid by each user group on the others, and the phenomenon is more comfortably attributed to circumstances beyond our control than to human mismanagement. At first glance, the shimmering waters of Lake Erie give little evidence that we have so polluted the Great Lakes and St. Lawrence River that fish and beluga whales are riddled with tumours, and human health is threatened.

Since 1989, the World Wildlife Fund (WWF) has been urging a fundamental change in attitudes and actions concerning the use of our lands and waters. We have called for a two-pronged approach to safeguarding our natural heritage: establishment of protected areas that represent the natural diversity of our lands and waters, and environmentally responsible use of the remaining land and seascapes. On land, the campaign has made progress, although slowly. On water, progress in protecting our marine and aquatic natural regions has been virtually non-existent.

Responsibility for protecting representative marine ecosystems is shared by federal, territorial, provincial, and aboriginal governments. Regrettably, most have been slow to even acknowledge their responsibility. The federal and B.C. governments have developed ecological classification systems for establishing representative marine protected areas, but the few areas designated to date are small-scale recreation sites that do little to conserve the larger marine environment. Other provincial and territorial governments have made little or no measurable progress in establishing marine protected areas. Not one of the commitments to marine protected areas made by any government since the launch of the Endangered Spaces campaign has been fulfilled.

Why has there been so little progress? The answers can be grouped into three broad categories: public attitudes and perceptions, scientific uncertainty, and jurisdictional and legal issues.

OUT OF SIGHT, OUT OF MIND

One of the major obstacles to safeguarding our marine environment is the depth of our ignorance about it. Most Canadians know the oceans only from the shore, or perhaps occasionally from a boat. From this perspective, the seas can appear deceptively featureless, homogeneous, even lifeless. Most of us have learned what we do know from watching television programs. So we are aware to some extent that there is another world beneath the waves, but our sensory experience is limited mostly to catching or eating fish, and perhaps taking a vacation to see whales and seabirds. A lucky few may have snorkled, although likely in the southern oceans during our winter. Our country's dizzying array of plants and fish, and the ecological processes that sustain them, remain largely unknown to us.

Because we're less attuned to the marine environment, we're less aware of changes, and signs of degradation. Somehow we have missed or ignored the signals that we must protect the oceans and their inhabitants, despite the fact that the future of entire fishing economies and the survival of Native cultures are at stake. Today, indications of declines in marine-life abundance and of widespread environmental damage are reported frequently and are becoming more dramatic. Those Canadians who have noticed have called on governments to take action. Yet, nowhere in this country have the political commitments prompted by such calls been converted into actual protection of any significant marine ecosystems.

Slowing, and ultimately reversing, this trend will require a massive improvement in our understanding of marine and aquatic environments. We need to make a collective effort to educate ourselves about the diverse habitats and biological communities that surround and sustain us, as well as the effects of our activities upon them. And it will take a significant shift in the focus of our political decision makers — away from simply allocating the economic pie, and onto the level of protection that ecosystems and economies need to survive. In the end, Canada "from sea to shining sea" cannot sustain itself without healthy and productive marine and aquatic environments.

THE SCIENTIFIC-UNCERTAINTY FACTOR

Other authors in this book describe the necessity of basing conservation efforts on science, of using our best understanding of how ecosystems function to guide decisions about what places to protect and about land-use policies in adjacent areas.

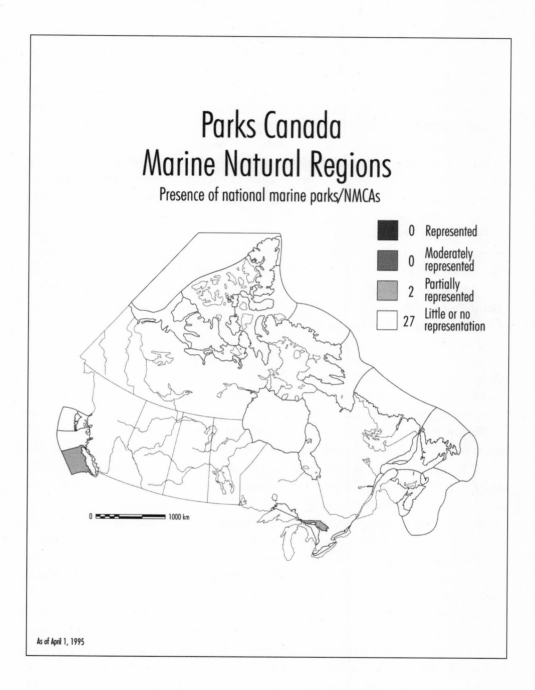

Parks Canada
Marine Natural Regions
Presence of national marine parks/NMCAs

0 Represented

0 Moderately represented

2 Partially represented

27 Little or no representation

0 ▰▱▰▱▰▱▰ 1000 km

As of April 1, 1995

The very same arguments apply to marine conservation. But because we know far less about marine ecosystems than terrestrial ones, arguments are often mustered against establishing marine protected areas based on this scientific uncertainty: "We don't know where to put marine protected areas, or how big they should be, or how many we need."

This is not sufficient reason for further delay. We do know enough to take the first steps now. For example, we understand the fundamental differences between marine and terrestrial ecosystems. Marine ecosystems are generally much larger than their land-based counterparts. They are made up of both fixed habitats, such as reefs, and mobile habitats, such as water masses that contain travelling biological communities.

Of particular importance for conservation is the way ocean ecosystems are connected. On land, a protected area can become an isolated "island of green" unless special provisions are made for corridors and linkages to other protected areas. As the preceding chapter described, maintaining this connectivity is crucial for maintaining the biological diversity of terrestrial ecosystems. In the sea, conservation efforts face the opposite problem: the high degree of connectivity within oceans means that marine protected areas are especially vulnerable to "downstream effects." A carefully planned marine protected area may be devastated by pollutants entering the water hundreds or thousands of kilometres away. Schools of juvenile salmon can vanish from an estuary because of fishing in the open ocean or because of logging debris that smothers distant spawning habitat. Destruction in one place can go a long way in the water.

But there are also conservation benefits to this connectivity. A protected spawning ground or ocean reef can act as a "seed bank," with larval fishes and invertebrates, such as scallops and lobsters, dispersing from the protected area into surrounding regions. So, protection in the right place can go a long way too!

We know other ways in which marine and terrestrial ecosystems differ, and future research will doubtless reveal many more. Our conservation efforts must recognize these differences; for example, by making marine protected areas generally larger than terrestrial ones, and by providing buffer zones and other means of guarding against downstream effects.

Marine conservation programs can also benefit from considering the similarities between marine and terrestrial ecosystems. For instance, the gap-analysis technique which WWF uses to assess ecological representation in protected areas is based on the relationship between the physical (enduring features) and biological (flora and fauna) components of an ecosystem. By analysing the physical features of a terrestrial ecosystem, such as climate, topographic relief, and soil type, we can to some extent predict the kinds of plants and animals that live within it. Ecological studies of marine environments have revealed analogous relationships between physical and biological components. Physical characteristics — water depth, bottom type (sandy or rocky), salinity, temperature, and current — partially determine what kinds of organisms live in a marine ecosystem. As on land, protecting a diversity of physical habitats or enduring features will also protect a diversity of biological communities.

WWF is adapting the technique of terrestrial, landscape-level gap analysis for application to the design of marine protected areas. Because the data available on the physical characteristics of our marine and Great Lakes environments are limited, marine gap analysis is less sophisticated than our terrestrial methodology. Nevertheless, it is also based on the concept of "enduring features" and is applied at a "seascape" level. Although it does not give precise answers to questions such as exactly where protected areas should be located, or how big they should be, or how many we need, it does provide a viable framework for beginning to establish a system of ecologically representative marine protected areas.

The benefits of a systematic approach are fourfold. First, protecting representative examples of many different marine habitats will help safeguard various life stages of many marine species. Even highly mobile species such as cod or whales will benefit from the elevated levels of protection afforded them as they travel through various conservation areas.

Second, assuming that all habitat types (or marine enduring features) are equally worthy of protection means that we don't have to rely on human judgments of which are "most important" and for which species. The representative approach thus helps compensate for our terrestrial bias and limited understanding of marine ecosystems.

Third, marine protected areas can serve as "control" areas for gauging the effects of human activities and environmental trends, such as global climate change, in relatively undisturbed marine habitats. For example, to assess the magnitude and persistence of the environmental effects of bottom-trawling in one habitat, we need to compare it to a similar habitat that has been left undisturbed.

Finally, a system of marine protected areas can be an excellent educational tool, providing a focus for recreational enjoyment, alerting people to the fragility and diversity of our marine environments, and building support for effective conservation programs.

There are, indeed, many scientific uncertainties about the structure and function of marine ecosystems, and about how best to establish and manage marine protected areas. Until we find the answers, we will have to rely on our best current understanding of the similarities and differences between the marine and terrestrial environments. *But let's get on with the job.*

JURISDICTIONAL INTERESTS AND LEGAL ISSUES

One last-ditch excuse for failing to establish marine protected areas is the complexity of jurisdictional interests and the current legislative/legal framework. With few exceptions, existing laws related to protected areas do not clearly or sufficiently extend to marine areas. For example, until 1986, Canada's National Parks Act made no mention of marine parks.

Federal and provincial or territorial legislation often coexist in coastal areas, blurring the lines of authority and diluting the burden of responsibility. The legislative gaps, uncertainties, and outright conflicts present complicated obstacles to the designation of marine protected areas. Conservationists have argued for over a decade that Canada needs to streamline and coordinate legislation to manage our marine environments effectively, including establishment of protected areas.

But we cannot afford to wait for new or amended legislation before proceeding; we must begin immediately to help compensate for years of neglect. Imperfect though the current legislation may be, it still contains sufficient legal mechanisms to begin designating protected areas and managing our activities in adjacent waters.

In much of Canada, a new yet historic jurisdictional interest is being reasserted: that of First Nations. In the North, treaties are already taking effect. In the not-so-distant past, Canada's oceans, lakes, and rivers were the sole domain of the First Nations, many of whom exercised hereditary and highly personal responsibilities for the precious ecosystems in their care. The federal government's inability to sustain important fish stocks has opened the door for First Nations to reassert time-tested principles of local stewardship over marine resources. In British Columbia, treaty negotiations with aboriginal people are just beginning to consider both freshwater and saltwater fisheries. It is hoped that this historical record of sound environmental stewardship can be revived and will result in effective marine conservation, including the establishment of marine protected areas.

DESIGNING MARINE PROTECTED AREAS

Thirty-five terrestrial national parks have been established across Canada, and the objectives of our National Parks Policy have grown beyond tourism development to include conservation and, most recently, maintenance of ecological integrity. By comparison, there is currently just one national marine park — Fathom Five in Lake Huron. A scattering of small provincial marine parks, migratory-bird sanctuaries, and other designations protect local marine features, but there are very few significant areas established and managed expressly for marine conservation.

The one and only advantage of starting from scratch is the opportunity to consider how a system of marine protected areas should be designed, based on our knowledge of marine ecology. Because marine ecosystems are generally bigger and more mobile than terrestrial ones, larger protected areas are likely to be more effective than smaller ones for maintaining species and ecological processes. To an even greater extent than for terrestrial protected areas, bigger is better.

This does not necessarily mean that we need large "off-limits to fishing" areas in our oceans and Great Lakes. Marine conservationists worldwide are increasingly advocating large, marine protected areas containing management zones in which human activities compatible with the conservation objectives of the area are permitted. Zoning is used to establish appropriate levels of protection in different parts of the protected area, and to separate mutually incompatible human activities. For instance, in a coastal protected area, core zones could be designated to protect a fragile salt marsh or a shellfish bed. In less sensitive parts of the protected area, one zone may be established for scuba diving and non-extractive activities, and another zone for fishing. This would allow both divers and fishers to use parts of the protected area, while ensuring divers are not snagged by fish hooks. A zone can be either seasonal — for example, to protect a spawning ground during spawning season — or year-round.

One example of this concept is called a Marine Biosphere Reserve. Biosphere reserves have three types of zones: core zones, buffers, and transition zones. Core zones provide a high level of protection to particularly sensitive parts of the ecosystem, such as spawning grounds, reefs, or upwelling areas. Buffer zones are established to protect core areas from deleterious human activities nearby. The outermost transition zone is the least protected part of a biosphere reserve and is the zone where the greatest level of human activity occurs. The key to this approach is tailoring the management of the entire area to protect ecosystem functions, rather than just individual species or stocks. (Ecosystem functions include physical processes, such as sediments and nutrients flowing from a river into the sea, and biological events, such as spawnings and migrations.)

The size and configuration of a candidate protected area should be based on an ecosystem perspective, with critical system functions and linkages afforded maximum protection. Our current knowledge of marine ecosystems allows at least preliminary identification of such critical ecological components, particularly in the coastal zone, where estuaries, salt marshes, and other shallow waters provide critical spawning and rearing habitats for a great many fish species. The design of protected areas must incorporate this knowledge, and must also take a precautionary approach, erring on the side of conservation to compensate for our limited understanding and for unpredictable environmental changes.

Zoning multiple-function protected areas does require fairly complex management plans and regulatory frameworks. However, the alternative approach — namely, protected areas with uniform restrictions — has at least two disadvantages. First, the size of the area will inevitably be traded off against the level of protection — the resulting area will tend to be either highly protected and small (a "no-take" zone) or large but lacking any meaningful protection. Second, managing a protected area as a homogeneous unit is inconsistent with our understanding of marine ecosystems; we know, for example, that certain ecological features and processes are more vulnerable than others, and therefore management of a protected area should reflect this. Perhaps the most famous example of a zoned marine protected area is the Great Barrier Reef Marine Park in Australia, which, at nearly 350,000 square kilometres, is one of the largest marine protected areas in the world. In the United States, the draft management plan for the 9600-square-kilometre Florida Keys National Marine Sanctuary proposes a variety of different zones, covering a broad range of protected levels. This will be the first of the U.S. National Marine Sanctuaries to employ zoning. These and other examples offer Canadians the opportunity to examine and learn from experiences elsewhere.

Once a marine protected area is established, a comprehensive management plan for human activities is essential. Activities compatible with the conservation objectives of the entire reserve would obviously be permitted within some or all zones. Although we have little data on the specific environmental impacts of most of our marine activities, some are known or suspected to cause large-scale, long-term habitat disruption. These activities, which include non-renewable resource exploration and extraction (e.g., underwater mining), large-scale dredging, dumping, and bottom trawling or dragging, should be prohibited, certainly within core zones and likely throughout marine protected areas. Such exclusions are analogous to our "no logging, mining, or hydro-electric development" approach in terrestrial reserves. Other activities should be considered on a case-by-case basis. It is also important that management plans allow for regular evaluation and modification as we gain experience and understanding of each area.

It [the national marine protected areas system] is not moving forward fast enough, and somehow or other we've got to persuade the people who take decisions that they have simply got to get on with it before it is too late.
PRINCE PHILIP, 1993

The time is past for polite discussions on marine protected area policy. In Atlantic Canada the scale of the marine conservation tragedy requires unprecedented action to identify areas requiring protection . . . . Similar action must be taken on our other coasts and in the Great Lakes to avoid further crises. We must urgently proceed to protect and represent our marine natural regions under the variety of legislation available.
JON LIEN, Memorial University, Newfoundland, 1993

NEXT STEPS

Across Canada, public awareness and concern are mounting over the degradation of our marine environments. Whatever the excuses offered for our failure to establish marine protected areas, they must now be firmly put aside. As with any big job, the key is to proceed one step at a time. Here, then, are a few next steps.

1. *Get going!* Marine protected-area initiatives are under way for each ocean, as well as for the Great Lakes and St. Lawrence waterway. These include: Gwaii Haanas in Haida Gwaii off the British Columbia coast; Igalirtuuq National Wildlife Area off Baffin Island in the Northwest Territories; West Isles National Marine Park in the Bay of Fundy in New Brunswick; and Saguenay–St. Lawrence Marine Park in Quebec. If governments completed the designation of these specific areas, they would establish a "psychology of success" by demonstrating the feasibility of establishing conservation-based marine protected areas, by providing models for new initiatives, and by building momentum for expansion of the system.

2. *Plan the work, and work the plan.* Establishing a system of representative marine protected areas requires planning, such as developing a natural-regions framework and defining criteria for representation. To date, only the federal and B.C. governments have taken this first step. The remaining provincial and territorial governments could begin with one of these schemes and adapt it for their own marine regions. Once the basic plan is in place, a timetable for site-level action must follow. The federal government promised in the 1990 Green Plan to establish six new national marine conservation areas by the year 2000. The succeeding government promised to accelerate the pace. These commitments must be met, if not exceeded, if we hope to create an effective system of protected areas.

3. *Make the tools fit the job.* Current legislation, while imperfect, can nonetheless be used to designate marine protected areas. On the federal level, the National Parks Act, the Canada Wildlife Act, and the Fisheries Act provide adequate authority. New legislation currently under development, such as a National Marine Conservation Areas Act and a Canada Oceans Act, should accommodate the specific needs of marine conservation programs, and should integrate protected areas within a larger planning framework or "sea use" policy. In B.C., treaty negotiations with First Nations could readily address core zones, buffers, and transition zones in proposed marine protected areas.

The goal of the Endangered Spaces marine campaign is to get at least one-third of Canada's marine and Great Lakes natural regions adequately represented by the year

2000, with a completed system of protected areas in place by 2010. The specifics for getting started in each jurisdiction are described in Section Two of this book.

To accomplish our goal, we will have to reach out to those with a common interest, get organized, then work together. The stakes are high, and it will not be easy to overcome the obstacles raised by commercial interests or to break through the political foot-dragging. But conservationists, fishing interests, shippers, government agencies, and concerned communities, will all have to find a way to raise marine conservation high on the political agenda, then keep it there until the job is done. Our marine heritage is rapidly deteriorating, and the biological legacy we will pass on to future generations of Canadians is hanging in the balance.

3 / Aboriginal Interests

JIM MORRISON

The preamble to the Canadian Wilderness Charter states: ". . . Canada's aboriginal peoples hold deep and direct ties to wilderness areas throughout Canada and seek to maintain options for traditional wilderness use . . ." This eloquent wording suggests that conservationists and aboriginal people share common objectives with regard to protected areas.

But, as Georges Erasmus points out in his contribution to the book *Endangered Spaces*, aboriginal interests are not identical to those of the conservation community. For the Native leadership, wilderness protection is only one part of a larger political question — one "bound up with the thorny issues of treaty rights, aboriginal title, and land claims."

Since the publication of *Endangered Spaces*, the broader implications of aboriginal political goals have caused cracks in the façade of common interests. Should Native rights take precedence over wilderness protection, or vice versa? What would happen, some environmental activists ask, if aboriginal people gained title to old-growth forests and then decided to log these areas themselves?

Nowhere has the issue been debated with more fervour than in Ontario. In 1991, the province entered into negotiations with the Lac la Croix Ojibway of northwestern Ontario, who were seeking increased motorized access to Quetico Provincial Park for fishing purposes. Many of the perceived differences between a conservationist view of protected areas and one based on aboriginal rights were summarized in an exchange of correspondence about Quetico in the *Globe and Mail*. On May 18, 1992, journalist Robert Reguly accused the Ontario government of giving the Lac la Croix Ojibway privileges which violated the park's status as a protected area. Like many wilderness advocates, he particularly objected to opening up the park to motorized travel.

Law professor Kent McNeil was quick to respond. He argued that the creation of Quetico Park had actually violated an 1873 treaty with the local Ojibway by excluding them from hunting and fishing within park boundaries. Canadians, he said, ought to reflect on the fact that only 0.3 per cent of the country had been set aside for indigenous people. "I am not against the creation of parks or wilderness areas, but surely the few rights the aboriginal people have left should take precedence over the pleasure of canoeists and campers."

This was too much for Kenneth G. Beattie of Toronto. Accusing Professor McNeil of shallow thinking on aboriginal rights, he insisted that the Lac la Croix people simply wanted expanded access to the park because they had depleted fish stocks elsewhere. Treaties, he argued, should be interpreted in the light of modern principles of resource management — for "uncontrolled exploitation of natural resources results in the destruction of those resources, regardless of the racial origin of the exploiters."

These positions have major consequences for the Endangered Spaces campaign. WWF's visionary goal of increasing the number of protected areas in all of Canada's natural regions will inevitably be caught up in the constitutional crossfire over aboriginal self-government. Not only are some proposed areas likely to fall under Native jurisdiction, but more and more existing parks and protected areas throughout the country will become the subject of claims to aboriginal or treaty rights. Sorting out these questions of jurisdiction and title could slow governmental action on new protected areas — and make it that much more difficult to complete the *Endangered Spaces* agenda by the year 2000.

Will the differences between conservationists and aboriginal people make it impossible to ensure the protection of vanishing wildlife and wilderness areas? The short answer is that there is already a great deal of common ground. In various parts of the country, especially the Far North, there have been many recent examples of cooperation among aboriginal people, conservationists, and different levels of government with respect to protected areas. These could serve as a model for future joint action.

But before looking at those examples, we need to examine what Erasmus calls "the profound philosophical cleavage in cultural points of view between indigenous and non-indigenous people in Canada." These differences have a history. If they are not understood, long-dormant hostilities could overwhelm efforts on both sides to protect endangered spaces.

A WILDERNESS ETHIC

Although there is no single definition of wilderness, many conservationists would acknowledge the philosophy expressed by American naturalist John Muir. He argued that there had to be spaces free from urbanization and industrial development, where the human species could recognize its own insignificance and retain a sense of awe at the wonders of creation.

Muir was reacting to the modern concept of nature as an enormous reservoir of energy and resources that the human race can exploit with impunity. In this, he had much in common with the views of indigenous societies, who have consistently placed mankind in a subservient position to the rest of creation. To aboriginal people, the idea that humans are a superior species which can dominate the natural world is blasphemous.

But, despite their apparent similarity, there are fundamental differences between the ways indigenous people and most conservationists view nature. A major part of the conservation movement sees the human species as an intruder, not as a part of the natural world. Protected-area management on this continent has tended to reflect that philosophy. Canada's National Parks Policy, for example, speaks of protecting and managing natural resources in parks "to ensure the perpetuation of naturally evolving land and water environments and their associated species." The term "associated species" does not necessarily include humans.

By contrast, indigenous societies place mankind at the axis of the natural world — subordinate to the whole, but essential. To aboriginal people, wilderness, in the sense of areas "untrammelled by man," does not exist. Even the wildest parts of this country are far from being empty spaces. They are occupied by indigenous people on the basis of detailed knowledge going back hundreds, even thousands, of years. Graves and habitation sites dot the landscape. Mountains and hills, lakes and streams, trails and portages — all have names and legends associated with them.

At the core of the indigenous people's relationship with nature is a reciprocal connection with the plant and animal world. Because of this, many aboriginal people share with conservationists what can reasonably be called a wilderness ethic. A clear, deep, spring-fed lake is valued as highly by an Ojicree trapper in northeastern Manitoba as it is by a recreational canoeist from Winnipeg. And an eagle is as worthy of respect and awe — both for its innate beauty and for its connection with the thunderbird of Native legend. In aboriginal communities across Canada, physical well-being is closely associated with nature. "Country food," such as wild fish and game, is uniformly perceived as healthy; store-bought food as unhealthy.

Like many indigenous leaders today, Erasmus insists that Native peoples "have a keen interest in preserving areas as close as possible to their original state." Without renewable resources to harvest, he says, aboriginal people lose both their livelihood and their way of life.

In one important respect, however, the subsistence economy is anything but traditional. Native people everywhere now use outboard motors, and snowmobiles or all-terrain vehicles in their hunting and fishing activities, much as in earlier generations they adopted canvas canoes in place of bark or skin boats. Indigenous people, then, do not share the antipathy felt by many in the conservation community towards technology — including mechanized forms of wilderness travel — because boats or snowmobiles are not really used for recreation. These modern devices simply make it easier to earn a living.

For their part, conservationists raise legitimate fears about the long-term effects of new technology on wildlife survival. This is the real nub of much of the current conflict between the two sides. Do modern methods, by making them easier to harvest, threaten or eliminate wildlife species?

Despite such questions, aboriginal people are only a small part of the perceived problem. Most of the anger and frustration voiced by conservationists is related to the diminishing supply of wild places throughout Canada. Urbanization is an obvious target. In much of southern Ontario, to give the most prominent example, there is no longer sufficient wild country to allow for the creation of fully representative protected areas.

Aboriginal people have not responded directly to many of these issues or questions. Instead, they have tended to concentrate on issues of title and rights. Their experience with parks and protected areas, as well as with fish and wildlife regulations, has made many of them deeply sceptical of both government and the conservation movement. Too often over the past century, say Native leaders, governments have either ignored or violated their aboriginal and treaty rights — sometimes at the urging of conservationists.

FORMATIVE NATIVE VIEWS ON PARKS AND PROTECTED AREAS

In the same year that Algonquin Provincial Park became Ontario's first genuine protected area — 1893 — the administrative head of the Crown Lands Department received a report from a fire ranger on the Petawawa River. He had spotted several Indians setting up camp within the new park, where they intended to hunt and trap; already, he said, they had moose meat, and beaver and otter pelts in their possession.

In reply to the report, Assistant Commissioner Aubrey White acknowledged that aboriginal interests were not among those considered by his government when the park reserve was being created. But he decided that it was far too late to make any special exceptions for Indians. He instructed his officials to explain to the people concerned — as carefully and tactfully as possible — that hunting and trapping were no longer permitted within the boundaries of Algonquin Park.

In fact, the creation of most early protected areas in North America involved the exclusion of aboriginal people. The most obvious example is Yellowstone National Park — that famous tract of hot springs and geysers in northwestern Wyoming. The park was established by Congress in 1872, during the post–Civil War campaign to subdue the Sioux and other plains tribes. The inhabitants of Yellowstone — mainly Crows and Shoshones — either left for reservations or were driven out by the U.S. Army.

In Canada, the boundaries of the 1877 Treaty Number 7, by which the Siksika (Blackfoot) and Nakoda (Stoney) tribes ceded much of southwestern Alberta to the Crown, extend into the Rockies. Although the treaty stipulated that participants could continue to hunt over the ceded tract, the federal government decided that this guarantee would not apply to Banff National Park when it was established in 1885. Aboriginal interests were also ignored when Riding Mountain National Park was established in southwestern Manitoba in 1933. The Keeseekoowenen Band were evicted, and their houses burned.

Provincial governments behaved no differently. Quetico became a provincial park in 1913. Since protection of game was the park's chief objective, the Ontario government forbade local Ojibway to hunt or trap within park boundaries. As well, park fishing licences prohibited the use of nets or spears, the usual Native fishing techniques at that time. In 1925, Ontario banned all hunting and trapping within the Chapleau Crown Game Preserve, a tract of several thousand hectares in northern Ontario, which was used by local Ojibway and Cree.

The postwar period saw an exponential increase in the number of protected areas across the country. But the various jurisdictions were no more solicitous of aboriginal interests than their predecessors had been. Tweedsmuir Provincial Park in B.C. was created despite a long-standing Native claim to portions of land within its boundaries. And both Bruce Peninsula National Park and Fathom Five National Marine Park in Ontario include lands and waters which have been claimed by the Saugeen and Cape Croker First Nations since the nineteenth century.

In 1974, the National Parks Act was amended to recognize aboriginal hunting, fishing, and trapping in parks north of the sixtieth parallel. With the exception of Pukaskwa in Ontario, the same recognition has not been extended to southern properties. Until recently, provincial jurisdictions have refused for the most part to consider such Native access to parks and protected areas.

North American parks and protected areas have generally been created in the name of the "public interest." Most conservationists fully support this concept, insisting that it is a governmental responsibility to protect significant regions of the country for the benefit of future generations. Aboriginal people, however, dispute the inclusiveness of the term "public." In their view, it automatically places the interests of the general society above those of minorities.

It is fair to say, therefore, that indigenous people have borne the costs of protecting natural areas, through the loss of access for hunting, trapping, and other harvesting activities. As Erasmus puts it, the doctrine of the public interest made "an ancient way of life subject to the apparent modern-day whims of an alien culture, all in the name of conservation."

Conservationists argue that the fundamental choice was never between protected areas and aboriginal interests, but rather between protection and industrial development. If anything, they say, the situation would have been infinitely worse without the skilled political lobbying of conservation groups. The damage to the habitat of the fish and wildlife sought by aboriginal people would have been that much more severe.

LAND-CLAIMS SETTLEMENTS AND PROTECTED AREAS

In Canada's north, the federal government has been negotiating with various Native organizations for the surrender of aboriginal title under its "comprehensive claims" policy. As the results of these negotiations become known, it is clear that land-claims settlements have provided a major vehicle for expanding the network of protected areas.

Inuvialuit Claim   In 1984, Canada reached a land-claims settlement with the Inuvialuit, the Inuit inhabitants of the western Arctic. In July 1992, an agreement was reached to establish a new national park on Banks Island. This had long been a goal of Parks Canada. The stated purpose of the park is to protect a representative natural area in the Western Arctic Lowlands and "leave it unimpaired for future generations while permitting subsistence usage and trapping by Inuvialuit."

The agreement gives the Inuvialuit exclusive rights to harvest wildlife in the park, and their fishing is given priority over sports angling. They will also have the power to screen archaeological research. The agreement recognizes the potential contribution by Inuvialuit traditional knowledge to planning and research. Other provisions give the Inuvialuit guarantees of employment and training, as well as priority in contracts and park business licences.

Conservation initiatives in the western Arctic are not limited to national park proposals. The Paulatuk community, for example, is now formally involved in managing the Bluenose caribou herd. And World Wildlife Fund Canada has been part of the Clyde River proposal for Igalirtuuq, a bowhead whale sanctuary at Isabella Bay on Baffin Island, based on the joint research of local people and WWF-funded scientists.

Yukon Claim   The long-standing land claims of Yukon Native people have basically been settled. An umbrella final agreement has been ratified by Canada and Native representatives, and First Nations final agreements are being implemented for Champagne and Aishihik, Nacho Nyak Dun (Mayo), Kluane, White River, and

Vuntut Gwitchin (Old Crow) First Nations.

The draft final agreements contain provisions for the creation of special management areas. These areas are to maintain important features of the Yukon's natural or cultural environment "for the benefit of Yukon residents and all Canadians while respecting the rights of Yukon Indian People and Yukon First Nations." They will include national wildlife areas, national parks or park reserves, territorial parks and national historic sites, special wildlife or fish management areas, migratory-bird or game sanctuaries, designated heritage sites, and watershed-protection areas.

Existing designated conservation areas will continue to be protected, though they will be identified as special management areas in accordance with the agreements. These include Kluane National Park Reserve, the McArthur Game Sanctuary, and the Horseshoe Slough Habitat Protection Area. Existing harvesting rights of Native people will be guaranteed.

The Inuit Tapirisat of Canada fully supports the national agenda for establishing protected areas by the year 2000. However, our support is contingent on this protection being achieved through a process that involves Inuit directly from the earliest stages through to completion. ROSEMARIE KUPTANA of the Inuit Tapirisat of Canada, speaking to the Tri-Council meeting in Aylmer, P.Q., November 25, 1992

Included in the final agreement with the Vuntut Gwitchin is the creation of Vuntut National Park. This park will protect a "representative natural area of national significance" in and around the Old Crow Flats wetlands and surrounding foothills, which encompass critical parts of the Porcupine caribou range.

As in the Banks Island park agreement, the Vuntut Gwitchin will receive priority in employment and contract tendering. One of the stated objectives of the Old Crow area park is to "recognize and protect the traditional and current use of the park by Vuntut Gwitchin in the development and management of the park." Among other reasons, the Old Crow people wanted acknowledgement that harvesting takes place using modern methods. They will have exclusive rights to hunt and trap in the park, and priority of access over sports fishermen. The Vuntut Gwitchin Renewable Resources Council will make recommendations to the Minister of Heritage Canada on routes, methods and modes of access for harvesting, harvest limits and seasons, and locations and methods of harvesting within the park. If, for example, use of all-terrain vehicles becomes an issue, the council provides the forum for resolving the matter. Nevertheless, the federal minister has ultimate authority to accept or vary the council's recommendations.

Inuit Claim Canada's land-claims agreement with the Inuit of the eastern Arctic and subarctic — through the Tungavik Federation of Nunavut (TFN) — has been ratified by both parties. The most publicized part of the agreement is Canada's stated intention to create a new government out of the eastern half of the Northwest Territories, to be known as Nunavut.

Various provisions of the TFN agreement concern the establishment of new protected areas; for example, three national parks, at Auyuittuq, North Baffin, and Ellesmere Island. It was the Inuit themselves who pushed for the creation of these protected spaces. Once again, there are provisions for Native employment and for preferential hiring and training.

There is . . . a need for an alliance between the First Nations and others who, for whatever reason, care enough for the "wilderness" to safeguard those areas for the benefit of all our succeeding generations on this planet, which we share.
GEORGES ERASMUS, National Chief, Assembly of First Nations, in *Endangered Spaces: The Future for Canada's Wilderness*, 1989

The Inuit will have exclusive harvesting rights and renewable-resource use within the parks. Any restrictions on the technology used in harvesting will require the consent of the Inuit themselves. The agreement talks about managing all resources, using both modern science and traditional knowledge.

The most interesting clause of the TFN agreement — one which does not appear in the other land-claims settlements — states that, prior to the establishment of any national park, an Inuit Impact/Benefit Agreement will have to be negotiated. From the Inuit perspective, this ensures that, because ultimate management authority will continue to reside with the Minister of Heritage Canada and Parks Canada, their rights will be respected in both park planning and management.

PROVINCIAL FERMENT: AN ONTARIO EXAMPLE

Ontario — where the names Temagami, Algonquin, and Quetico have made headlines — ranks next to British Columbia in controversy over wilderness values, parks, and protected areas.

In September 1991, Premier Bob Rae formally signed a Statement of Political Relationship with representatives of Ontario aboriginal organizations. In keeping with the principles of this statement, Ontario has announced that the "creation of all new provincial parks and protected natural heritage areas will respect all treaty and aboriginal rights." A consultation process has been undertaken to that end.

How the consultation will work out in practice is still unclear. Relations in the past between parks personnel and the Native community have ranged from cool to hostile. Although some aboriginal people have been employed within the system, Ontario is typical of the provinces in never having acknowledged treaty or aboriginal rights to harvest wildlife within parks. In the remote north of Ontario, it is government policy, not legal recognition, that has permitted Native hunting and trapping.

Aboriginal people are already demanding access to existing parks for subsistence pursuits and community purposes. The ministers of Natural Resources and Native Affairs, however, have publicly assured conservationists that certain wilderness or conservation values will be protected in any settlements with aboriginal people.

At the 1992 Tri-Council meeting of all ministers of parks, wildlife, and environment, then Natural Resources minister Bud Wildman announced the creation of several new provincial parks and the enlargement of others, as part of Ontario's commitment to the goals of the Endangered Spaces program. His statement also reassured aboriginal people that their interests would be considered before any final decisions were taken.

THE WAY FORWARD

Regardless of its exact contours, a new level of authority — Native self-government — is being created in Canada. When it is complete, the aboriginal people of Canada will arguably have more powers than any other indigenous group in the world. The recognition of their inherent right to self-government is a crucial goal for aboriginal people. It is part of their path to self-respect and community control. This explains the frequent insistence by aboriginal leaders that talks now be conducted with them on a "government to government" basis.

The combination, therefore, of self-government initiatives, the settlement of Native claims, and constitutional recognition of treaty and aboriginal rights will have an obvious impact on both the Endangered Spaces campaign and on protected-area management in general. As we have seen, this has already happened in some areas — particularly those under federal jurisdiction. The results in the Yukon and Northwest Territories have been generally positive. Both Canada and aboriginal groups have agreed to provide for new protected areas as part of land-claims settlements. The Inuvialuit, Inuit, and other groups have also ensured that their interests, including employment opportunities and cultural survival through continued harvesting rights, are met.

We should look at this whole world that we live on as being a protected area. It's only through that kind of thinking, all as one people, that we are going to have a land seventy-five years from now that our grandchildren, our great-grandchildren, will have to live on.
MARY JANE JOHNSON, Kluane First Nation, 1994

Within the provinces, however, the situation is much more problematic. It has been hard enough to reach land-claims settlements between aboriginal people and the federal government. The addition of the provinces and private or third-party interests makes agreements that much more difficult. And, in provinces like Ontario, the hostility of angler and hunter groups to treaty and aboriginal rights has greatly complicated the task.

Virtually all of British Columbia is subject to Native claims of one sort or another. The same is true of large portions of Québec and the Maritimes, which also have few, if any, treaties with their Native inhabitants. The Prairie provinces are blanketed with claims based on treaty entitlement. Some lands with conservation potential may well be selected by First Nations as reserve lands. In Alberta and Manitoba, claims have been advanced to parcels of existing national parks. Ontario, too, has outstanding claims issues.

Obviously, in much of the country, it is the Native political agenda that will influence protected-area programs, not the other way around. In northern Québec, for example, the Cree are interested in park proposals because they see them as one means of permanently halting the James Bay II hydro-electric project. If parks or protected areas will prevent further development on rivers leading to the bay, then they are in favour of them.

In other regions of the country, it is possible that the claims process will slow, rather than speed up, progress towards the year 2000 target date for the Endangered Spaces program. This has certainly been happening in Ontario, where tensions between aboriginal groups and environmentalists are rising, as each side pursues its own goals.

These tensions flow from fundamentally differing viewpoints, as is highlighted in the exchange of letters in the *Globe and Mail* with which we began. However, so long as these arguments pit Native subsistence against the recreational needs of an urbanized society, aboriginal people will always have the moral upper hand. Indeed, their message to conservationists is that, without respect for existing treaty and aboriginal rights, new conservation agreements will not be possible. They will no longer allow their rights to be sacrificed on the altar of some larger public interest. In the planning of new protected areas, aboriginal people also expect to be involved from the very beginning. They want protected-area managers to realize that their participation in planning and management is not a threat, but a guarantee of their own livelihood and a positive contribution to the preservation of wild spaces.

Conservationists and aboriginal people should not always be expected to agree on goals or tactics. What is needed is respect for alternative positions so that gains can be realized. While the two sides may differ on their ultimate objectives, they do have common interests. To paraphrase a popular saying used by aboriginal leaders, both groups do not have to travel in the same canoe. But they can certainly share a waterway — and even arrive at a common destination.

4 / Business, Economics, and the Wise-Use Movement

MONTE HUMMEL

The Endangered Spaces campaign has simultaneously attracted some of its strongest support and its most bitter opposition from members of the Canadian business community.

If nothing else, this may indicate that business is not some monolithic entity, but a part of Canadian society made up of diverse individuals and economic interests. Some of them clearly feel threatened by the goals of the campaign, some do not. Others, far from feeling threatened, believe their future is closely tied to its success. As a result, rather than assume that everyone in business is either for or against us, WWF has deliberately chosen to recognize this diversity, by actively taking on our critics, and by drawing support — both financial and moral — from those who are with us.

At this point, lest the tough-minded reader anticipate some syrupy rhetoric about "all of us really sharing the same objectives" or "environment and the economy simply being opposite sides of the same coin," it is important to clarify the extent to which the Endangered Spaces agenda truly does challenge the status quo. It does this, first and foremost, by requiring that some things be left alone. It suggests that some things have value in a natural state, not only because a growing number of people want them that way, but also because they have worth in and of themselves, regardless of the value we humans place on them.

For some people, this premise amounts to a needless waste of otherwise useful natural resources which could and should serve as stock or inventory for industry. For others, such a viewpoint is out-and-out heresy which flies in the face of such sacred cows as economic growth, technological innovation, and human progress. They have accused wilderness advocates of being everything from left-wing "Neo-Luddites" who want to throw modern society back into some primitive pre–high-tech state, to right-wing misanthropes, and even "Neo-fascists" who care more about trees than people.

These are strong words, indicating strong reactions to what at first blush seemed a relatively harmless idea: to simply leave some things alone, more specifically, to reserve large ecologically self-sufficient, representative samples of our lands and waters, and let them change at the hand of nature. This idea stands uncompromised, and continues to drive the Endangered Spaces campaign.

Now, lest the fair-minded reader suspect some cynical anti-business polemic, it is important to give examples of how business people have rallied to our cause.

Canadians still have a chance to complete the network of protected areas which represent the tremendous biological diversity of this country. . . . The federal government, the private sector and the public at large (should) work cooperatively to establish a system of protected areas . . . to represent all natural regions of Canada by early in the new century.
THE CANADIAN CHAMBER OF COMMERCE, 1990

After all, WWF Canada was founded in 1967 by prominent members of the business community, in partnership with leading scientists from across the country. Both groups shared a concern about Canada's environment at a time when there was no Department of the Environment or Environmental Protection Act. Since then, more than 500 Canadian corporations have financially supported our work, and more than 100 business men and women have provided volunteer leadership to WWF Canada by serving on its board.

As far as the Endangered Spaces campaign is concerned, it has been supported by two successive resolutions passed in 1991 and 1993 by the Canadian Chamber of Commerce, whose membership, as one would expect, is broadly representative of the business community. Our goal has also been supported by the Canadian Bar Association, not exactly an anti-business crowd. Financial supporters have included more than twenty of the country's blue-chip companies and a dozen private foundations. To date, their combined financial commitments to the Endangered Spaces campaign exceeds $5 million.

In addition to financial support, we know of many occasions when moral suasion has been exercised on our behalf. Some of our corporate supporters have questioned their peers about their environmental practices, some have openly refused to join coalitions organized to defend indefensible industry practices, some have gone to bat for us by advocating change in their own business sector, some have accompanied us to lobby politicians, some have risked losing business because of their support, some have backed controversial local activist projects, and virtually all of them at one time or another have had to answer tough questions about why they have decided to plant their flag on our side of the fence.

This kind of support goes far beyond "green-washing," or simply trying to get as much public-relations mileage as possible out of appearing to be a "good corporate citizen." The fact is that many influential members of the Canadian business community believe in the Endangered Spaces goal every bit as much as do those of us on the front lines.

Such support has not compromised the campaign in any way, but it does bring with it a responsibility on our part to do our homework, to be sure of our numbers, and to be sensitive and sensible with people who stand to be affected negatively by our agenda. Fair enough.

Business support is an element of the Endangered Spaces campaign, which, as far as we know, makes the campaign unique in the world. Certainly it has surprised and earned some envy from wilderness advocates in the United States. It's one thing to rally support from kindred spirits, the kinds of groups and individuals that would normally be *expected* to back such a campaign; it's quite another to rally support from unexpected quarters.

Finally, strong business support allows us to respond to critics from the business community by suggesting that perhaps *they* are the ones who are out of step when so many of their colleagues have come aboard. This support should not be attributed strictly to the persuasive abilities of those of us leading the campaign; rather, it is a tribute to the far-sighted nature of our business partners, and the degree to which they have been willing to stand and be counted.

ECONOMICS

Despite the power and pervasiveness of economic analysis today most of us still resist the thought that absolutely everything can be reduced to a matter of dollars and cents. Drafting the Canadian Wilderness Charter was an interesting case in point.

The idea behind the charter was to produce as inspiring a document as possible. It would first be signed by all twenty-one authors of the 1989 *Endangered Spaces* book, then taken to the streets as a kind of petition for signature by Canadians in general. The charter begins with a number of different reasons or motivations for protecting wilderness (see page xii). In anticipation of being asked to sign the charter, some of the original authors warned that, if the document included all kinds of hard-nosed, utilitarian, economic reasons for protecting wilderness, they would not sign. In their view, it was the spiritual, aesthetic, and emotional arguments that really moved people. Other authors indicated that, if the document simply waxed inspirational with all the poetic arguments for preserving wilderness, *they* would not sign! They felt that tough economic arguments were needed to move decision makers and advance the agenda in practical terms. As a compromise, both sides agreed (a) to sign if the arguments that appealed to them were included and (b) not to worry if other points of view were there as well.

This experience nicely demonstrates both the power and the weakness of economic arguments. They turn some people off, and some people on. However, even non-believers would likely agree that, in today's economic climate, any cause ignores economic arguments at its peril. As a result, in September 1993, WWF Canada produced a discussion paper called *The Economic Benefits of Conserving Canada's Endangered Spaces*, which is now available as part of a series of Endangered Spaces publications.

What became clear from this paper is what economists have long (and somewhat smugly) argued: that people who value wilderness from a spiritual, artistic, or even scientific perspective are often the ones willing to pay a great deal for it, precisely because they *do* place a high value on it. Furthermore, when asked to give up wilderness, Canadians are entitled to ask for a convincing argument indicating that the full range of economic benefits wilderness provides are outweighed by the economic benefits associated with its loss. In most cases, we hear only the latter.

On the first point — what people are willing to pay for wilderness — the data are strong enough that we and other wilderness advocates should feel confident about our economic arguments. In fact, more times than we realize, we have an overwhelming case, and we should be much more aggressive in making it. For example, a 1987 study by StatsCan called *The Importance of Wildlife to Canadians* indicated that 90 per cent of us participate in some form of "wildlife-related activities." The annual value of these activities, including expenditures by U.S. tourists in Canada, is $9 billion per year, accounting for 150,000 jobs.

In one year, 1990, the Canadian Parks Service and park visitors spent $700 million in eight provinces and the Yukon (excluding British Columbia, Québec, and the Northwest Territories). This resulted in 18,000 jobs and over $1 billion in labour

It's called the Endangered Spaces campaign, and its aim is to protect wild lands and wild waters representative of the ecological nature of Canada's more than 400 natural regions by the year 2000. Now, with funding to this World Wildlife Fund (Canada) program from IBM Canada to develop scientific criteria for determining endangered areas, that aim will be more readily accomplished.
IBM, *IBM and the Environment
— A Progress Report*, 1993

income and contribution to gross domestic product. These numbers are for only part of our national park system, which in total represents fewer than 200 parks and historic sites. Provincial and territorial agencies account for an additional 11,000 protected areas of one kind or another, so a similar analysis for this sector would considerably boost the calculation of annual economic benefits provided by parks.

The above figures are indications of "willingness to pay" in the form of actual expenditures and direct contributions to the Canadian economy. However, such numbers exclude what people would pay to avoid losing wilderness, or to protect more. The StatsCan national survey indicated that "over 60% of Canadians are willing to pay increased taxes or higher prices if these were needed to conserve wetlands, forests and other habitats on which wildlife depends." We need to better understand how much Canadians are willing to pay, not just for direct wilderness experiences, but to simply know it's there ("existence values"), or to pass wilderness on to future generations ("bequest values"). There's every reason to believe that Canadians are willing to pay for these indirect values, often assumed to be priceless, unquantifiable, or beyond dollars or cents. Without such an assessment, we are missing a significant entry on the balance sheet when we are asked to surrender wilderness for the alternative economic benefits of activities such as logging, mining, and hydro-electric development.

Additional benefits provided by wilderness which do have an economic value, although seldom estimated, include nutrient cycling, climate regulation, watershed protection, and other biological functions. When lost, these "ecological services" cost billions of dollars in reduced fertility or in drought and flooding, yet we rarely place an economic value on their contribution while they still exist. Instead, we take them for granted.

We must also sharpen our pencils when considering the time period over which economic benefits are calculated. For example, when considering the value of a boreal forest stand converted to pulp, the value of the pulp and the jobs created is usually stated only for the two to three years when logging and processing take place. Not surprisingly, this renders a high annual value. But it may be fifty to eighty years before that same forest can be cut again to provide another pulse of pulp dollars. In considering the economic value of that forest cut for fibre, the benefit should be costed over the full fifty- to eighty-year harvest cycle of the forest. This makes the annual economic benefit of the exploitation option considerably less than might first appear to be the case. Once exploitation benefits are calculated on this basis, a meaningful comparison can be made with the annual economic benefits provided by that forest left in an uncut state (tourist revenues, ecological services, etc.), also for fifty to eighty years.

One further concern is the uneven distribution of economic benefits. Often a local community is asked to forgo immediate revenues and jobs — for instance, from timber cutting — so that society in general can enjoy more long-term benefits

— for example, from a wilderness park. This has been tersely expressed as "providing public benefits at private expense." The "resource," in this case forested land, is often publicly owned; therefore, it can be argued that the broader public has a right to determine its future, even at the expense of a local community. Furthermore, a case could be made that society as a whole is better off in every way by protecting the area as a park rather than logging it. Is the majority supposed to suffer so that a minority can benefit? On the other hand, the local community may have to pay a higher price than anyone else right now, so that others may enjoy wilderness benefits in the longer run.

Our goals . . . To create and set aside from industrial development by the year 2000 those protected areas required to achieve representation of Canada's land-based natural regions.
THE WHITEHORSE MINING INITIATIVE, 1994

In cases like this, we have to find a fair way for those who benefit to compensate those who lose. In many cases, those who claim to be losing when wilderness is protected have organized under the banner of "wise-use."

THE WISE-USE MOVEMENT

In *Endangered Spaces*, we predicted that "the next ten years in Canada may not be characterized so much by a win/lose, extremist, fight-to-the-death over wilderness, but by a more professional competition as to who can sound the most reasonable." We guessed that our chief competitor in this regard would be the "wise-use movement."

History has proven us correct, but has not yet declared a clear winner.

The contemporary wise-use movement was born in the western United States in the mid-1980s. It was part of a backlash against big-city environmentalists, who, it was claimed, didn't understand or care about the concerns of local ranchers, loggers, miners, or the residents of small, resource-dependent towns. One of its gurus was Ron Arnold of the Center for the Defense of Free Enterprise in Washington, D.C., who, in a previous life, had served on the board of the Sierra Club. Using his insider knowledge, Arnold borrowed a page from the environmentalists' book to fight them. He and his friends advised big resource companies not to launch glitzy advertising campaigns against wilderness advocates but, rather, to organize at the grass-roots level, taking advantage of local fears about unemployment and feelings of being dictated to by outsiders. The goal? "To destroy environmentalism once and for all," said Arnold.

In the United States, the wise-use movement has attracted a strange, sometimes violent group of property-rights and family-values advocates who support "not only unrestricted timber cutting on public lands but also off-shore 'energy development'; mining and drilling in National Parks and Wilderness Areas; abolition of the Endangered Species Act; a roll-back of clean air, water-quality and pesticide legislation; and cost-plus compensation from the taxpayer whenever a property-owner or corporation is prevented from filling in a wetland, mining a river-bottom, or grazing cattle on public range-land." This quotation is from *The War Against the Greens*, a 1994 book by journalist David Helvarg, which exhaustively documents the rise of the wise-use movement in the United States. Reading Helvarg's book can only leave more moderately inclined Canadians with the hope that it never happens in this country.

But it has. Not with the same zany extremist personalities, the alleged murders,

Protecting Canada's wilderness heritage must become an urgent priority for all of us. The OCNA strongly endorses the efforts of the World Wildlife Fund to ensure a future for the country's wild lands and wild waters.

JOHN MORRIS, President of the Ontario Community Newspaper Association, 1990

the bombings, or the flamboyant exhortations to "pick up a sword and shield and kill the bastards." No, here in Canada, the wise-use movement uses lower-key, more insidious tactics. They gradually wear down wilderness advocates in their home communities until they have to choose between staying as social outcasts or leaving town.

Such seedy tactics hide behind a more respectable front, both philosophically and institutionally. Philosophically, wise-users use the code-word "balance" to describe their position, arguing that what's needed in everything from clear-cuts to national parks is "a proper balance between sustainable-use and environmental protection." How could anyone argue with *that*! By implication, of course, anyone who disagrees doesn't believe in "balance."

Institutionally, wise-users form organizations that often incorporate other code-words, like "share" or "care," in their names. Examples are Share B.C. and NorthCare in Ontario. The idea here is that we can all "share" the land by permitting all kinds of uses on virtually all of it, or that we best "care" for the land by using it (always in some commercial manner). Some of the groups' names deliberately obscure their motives. The Forest Alliance of B.C. is an industry-initiated lobby which aggressively defends clear-cutting, and the Association for Mountain Parks Protection and Enjoyment (AMPPE) is a coalition of local tourist-industry interests who promote intensive recreational use of our western national parks.

To help project the image of balance and rational middle ground, such organizations employ high-profile, reasonable-sounding spokespersons: in the case of the Forest Alliance, Jack Munroe, a former leader of the International Woodworkers Association, and Patrick Moore, one of the founders of Greenpeace; in the case of AMPPE, Dave Day, a former superintendent of Banff National Park, and Ken Read, a former member of Canada's national ski team.

Given this kind of shrewd organization, it only helps the wise-use movement when a small minority of wilderness activists burn bridges on logging roads, spike trees, or sabotage heavy equipment. Because these are not the kind of tactics supported by the majority of Canadians, they serve only to drive more support into the apparently moderate wise-use camp. Instead, those of us trying to defend wild Canada would do better by demonstrating real sensitivity to those at the local levels who may feel threatened by our cause, by doing our statistical homework well enough to argue the economic benefits of our cause, and by using solid science to document what happens when we protect wilderness and what happens if we don't.

In any case, the sharing and caring wise-use movement has proliferated so extensively in Canada at the national, provincial, and local levels that a citizens' guide would be a useful tool for a confused public trying to sort out who's who. Clearly, the predicted competition for the hearts and minds of Canadians is under way, and it will be up to each of us to decide who speaks truthfully and who doesn't. No doubt this is as it should be in a participatory democracy, keeping in mind that such a democracy works only if people actually do participate. The cost of not getting involved will be the loss of our wilderness heritage by default.

For now, however, let us not lose sight of where Canadians stand. A 1994 Environics poll indicated that seven out of ten Canadians believe that federal, provincial, and territorial governments should either "be held to their original commitments" to complete a network of representative protected areas or "be required to complete this goal even faster." So, although the wise-users may have a point in urging us to go about the job sensibly, there can be no doubt about whether or not the job should be done.

5 / Working with Government

ARLIN HACKMAN

Why is government important to the Endangered Spaces campaign? Approximately 95 per cent of Canadian territory is owned by the "Crown," that is, by you and me through our governments. What happens to these lands and waters is decided on behalf of the owners by our political leaders and their officials. Even the disposition of private lands in the southern, populated regions of Canada is strongly influenced by planning controls, taxation, and other government policies which encourage or discourage this or that use.

In other words, government sets the rules for land use. In so doing, it also defines the "tool kit" for conserving the natural values of our country. This tool kit includes various protected-area designations such as parks, ecological reserves, and wildlife areas, which can be applied to specific sites by a Cabinet decision. Therefore, the responsibility for actually achieving the Endangered Spaces goal rests, by and large, with governments. It follows that the Endangered Spaces campaign is largely an effort to influence public policy.

WHERE IN GOVERNMENT DO WE FOCUS?
The federal and provincial governments dominate the field of land-use and protected-areas decisions. True, thousands of local governments can promote or stymie conservation on private lands, which typically include some of the most biologically rich and threatened habitats in the country. In the North, the new regional government of Nunavut, as well as other First Nations governments empowered through comprehensive land-claims settlements, will soon direct conservation on vast areas of globally rare wildland ecosystems. Yet the thirteen senior jurisdictions — the federal, provincial, and territorial governments — have the mandate and capacity to contribute the most to our campaign goal. Consequently, they remain the primary focus of our advocacy and expectations.

More specifically, it is ministers responsible for parks, wildlife, and other natural resources or land-use programs; their political aides; deputy ministers; assistant deputy ministers; and parks and wildlife directors, planners, and natural scientists who are the focus of our efforts. More than anyone else, they are responsible for ensuring that new protected areas are designated quickly enough to reach the year 2000 goal. Despite their day-to-day role as landlords to so much of Canada, these ministers and officials are often of second rank within the government. Most are all but unknown to the general public, especially to big-city dwellers.

HOW IS GOVERNMENT MOVED TO ACTION?

Although ministers responsible for protected areas may not have sufficient authority and resources to get the job done all by themselves — we also need premiers and finance ministers on side — their leadership within government is essential. Without this we will not succeed. Fine, but how do we get such leadership?

At first glance, the answer seems simple: public pressure. But that pressure can take many forms. Which ones are best? Ideally, the Endangered Spaces goal would be achieved by simply persuading the appropriate minister in each province or territory to agree over lunch to protect all the necessary sites. After all, with a conservation goal measured strictly in terms of on-the-ground protection, not some ideological agenda, there's no special virtue in mass rallies and heroic speeches, letter-writing campaigns, and the like if a simple face-to-face conversation with one decision maker will get the job done. But don't count on that.

Even if a minister has no responsibility other than protected areas, he or she will not want to appear captured by any special interest, let alone be told how to do his or her job. Experience shows that the kind of leadership we seek will come about only if ministers (and their officials) develop a sense of ownership and accountability regarding the Endangered Spaces goal. As well, they need resources to carry out their role, and some sense of political benefit when they do. However, even if the current Parks minister promises action, he or she may not hold the portfolio long enough to follow through and deliver. Not a single minister, and only a few senior officials, responsible for parks when WWF launched the campaign in 1989 remain in the same jobs today.

These are just a few reasons why the Endangered Spaces campaign has devoted considerable effort to confirming broad public, institutional, and scientific support. Altogether, the 600,000 signatures on the Canadian Wilderness Charter, the endorsements from 280 groups, and the support from resource industries for a scientific approach to siting new protected areas provide a basis for sustaining ministerial leadership over the decade.

Just because we can't snap our fingers and get government action does not mean we have to relate to government officials as adversaries, relying on public protest to convey our message. At times protest is necessary to highlight a problem or depth of concern. But it is preferable to resolve problems through partnership rather than polarization. Governments are made up of individuals, and it is simple human nature to respond more favourably to encouragement rather than criticism or abuse, especially if the criticism isn't backed by sufficient power to compel action. Bad personal relations between the government and Endangered Spaces campaigners have never helped to gain ground for conservation. Confrontation and personal antagonism often consume enormous energy, without yielding any positive results. A goal as ambitious as ours will not be accomplished if it depends on dragging governments kicking and screaming to the right decision on a site-by-site basis.

That's not to say chumminess is good. Relations can become too familiar and comfortable, whereby process (meetings, consultations, studies and more studies) substitutes for real on-the-ground progress. Being constructive and fair is not the same thing as being compromising, and the Endangered Spaces campaign has been designed to keep this distinction in full view every step of the way. At year end, our progress reports measure results in ecological, not political or emotional terms. Protected hectares, not good intentions, count as progress.

HOW HAVE WE ACTUALLY WORKED WITH GOVERNMENT?

While always an advocacy campaign, Endangered Spaces was launched in a spirit of cooperation, with a view to working with government in support of a *mutual* goal. After all, the notion of completing a network of representative protected areas was already well established in many jurisdictions before the Endangered Spaces campaign was launched. The only new ingredient WWF provided was the year 2000 deadline. So we had every reason to hope for cooperation.

It is one thing for two people to agree informally that they share a goal and will work together to achieve it, and quite another for a multitude of agencies across a country to do the same. We clearly needed an official commitment to the campaign's goal from each jurisdiction to sustain effort and results over the rest of the decade.

"Getting to yes" took somewhat longer than anticipated, but relatively little hard negotiation was necessary. There was almost a domino effect as one jurisdiction after another signed up, an effect no doubt spurred on by elections in which politicians were eager to respond to their constituents' "top-of-mind" environmental concerns in the 1980s. In three years' time, each jurisdiction except Québec and Alberta had individually promised WWF, over the signature of the premier or minister, that they would do their share to contribute to the national Endangered Spaces goal.

As a result, the federal government was able to pull together the November 25, 1992, Tri-Council meeting of federal and provincial parks, environment, and wildlife ministers. At the meeting, held in Aylmer, Québec, the governments collectively signed a contract with Canadians entitled *A Statement of Commitment to Complete Canada's Networks of Protected Areas*. WWF symbolically represented Canadians by delivering more than half a million signatures on the Wilderness Charter to the ministers' signing ceremony.

While Alberta and Québec held out for some time before providing individual commitments, both were represented, and signed, at Aylmer. Significantly, this meeting drew the first official representation at a federal-provincial meeting from the government of Québec after the failed Meech Lake Accord, signalling that conservation interests transcend political differences. The Endangered Spaces goal will be pursued in Québec regardless of its place in or out of the Canadian family.

After this turning-point for the campaign, high-level diplomacy gave way to more operational discussions with senior officials, the people who have to carry out the promises made by their political masters. And they can do this with enthusiasm, or find a thousand reasons for delay and inaction. It was no accident that the first people to hear about the launch of the campaign in 1989 were the parks agency directors from the federal, provincial, and territorial governments at their annual meeting. We pointed out that our goal was really one *they* had defined, and we outlined an overall approach to meeting it which mirrored the type of program planning with which they were already familiar. First, the goal is defined; then, the policy framework is established, the program resources are assembled, the gaps in the existing protected areas system are identified, candidate sites to fill the gaps are identified; and, finally, decisions are taken to designate candidate sites as new protected areas.

WWF has since contributed its own expertise and resources to aid this approach by way of technical studies on representation criteria and protection standards, gap analysis to identify where new protected areas are needed to achieve representation, support for local projects by conservation groups to advance individual sites towards protection, and reporting on progress nation-wide every year. Our overall strategy has been to identify science-based action steps and to build sufficient consensus behind them, both within and outside government, to ensure that they are taken. This approach was driven by pressure from governments themselves, who asked that we use consistent standards nation-wide to measure their progress and define the geographic requirements to meet the year 2000 goal.

A systematic approach must still reflect the policy and program structure in each jurisdiction. One province may do all its planning, then make designation decisions for the entire province in the last year of the decade. Another might complete the work region by region, designating new areas in batches. As well, top-down planning can be taken only so far before it prompts legitimate concern from people at the local and regional levels that they are being disenfranchised. These might be local residents worried about the potential impact of protected-areas decisions on their communities, as well as conservation groups who have worked long and hard to protect particular sites.

To address this need, WWF recruited a regional coordinator for the campaign in each province and territory. This person is charged with adapting the campaign to the political culture and specific programs in his or her jurisdiction. Although we are as flexible and cooperative as possible, and encourage local innovation and pragmatic partnerships, we have held to meaningful representation and protection standards as a baseline for the campaign nation-wide. As a general rule, we have said it doesn't matter what kind of official designation is used to establish the protected area, or who owns or manages it, so long as it is representative, and enjoys long-term legal security from industrial activity. Equally important, we don't really care how jurisdictions choose to design their planning process and schedule, so long as there is a "game plan," and it *does* get the job done by the year 2000. Still, anyone who expects to push all the new sites out the end of the pipe on December 31, 1999, is playing a high-stakes game.

The day-to-day level of working in partnership has involved regular personal contact with a small number of key officials in each jurisdiction so that a trusted channel of communication is available when problems or special opportunities develop. Typically, this network consists of a ministerial assistant, the assistant deputy minister, the parks or wildlife agency director, and the protected-areas system planner. With the Endangered Spaces regional coordinator at the centre, this network is used to review and revise draft materials being prepared under campaign auspices, especially the annual progress report, gap maps, and other documents which report on the status of protected areas in the jurisdiction.

Completing Canada's basic system of protected areas is our most critical environmental project. Achieving that objective by the year 2000 will take all the energy and skill we can muster. Government commitments, however, are now in place, we know what needs to be done, and largely how to do it. We must get on with it with energy and dedication at every level.

AL DAVIDSON, former Assistant Deputy Minister in charge of the Canadian Parks Service, 1993

It is essential to keep in touch with both politicians and civil servants every step of the way towards our goal, because neither the minister nor the official can do the job alone. Ministerial direction enables officials to move ahead by identifying and releasing candidate sites for public comment. At the same time, actions undertaken or recommended by officials regarding those sites enable ministers to make designation decisions. This relationship produces a kind of ratcheting-up process, each step taken by one party making the next step easier for the other. As a partner, WWF has assisted the process by standing ready to recognize and join with a government in announcing new protected areas. But we must play this role with care. Sometimes our offer to support announcements publicly is gladly accepted as helpful, sometimes it is not, both by the government and by other conservation groups who may be critical of the government for other reasons. However, on balance, we must be ready to support government when it does make progress; otherwise, our claims to partnership are hollow.

In addition to working directly with government officials, we have helped indirectly by mobilizing a strong constituency to support their efforts, especially from the business and labour sectors. While land-use conflict persists in many areas today, even rhetorical support from the Canadian Chamber of Commerce, Canadian Association of Petroleum Producers, and Canadian Labour Congress would have seemed impossible ten years ago.

Finally, the WWF has brought financial resources to the partnership. Although these in no way rival government program budgets, our financial support for campaign professionals across the country, policy research and database development, as well as grants to local groups and even land acquisition, could easily reach $20 million by the end of the decade, virtually all from private sources. This includes funds to hire the first non-government professional working full-time on marine protected areas in Canada. All in all, the campaign has brought substantial non-government support to help government accomplish objectives it has set for itself — an impatient partnership, but a partnership all the same.

IS THE PARTNERSHIP WORKING?

On a national basis, it's no coincidence that in the last five years we've more than doubled the area of Canada protected to Endangered Spaces standards over the previous century. Goals, program design, and on-the-ground decisions have been tuned up and accelerated, at least relative to what might have happened otherwise in Canada's present economic and political climate. Endangered Spaces has become *the* protected-areas agenda in some regions. Yet, progress must still quicken dramatically if we are to achieve our year 2000 goal. What type of approach to government will bring this about?

That question is best answered by looking at each jurisdiction, as this book does. Apart from the Tri-Council meeting, the annual federal-provincial parks directors' conference, and some jointly sponsored public-awareness activities on the annual Parks Day, governments themselves are not really working together at the national level. Efforts to form strategic partnerships — for example, between federal and provincial parks agencies in Atlantic Canada — have not progressed beyond early good intentions. The one unifying principle at the national level, it seems, is competition. Jurisdictions are all anxious to be doing better than their neighbours, and the Endangered Spaces "report card" has been a very effective motivational tool.

Good day-to-day working relations have developed between Endangered Spaces campaigners and parks planners in virtually every jurisdiction, enabling the exchange of basic information about protected-area systems, sites, policies, and so forth. This is essential for maintaining a useful understanding of each other's activities. However, close, ongoing cooperation in policy development, strategic planning, program implementation, public communications, and decision making about specific sites has been much more difficult to achieve, for a number of reasons.

First, although governments speak constantly of partnership, they have trouble actually forming true partnerships. Too often it simply means looking to the private sector to help share the costs of programs or services, with as little sharing of related decisions as possible. At the same time, few conservationist non-government organizations (NGO's) have the human resources or organizational stability to maintain a close working relationship with a government agency. And because they have often been suspicious of government, these NGOs haven't made attractive partners.

Second, Endangered Spaces is not primarily involved in delivering a service, but in lobbying government. It is not too surprising that government would be reluctant to join forces with a partner that is also mobilizing public pressure to tell it what to do.

Third, as the recession, deficit reduction, and other forces combine to shrink the size and role of government, even officials who were keen boosters of the campaign goal a few years ago are becoming guarded or defensive. They don't want to "set up" their minister by making promises they can't keep. Any agenda with the remotest potential to worsen, rather than relieve, economic hardship is an agenda they don't want to touch.

Notwithstanding these problems, relations with some jurisdictions, such as British Columbia, Manitoba, Nova Scotia, and the federal government, have been relatively fruitful. Those with New Brunswick, Ontario, Alberta, and the Yukon have been more challenging. What explains the differences?

Viewed up close, some of the variation can be attributed to the individuals involved, in both government and non-government organizations, and their working relationship with each other. But from a decade-long rather than a moment-by-moment perspective of the national campaign, other factors come into focus and must be addressed if we want to increase the pace of action by the orders of magnitude necessary.

In general, jurisdictions with positive records have had high-level political direction that has enabled them to move ahead on a systematic basis. For example, in both B.C. and Manitoba, the premier's public leadership on the Endangered Spaces agenda has made a noticeable difference. When a premier becomes involved in an issue, it gets drawn to the centre of government. Here it can be addressed comprehensively by

W**ill you complete the national terrestrial parks system by the year 2000 by establishing at least ten national parks by 1997, and reserving the remaining six by 2000?**

Yes. Liberals are committed to completing the national terrestrial parks system by 2000. To meet this goal, an acceleration of the timetable, established by the Conservatives in the Green Plan, will be required. PRIME MINISTER JEAN CHRÉTIEN, in a pre-election questionnaire, 1993

officials who have all the levers of power at their disposal. Typically, a parks minister or director has to push a protected-areas proposal against the grain of much more powerful economic and social interests around the Cabinet table. However, when the leader of the government puts forward conservation decisions as part of a total government program, this enables the protected-areas commitment to appear, rightly, as part of a balanced policy agenda. Specific site designations are supported as measures to address changes in the socio-economic conditions in the region. In other words, it makes it possible to fashion and undertake a planned transition in the pattern of land and resource use, which is required to achieve sustainability.

Leadership on this issue stems from a combination of factors, including: pressure from within the political party; intense public protest and conflict; the desire of business for a stable operating environment; the possibility that a positive conservation record might provide an edge in a tight race on voting day; the work of skilled officials who can put all the pieces of a land-use puzzle together into an effective policy package, and then sell it. In the end, leadership has little to do with whether or not the politicians are "true believers" in the Endangered Spaces goal.

Another key factor is money. Premier Mike Harcourt of B.C. went on province-wide television in 1994 to sell controversial land-use decisions involving major new protected areas, with the claim that no one working in the forest sector would be out of work as a result of these decisions. He was able to do this because record profits in the forest industry had made it possible for the government to set up a Forest Renewal Plan, which would finance reforestation and research into value-added forest products, retraining programs for forest workers, investments in intensive forest management, and so forth. In other words, profits from the forest are helping communities adjust to a more balanced forest land-use regime.

B.C.'s approach may or may not be a model for others. On the prairies, a comparable strategy might be to remove or redirect agricultural subsidies so that they would support, rather than hinder, prairie protection and restoration. In Atlantic Canada, a portion of the vast sums being spent to address the fisheries collapse and support new enterprise, such as aquaculture, could be channelled into setting up a marine protected-areas agenda. The point here is that: (1) There *is* money in the economy which can be directed to aiding the transition to sustainability, including the short-term costs of protected-area decisions; (2) Governments can accomplish their objectives by using their fiscal and regulatory powers to direct how this money flows through the economy; they don't have to rely on putting it in their annual operating budgets to fund new programs and bureaucracies; and (3) Most important, without this approach of combining conservation and development policies, there is little likelihood of protected-area decisions being taken quickly enough, and on as large a scale as necessary, to reach our representation goal on time.

This is not a partisan political issue. There are Conservative, Liberal, and New Democratic Party governments in Canada today which are making headway in this area, and others which are not. Rather, it is a matter of good public policy and good government, something increasingly difficult to find as government struggles to reinvent itself in response to changing public expectations and fiscal realities.

If there ever was a day when parks ministers could spend their way to a completed protected-areas system using their operating budget, it is long past. But that doesn't mean the job cannot be done.

LOOKING AHEAD

How will we work with government over the latter half of the Endangered Spaces campaign to actually accomplish our goal?

The answer, as we move from rhetorical commitments into more and more site-specific action, is going to be increasingly dependent on the plans of each province and territory, and to a considerable degree, on how similar our views are of the geographic requirements of meeting the year 2000 goal. Hence, government response to the regional blueprints in this book, and associated gap-analysis maps, will be a key factor. At the same time, on a national basis it is likely that the going will get tougher simply because the easy sites have now been protected. As a result, our approach will need to be multifaceted. We must maintain a credible, science-based framework for measuring progress, and obtain agreement on its merits from technical specialists in government.

In addition, along with inspired pleas to protect individual sites, we need to bring our agenda closer to the centre of government decision making in most jurisdictions. That means finding ways to link economic and conservation policy in order to create a favourable environment for accelerating new protected-areas designations. To do this, given the entrenched forces restricting progress today, there may well need to be more marketplace pressure, including from foreign consumers. Like it or not, there is no doubt that protest and court challenges have been a factor in changing the yardsticks for conservation in, for example, B.C. and Québec.

Finally, we need to be on the lookout for opportunities to strengthen the business support for our goal and for quick action by government to reach it. We must keep an open mind and be willing to work with anyone who will lend a hand, assuming goodwill rather than ulterior motives. Ultimately, protecting our natural heritage has to make economic as well as ecological sense. The sooner we find more partners in business and government to promote this fact, the quicker we'll reach our goal, and the longer that achievement will endure.

6 / Using the Law to Protect Wild Places

HARVEY LOCKE AND STEWART ELGIE

 There was a time, not long ago, when there was no legal way to ensure that protected areas stayed protected in Canada. The National Parks Act has clearly stated since 1930 that all parks "shall be made use of in a manner that leaves them unimpaired for future generations." But there was no way a private citizen could go to court to ensure that park administrators and politicians obeyed that law. Fortunately, all that is changing. Now legal action can be taken in appropriate cases to ensure that protected areas are not defiled.

To understand the present state of legal recourse for protected areas, we must understand the past. Historically, English Common Law, which is the source of Canada's law (except in Québec), had two biases; first, Parliament was supreme, so public policy should be left to the politicians and not the courts; and, second, the promotion of commerce and protection of private property rights were perceived to be inherently good. These nineteenth-century world-views were firmly entrenched in the Canadian judicial mind until the late 1980s.

As a result, Canadian courts refused to allow private citizens, or environmental groups, the right to defend protected areas. They would not even give them "standing" — the right to raise a legal issue in court. Without standing, it doesn't matter how right you are in law; the courts won't hear you. According to the traditional standing rule, only those persons whose private property or economic interests were affected by a government decision had the right to sue over the decision. This ruled out actions to protect parks, which, by definition, were public property.

OPENING THE COURT-HOUSE DOORS

The restrictive laws of standing did not deter Larry Green from bringing Canada's first major park-protection lawsuit. In 1972, he brought an action against the Government of Ontario for allowing a commercial gravel operation on public lands next to Sandbanks Provincial Park — a park which had been created largely because of its spectacular sand dunes. Section 2 of the Ontario Provincial Parks Act states: "All provincial parks are dedicated to the people of the Province of Ontario and others who may use them for their healthful enjoyment and education, and the provincial parks shall be maintained for the benefit of future generations." Green contended that this section imposed a public-trust obligation on the government to preserve the park for future generations. Allowing some of the dunes adjacent to the park to be turned into a gravel pit, he argued, violated that trust.

The Ontario High Court emphatically rejected this argument. To start with, the Court decided that Green lacked standing, and should lose for that reason alone. Nonetheless, it went on to discuss the merits of his argument. It ruled that Section 2 did not create a public-trust obligation over parks. In the Court's opinion, the section merely meant that the public was free to use the parks, and the government was required to maintain them — nothing more. The evidence that the sand dunes were a unique ecological and recreational resource was rejected by The Honourable Mr. Justice Lerner as "clearly a statement of opinion as much as a comment that a particular *objet d'art* is good or bad aesthetically." To top it off the judge ruled that the action was "vexatious and frivolous" because the gravel lease predated the park, and he warned against bringing such "ill-founded actions for the sake of using the courts as a vehicle for expounding philosophy."

The *Green* case was tremendously discouraging for those interested in park protection. For one thing, it suggested that judges may not be very understanding when faced with environmental concerns. That fear was reinforced in 1976 when The Honourable Willard Estey, Chief Justice of the Ontario Supreme Court (who went on to become a Supreme Court of Canada judge), stated: "To teach environmental law, in my opinion, is a terrible waste of the taxpayers' money, and it's a waste of a guy's life."

The *Green* decision sent a strong signal that the courts were not prepared to reconsider the traditional rules of standing. In fact, it was just one of many cases in which environmental groups or individuals seeking to protect Canada's wilderness were denied standing by the courts. The result was that the court-house doors were effectively closed to environmentally concerned citizens in the 1970s and the 1980s.

South of the border, however, the situation was quite different. U.S. judges showed far less reluctance in censuring government officials who failed to comply with environmental laws. Perhaps the most important decision of all came in the *Sierra Club v. Morton* case. In 1969, the Sierra Club took the U.S. Forest Service to court over the agency's hasty decision to approve a massive ski resort on the edge of Sequoia National Park. The suit went all the way to the U.S. Supreme Court over whether the Sierra Club had standing to bring the action. The Court rejected the Sierra Club's broad argument that natural objects such as trees and valleys should have standing to sue in their own right. But some members of the court accepted the proposition that citizens who used a park should be able to go to court to see that it was lawfully protected. In an eloquent and oft-quoted judgement, Justice William O. Douglas proclaimed the effect of this decision:

> Before these priceless bits of Americana (such as a valley, an alpine meadow, a river or a lake) are forever lost or are so transformed as to be reduced to the eventual rubble of our urban environment, the voice of the existing beneficiaries of these environmental wonders should be heard. Perhaps they will not win. Perhaps the bulldozers of "progress" will plough under all the aesthetic wonders of this beautiful land. But those people who have so frequented the place as to know its values and wonders will be able to speak for the entire ecological community.

The Sierra Club ultimately lost the case, but during the eight-year court battle the tide of public opinion turned, and the resort did not proceed. This case marked the birth of public-interest environmental legislation in the United States. Henceforth, concerned citizens could go to court to ensure that U.S. environmental laws were followed. It would take many years for such a change to occur in Canada.

It was not until 1987 that the Canadian courts recognized public-interest standing. The change was initiated by an unlikely — and probably unsuspecting — hero. Robert Finlay was a welfare recipient who took the Manitoba government to court over the way it was applying its welfare laws. The case went all the way to the Supreme Court of Canada, and Finlay bought a secondhand suit and hitch-hiked to Ottawa to watch. It was worth his while. In a landmark decision, the Supreme Court ruled that, in appropriate cases, private citizens like Finlay could go to court as representatives of the public interest in order to ensure that government officials obeyed the law. In short, the Court recognized public-interest standing.

The *Finlay* decision meant that the court-house doors were finally open to Canadian environmentalists. But it still remained to be seen what kind of reception awaited them once inside.

The first major environmental case following the *Finlay* decision involved the huge Rafferty and Alameda dam projects in southern Saskatchewan, and the federal government's obligation to carry out environmental assessments. In 1984, the federal Cabinet adopted the Environmental Assessment and Review Procedure (EARP) Guidelines Order. The EARP Guidelines called on federal departments to assess the environmental impacts of all projects over which they had approval authority. Many departments, reluctant to change old habits, continued approving projects without doing environmental assessments. Everyone assumed that the EARP Guidelines were just another nice-sounding policy, without legal force.

Everyone, that is, except the Canadian Wildlife Federation. In 1989, it took the federal Minister of the Environment to court for approving the Rafferty and Alameda dams without conducting an environmental assessment. Government lawyers argued that EARP was just a guideline, not a law, so compliance was optional. However, the Federal Court of Canada disagreed. It ruled that EARP was legally binding. The environmental effects of the dam had to be assessed.

The ink was barely dry on the *Rafferty Dam* decision before the federal Minister of Transport was taken to court for approving the Oldman River dam in southern Alberta without an environmental assessment. This time, a different Federal Court judge ruled that the Minister of Transport did not have to comply with EARP, effectively undermining the precedent set in the *Rafferty Dam* case. This decision was appealed all the way to the Supreme Court of Canada, where the fate of the EARP Guidelines Order would be decided.

The case would be the first major environmental claim to be heard by the Supreme Court in nearly five years. Because many believed it would be an important bell-wether of where the Court's environmental sympathies lay, it drew a lot of attention. On one side of the courtroom was the federal government, supported by seven provinces and one territory, arguing that EARP was unenforceable. On the other side was the tiny Friends of the Oldman River Society and a small coalition of environmental groups. After deliberating for nearly a year, the Court ruled in favour of the environmentalists. EARP was an enforceable law, and all federal departments were required to comply with it.

The *Oldman River Dam* decision was a watershed event in the history of Canadian environmental law. The opening line of the Court's decision read: "The protection of the environment has become one of the major challenges of our time." This suggested that the highest court in the land viewed environmental concerns as very serious, and was prepared to censure government officials who failed to comply with their environmental obligations.

In the twenty years since Larry Green had gone to court to protect Sandbanks Provincial Park, the law had changed dramatically. The development of public-interest standing meant that environmentally concerned citizens could now gain access to court, and the *Rafferty* and *Oldman* decisions suggested that the courts were more willing to question government officials' interpretation of the law.

A POWERFUL TOOL FOR WILDERNESS PROTECTION

For conservationists, legal action represented a potentially powerful new tool to ensure that parks were properly protected. They first turned their sights to the problem of resource extraction in parks. Wood Buffalo, Canada's largest national park, is a United Nations World Heritage Site, but it wasn't being treated like one. Canadian Forest Products, a large logging company, held a lease that allowed it to log over 500 square kilometres of forest in the park. The lease included some of the oldest and largest trees in northern Canada.

For years the Canadian Parks and Wilderness Society (CPAWS), the Canadian Nature Federation, and the Alberta Wilderness Association had tried to put an end to the logging. CPAWS even met with federal Environment minister Robert de Cotret and his successor, Jean Charest, but to no avail. Tired of waiting, CPAWS consulted the newly created Sierra Legal Defence Fund (SLDF). SLDF is a non-profit organization, created in 1990 for the purpose of providing free legal representation to Canadian environmentalists. It advised that challenging the logging contract between the government and the company would mean breaking new legal ground, but it was worth a try.

CPAWS sued on two grounds: that the contract was a breach of the public-trust obligation created by the National Parks Act and, alternatively, that it was an illegal contract not authorized by the act. The public-trust argument was based on Section 4 of the National Parks Act, which reads: "The National Parks of Canada are hereby dedicated to the people of Canada for their benefit, education and enjoyment, subject to this Act and the regulations, and shall be maintained and made use of so as to leave them unimpaired for the enjoyment of future generations."

The trust is an ancient concept, derived from English law, that requires the administrator, known as "the trustee," to manage the trust property for the benefit of someone else, and to keep it from harm. Logging, it would be argued, damaged the trust property — the park — and therefore was forbidden by the National Parks Act.

The problem was that a similar public-trust argument had been made in the *Green* case, and had failed. True, that case had been based on Ontario's act, which had slightly different wording. However, in order to succeed, CPAWS would have to develop a stronger public-trust argument. Stewart Elgie, the founder of SLDF in Canada, came up with the idea of looking to United States cases for support. He had studied and practised law in the U.S. for several years, and was aware that the American National Parks Service-Organic Act had a section very similar to Section 4 of Canada's act. U.S. courts had interpreted that section to impose a public-trust obligation over parks. The strategy held promise.

The federal government initially filed a written response, defending logging in the park. As the trial date approached, however, the government changed its position. It agreed to consent to a judgment by the Court without a trial on the basis of the CPAWS's second argument, that the logging lease was an invalid contract unauthorized by the National Parks Act. The first lawsuit to protect the integrity of national parks in Canada had been won. However, establishing the public-trust doctrine in law would have to wait for another day.

Shortly after the *Wood Buffalo* decision, Environment minister Jean Charest announced that commercial logging would no longer be permitted in any of Canada's national parks. The implication was that no types of harmful resource extraction would be permitted. This was great news.

Sadly, however, resource extraction is not the only threat to the integrity of parks. These days, the greatest threat to some parks comes from the booming number of visitors and the growing array of facilities being built to accommodate them. Nowhere is this problem more apparent than in Canada's oldest national park, Banff.

More than 4 million visitors a year pour into Banff National Park. This influx has spawned a building boom. In the years 1980 to 1992, nearly $500 million worth of building permits were issued in the park, a figure that would make some urban areas envious. Pressures to expand facilities like golf courses and ski hills were unrelenting. Park wardens began warning the public that the park's black bear population might not survive the loss of habitat and that the park was no longer functioning as a secure sanctuary for grizzly bears. Not surprisingly, Banff National Park was the subject of the first lawsuit to challenge excessive tourism developments in a national park.

The case concerned plans to expand the Sunshine ski resort and the adequacy of environmental assessments. In 1992, Sunshine Village Corporation submitted a proposal to Parks Canada to proceed with a plan to log nearly 40 hectares of old-growth forest for ski runs and lifts on Goat's Eye Mountain. This idea had been approved in principle back in 1978, but was subject to environmental assessment. The hitch was that Sunshine argued that, in order to accommodate the additional 2500 skiers per day, the company should also be allowed to expand its hotel capacity by 50 per cent and construct a new 1100-space parking lot. The proposed parking lot would occupy virtually the entire width of the Healy Valley. These plans had not been approved.

In September 1992, Environment minister Jean Charest gave his conceptual approval to the expansion plan, which linked Goat's Eye to the new hotel and parking lot. CPAWS was shocked. It wrote to the minister, seeking clarification. What did "conceptual approval" mean? Had the minister really intended to approve the expansion before an environmental assessment had been done? And why had he called for a separate assessment of each component instead of assessing the environmental impact of the overall proposal? No answer came, despite numerous promises from the ministerial staff.

Then, in February 1993, Parks Canada completed an environmental assessment that looked only at the impacts of constructing the new ski runs and lifts on Goat's Eye and recommended they be approved. CPAWS again wrote to the minister, asking that no permits be issued until the environmental impacts of the overall expansion had been assessed. Again no response came.

On October 7, 1993, two weeks before the federal election that would see the Conservatives lose power, Parks Canada issued a permit allowing the company to begin clearing timber for its ski runs. CPAWS immediately contacted SLDF, who applied for a temporary injunction to stop the logging. (A temporary injunction is used to halt an activity, based on a brief summary of the parties' evidence and arguments, until a full trial can take place.) The Court ruled that CPAWS appeared to have a reasonable legal argument that environmental assessment of the overall proposal was required, but the injunction was refused.

One reason for refusing the injunction was that CPAWS, in the event that it lost after a full trial, could not afford to reimburse Sunshine for the damages it would incur as a result of the injunction. CPAWS had argued that this requirement should be waived for non-profit organizations suing to protect a public interest. This argument has been accepted by U.S. courts, recognizing that the requirement to pay the other side's damages would effectively prevent public-interest groups from seeking injunctions. However, the Federal Court judge in this case did not accept this argument, and denied the injunction. The Court ruled Sunshine could proceed with clearing runs and building lifts on Goat's Eye, but the rest of the proposed expansion would have to be assessed. The *Sunshine* case demonstrates that, even though the barriers to standing have come down, some impediments to public-interest litigation still remain in Canada, and should be changed.

Despite the denial of the temporary injunction, CPAWS and SLDF moved quickly to get the case to trial before any further permits were issued. They believed they still had a good chance of winning the case. Apparently the government agreed. In January 1994, with the trial date approaching, Heritage minister Michel Dupuy ordered a public environmental review of Sunshine's overall expansion proposal. In the end, the Court allowed the company to complete clearing of ski runs, which was well under way already, but the rest of the proposed expansion would have to be assessed. However, Sunshine has now challenged the assessment ordered by Minister Dupuy, and that suit remains outstanding.

On the other side of the country loomed the Great Whale project, the latest part of Hydro-Québec's grand scheme to dam the major rivers flowing into James Bay, eventually flooding over 10,000 square kilometres of northern Québec wilderness. In 1990, Hydro-Québec had applied to the National Energy Board for a permit to export large quantities of hydro-electric energy to the United States. The energy would be generated largely by the construction of new facilities, including the Great

The only hope for the persistence of species in parks and reserves is to view nature as having extrinsic worth everywhere. At the top of the environmental agenda must be the establishment of many more large parks and reserves and the forging of broad and strongly protective regional conservation strategies to buttress them. With all the environmentally destructive forces controlling resource and land management in Canada, there is little chance that we will ever protect too much.

JOHN THEBERGE, *Parks and Protected Areas in Canada*, 1993

Whale dam. However, the utility had refused to provide the board with any evidence about the likely environmental impacts of Great Whale, or any other new facilities it planned to construct. Despite this lack of environmental evidence, the board granted Hydro-Québec an energy-export permit. That decision was appealed by the Grand Council of the Crees of Québec, and the case reached the Supreme Court of Canada in 1993.

It was the first major environmental claim to reach the Supreme Court since the *Oldman River Dam* case, two years earlier. At the hearing, the Crees were joined by a coalition of environmental groups, represented by the Sierra Legal Defence Fund. They argued that it would be absurd to limit the National Energy Board to assessing only the environmental impacts of transmitting energy for export. That energy had to be produced somehow, and the environmental impacts of the production should also be considered. The Supreme Court agreed. In a unanimous decision, the Court ruled that energy-production facilities were an integral part of the export proposal. Therefore, it was proper for the board to consider the "overall environmental costs of granting the export licence."

The Supreme Court's decision was released on February 24, 1994, and had an immediate effect on the Great Whale project. Within a few weeks, two of Hydro-Québec's major U.S. customers pulled out. Nine months later, the Québec government announced the project had been shelved. The *Great Whale* case underscores the fact that litigation, in appropriate cases, can play an important role in the struggle to preserve Canada's wilderness. Nevertheless, the *Great Whale* case also underscores that the power of politics should not be ignored. When the EARP Guidelines were replaced by the Canadian Environmental Assessment Act, in 1995, energy exports were exempted from environmental assessment.

While litigation can achieve important results, conservationists should never lose sight of the fact that lawsuits are not an end in themselves. Litigation can be costly and time-consuming, and the results are not always positive. In *Peter Reese, Alberta Wilderness Association, Peace River Environmental Society, and Sierra Club of Western Canada v. Alberta,* the plaintiffs were granted standing, but lost their challenge that the Alberta government's forestry management agreement with Daishowa would not meet a statutory obligation to ensure that logging levels in Alberta's boreal forest were sustainable. The result was not only defeat for the environmentalists, but also a very significant costs award against them.

REGULATORY PROCEEDINGS

Quasi-judicial (court-like) regulatory proceedings can also contribute to the protection of ecosystems. One advantage of regulatory hearings is that they usually focus on the environmental and economic merits of a proposal, whereas court cases generally focus on technical issues of whether or not government officials acted legally in approving a proposal. However, one potential problem is that many regulatory boards have been viewed as having a pro-development bias. A trilogy of Alberta regulatory cases demonstrates that regulatory proceedings can be important to protected areas.

Alberta has two regulatory boards with significant jurisdiction over the environment. The Energy Resources Conservation Board (ERCB), soon to be renamed the

Alberta Utilities and Energy Board, and the Natural Resources Conservation Board (NRCB) are charged with determining whether the projects which come before them are in the public interest. They must take into account the social and economic effects of the project and of the project's effects on the environment.

The responsibilities and jurisdiction of these boards did not come about by accident. Environmental activists in Alberta, supported by citizen outrage over the sell-off of Alberta's boreal forest in 1989, demanded processes to ensure such things would not happen again without any consideration of the environmental consequences. The provincial government established a task force to review proposed environmental legislation and to tour the province, gathering public input on how Alberta's environmental laws could be improved. The result was resounding support for giving these regulatory boards jurisdiction to say no to projects on environmental grounds, if warranted.

The first big test for the NRCB came with the massive Three Sisters Resort proposed for the Bow Valley and adjacent Wind Valley, in Canmore, close to the eastern boundary of Banff National Park. The park's boundaries, like most protected areas in Canada, do not reflect ecosystem reality. The Montane ecoregion, which comprises low-elevation areas blown snow-free by Chinook winds in winter, extends from Banff Park down the Bow Valley through to the Wind Valley. The Montane is, for many species, the ecological heart of the Canadian Rockies.

The Three Sisters project proposal to the NRCB consisted of recreational facilities and thousands of housing units and hotel rooms. It would cover several kilometres of the Bow Valley and then turn into the Wind Valley, a scenic jewel and ecological crossroads in the heart of the regional ecosystem. The Wind Valley would be the resort's centrepiece. A coalition of the Alpine Club of Canada, CPAWS, and the Sierra Club of Western Canada appeared before the NRCB to save the Wind Valley.

The environmental evidence was compelling. Internationally renowned grizzly bear biologist Dr. Stephen Herrero testified that, in terms of large carnivores, the Wind Valley had the greatest biodiversity of any place within an hour's drive of a major city in Canada. He said the valley was also important to the regional grizzly bear population which used Banff National Park. Dr. Valerius Geist, a noted ungulate biologist, described it as an ecological jewel and the best single site he knew of in North America to view bighorn sheep. Monte Hummel, president of World Wildlife Fund Canada, described the possible loss of the Wind Valley as the kind of event that has led to the decline of large carnivores throughout their range in southern Canada. John Weaver, former U.S. National Forest grizzly bear habitat coordinator, described the Wind Valley as having greater large carnivore diversity than Yellowstone National Park.

On the other hand, Three Sisters proponents described the Wind Valley as the heart of their project. They planned a world-class eighteen-hole golf course, a five-star Marriott hotel, attractive housing units, and a shopping plaza. The economic impact would be significant.

For the first time in Alberta history, a regulatory tribunal said no to part of a project on ecosystem grounds. The Wind Valley was spared. In its decision, the NRCB determined that "because the value of wilderness appears to be increasing worldwide, the importance of protecting the wilderness which we have is all the more pressing."

The NRCB reached another ecologically favourable decision in the case of the West Castle Resort expansion. A major resort was proposed to be built in a long thin valley in the Rockies of southwestern Alberta. The West Castle Valley is not far from Waterton Lakes National Park, both of which are part of the "Crown of the Continent" ecosystem which straddles Alberta, British Columbia, and Montana. A small, economically unsuccessful ski hill had operated in the area for many years. With promises of $20 million in provincial grants to support a $75-million expansion project, Vacation Alberta Corporation proposed a series of hotels and condominiums, two eighteen-hole golf courses, and an expanded ski hill.

A coalition of the Alberta Fish and Game Association, the Castle Crown Wilderness Coalition, CPAWS, the Federation of Alberta Naturalists, and Trout Unlimited Canada intervened, as did other groups. Their case was that the West Castle Valley formed part of an ecosystem that was under so much pressure from activities already that it could not bear this additional impact without losing its rich ecological qualities. The area is home to endangered bull trout and cutthroat trout populations, grizzly bears, grey wolves, moose, elk, and bighorn sheep, as well as the tiny wandering shrew. Of particular concern were the international consequences of degrading this ecosystem because of its critical importance to the survival of grizzly bears and grey wolves in the western United States.

The NRCB approved the project, but with a very significant condition. It said that, before its decision could come into effect, the Government of Alberta had to create the Waterton-Castle Wildland Recreation Area with a specific management regime which would exclude other uses that threaten the overall integrity of the ecosystem, like logging, four-wheel driving, and snow-mobiling. One year later, the government announced it would proceed with the protected area. Then, a few months later, it reversed the decision in response to the four-wheel drive and logging lobbies. The fate of the area remains unsettled.

The final case in the Alberta trilogy is perhaps the best known — the Whaleback. The stakes were enormous. Amoco Canada Petroleum Limited wanted to drill a sour gas well in the heart of the Whaleback area. It said there could be a sour gas field there worth $2 billion.

The Whaleback is the largest intact area of Montane left in Canada. The landscape is visually stunning. It contains abundant native grasses, ancient limber pine, Alberta's second largest wintering elk population, Alberta's largest cougar population, golden eagles, falcons, and habitats for grizzly bears, black bears, wolves, and mule deer. It has also supported sustainable cattle ranching for many years. The Alberta Wilderness Association, CPAWS, and local residents, under the name "The Whaleback Coalition," intervened in the hearing before the Energy Resources Conservation Board, as did another group of local residents who called themselves "The Hunter Creek Coalition."

A major issue in the hearings was the Alberta government's "made in Alberta" commitment to the Endangered Spaces campaign. Its "Special Places 2000" plan is described in more detail in Chapter 8. To meet its protected-areas commitment in the Montane ecoregion, the Government of Alberta has few choices. The Whaleback is the last large, relatively undisturbed tract in the country. However, the

Alberta government had sold oil and gas leases to Amoco, and was obviously supportive of drilling there. It even refused to send its wildlife biologist responsible for the area to the hearing, despite repeated requests for his evidence.

In its sixty-year history, the ERCB had never said no before on ecosystem grounds, but it did for the Whaleback. The decision was to refuse a drilling permit to Amoco. To do so, it said, would degrade this obvious candidate for protection under Special Places 2000 before it could be properly considered.

As the trilogy of Alberta cases shows, regulatory proceedings can be a useful forum for promoting a protected-areas agenda, especially where governments are quick to make rhetorical commitments to protected areas but slow to follow through. But as the West Castle case shows, politics remains important, regardless of the regulatory process.

Since the dark days of the *Green* decision, environmental law in Canada has made great advances. Litigation and interventions in regulatory proceedings have become an important tool in the conservationist's kit. When used thoughtfully, lawsuits can ensure that legal commitments to protection are not cast aside for short-term economic gain. Canada's courts have demonstrated they are now ready to give environmental considerations the attention they deserve. It's up to those dedicated to the protection of endangered spaces to use the courts to ensure that legal protection on the books means protection on the ground.

Thirteen
Blueprints for Survival

7 / British Columbia

BILL WAREHAM AND RIC CARELESS

More than one hundred years ago, Henry David Thoreau wrote: ". . . in Wildness is the preservation of the World." Today, these words echo with renewed meaning and urgency amidst the scenic mountains and landscapes of British Columbia.

B.C.'s many ecosystems and species make it one of the most biologically diverse areas on earth. This richness is the result of a climate that ranges from maritime to desert, to sub-arctic. The topography includes steep coastal mountains and deep fjords, ocean beaches, estuaries, dry interior plains, large river systems, and forested valleys containing an impressive variety of tree species. From the spectacular gardens of wildflowers in the alpine meadows of the Kootenays to the giant spruce and lush coastal rainforests of Vancouver Island, B.C.'s wild places are of global significance.

In Thoreau's time, virtually all of British Columbia was wild. Since then, development has significantly altered its natural landscape. World Wildlife Fund research indicates that 60 per cent of B.C.'s land base — 80 per cent in the southern half of the province — is either developed or committed for resource and industrial use. By 1990, two-thirds of Vancouver Island's ancient forests had been cut, with half logged since 1954. Of the remaining large unfragmented ancient forest blocks, two-thirds will be logged or have roads built through them by 1996.

Environment Canada says all of B.C.'s unprotected low-elevation coastal commercial forest will likely be logged out within sixteen years. Given this rapid rate of development, remaining pristine natural areas are at grave risk. We are caught in a race against time to protect this wilderness heritage. Accordingly, British Columbians have become keenly aware of the need to protect the full range of their province's natural diversity so that they can leave future generations a part of the wilderness heritage they themselves inherited. The Endangered Spaces campaign is an essential element in achieving this goal. The past five years of campaigning have helped protect many of B.C.'s ecologically significant areas.

THE EVOLUTION OF PROTECTED-AREA CAMPAIGNS IN B.C.

In the 1970s, publicly driven campaigns to preserve wilderness in British Columbia resulted in protection of Pacific Rim National Park (Vancouver Island), the Spatsizi Plateau (northwest B.C.), and the Skagit Valley (southwest B.C.). By the early 1980s, the Purcell Wilderness Conservancy and the Valhalla Wilderness were also protected. Due to industry opposition and limited public support, it took years to protect these areas. It was not until the campaign to save South Moresby in the Queen Charlotte Islands (Haida Gwaii) that the extent of ancient-forest loss became publicly understood. Subsequent campaigns to protect giant trees in the Carmanah Valley and Clayoquot Sound areas of Vancouver Island in the late 1980s served to heighten public awareness. These campaigns generated extensive media coverage, not only in the province but across Canada. The result in the case of South Moresby was the establishment of a National Park Reserve. The battle continued for the Carmanah Valley and Clayoquot Sound.

Towards the end of the decade, however, leaders in the conservation movement began to realize that valley-by-valley campaigns were consuming a disproportionate amount of energy, while lesser-known wild areas were being lost. As a result, conservation groups began developing a province-wide strategy to ensure that the full range of B.C.'s natural ecosystems would be represented in a system of protected areas. In 1988 the Valhalla Society produced a vision map outlining what a completed system of protected areas in B.C. should look like.

At this time, WWF Canada was also contemplating a completed national system of protected areas, and launched the Endangered Spaces campaign. In 1989, the combined efforts of national and provincial environmentalists led to the swift adoption of the Endangered Spaces campaign by B.C. environmental groups.

"Endangered Spaces" became part of the vocabulary of environmentalists and government officials. Essential elements of the B.C. campaign included assigning a WWF regional coordinator and developing public support through signing the Canadian Wilderness Charter. The initial campaign launch was followed by an Endangered Spaces conference, which was organized by the Earthlife Canada Foundation and held in Vancouver in December 1990. This event provided a forum for industry, academia, government, and environmentalists to discuss protected areas. The initiatives it sparked in both government and the environmental movement have served as critical milestones in the effort to complete B.C.'s protected-areas system. Committed individuals in the B.C. Parks Service encouraged government to launch "Parks Plan '90," the first provincial government initiative to identify the full range of areas required to complete a representative protected-areas system for B.C. This evolved into "Parks and Wilderness for the '90s," a comprehensive planning process which combined the interests of both the Parks Branch and the Forest Service. The process included extensive public consultation in communities throughout the province. As a result, numerous protected-area proposals were submitted to the government for evaluation.

Shortly before being elected to office in 1991, B.C.'s government made a formal commitment to the Endangered Spaces campaign. In January 1992, it launched the Protected Areas Strategy (PAS), which proposed a detailed agenda and set of criteria for establishing new protected areas. In May 1992, the government released a protected-areas proposal map. The principal goal of the PAS was almost identical to the Endangered Spaces goal — to complete a system of representative protected areas by the year 2000. The government's announcement that it intended to double the size of B.C.'s protected-areas system was strongly welcomed by the environmental community, although many groups responded by saying that more than doubling the protected-areas system would be required to truly protect B.C.'s diversity of plants and animals.

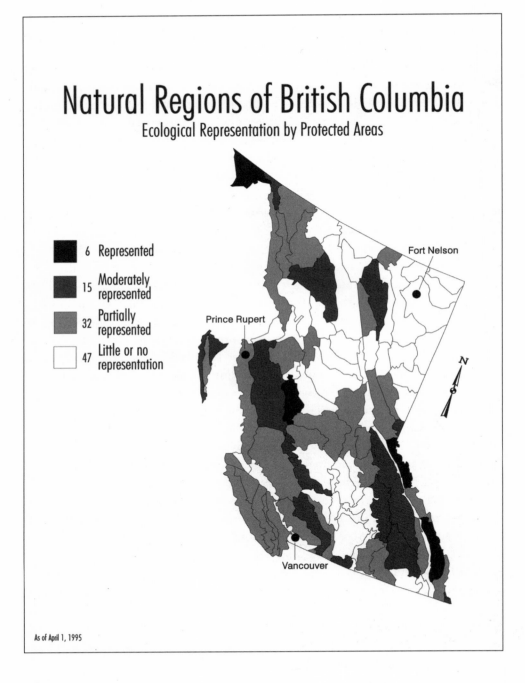

Natural Regions of British Columbia
Ecological Representation by Protected Areas

6 Represented

15 Moderately represented

32 Partially represented

47 Little or no representation

Fort Nelson

Prince Rupert

Vancouver

N

As of April 1, 1995

PROGRESS TO DATE

Following the announcement of the Protected Areas Strategy, the government acted. When the Endangered Spaces campaign was launched in 1989, 6.5 per cent of B.C.'s 94,780,000 hectares of land was protected. By mid-April 1995, the government had designated ninety-nine new protected areas, increasing the total to 9.2 per cent. Several long-standing candidate areas were now protected, including:

If we are to complete an adequate national (provincial and territorial) park and wilderness system, there is not a minute to lose. That's why I welcome the emergence of the Endangered Spaces campaign with its national scope and ambitious goals . . .
TOM PERRY, MLA, Vancouver–Point Grey, 1991

- Tatshenshini/Alsek (958,000 hectares), North America's wildest river. This park, combined with neighbouring parks in Alaska, completes the largest World Heritage Site on the planet;
- Khutzeymateen (44,900 hectares), on B.C.'s northwest coast, Canada's first grizzly bear sanctuary;
- Ts'yl-os (233,240 hectares), a magnificent wilderness area containing the spectacular glacial blue Chilko Lake in the Chilcotin Mountains;
- Kitlope (317,290 hectares), the largest intact coastal temperate rainforest in the world;
- Itchas/Ilgachuz (109,000 hectares), an extinct volcanic range in B.C.'s central interior, which supports the largest herd of woodland caribou in southern B.C.;
- Churn Creek (36,100 hectares), B.C.'s most extensive undeveloped interior grassland, which supports a herd of more than 1000 California bighorn sheep, mule deer, cougars, and numerous rare and threatened grassland species;
- Complete Vancouver Island watersheds, including the Carmanah, Power, Battle, Silburn, and Nasparti. These areas total more than 30,000 hectares and protect some of the best remaining ancient forests on the West Coast;
- White Grizzly (78,000 hectares) in the West Kootenays, which protects a large portion of the critical habitat for the rare white-phase grizzly bear.

New protected-area designations included: twenty-three new areas totalling 78,000 hectares on Vancouver Island; seventeen new areas totalling 460,000 hectares in the Cariboo-Chilcotin; and fourteen new areas totalling 389,900 hectares in the East and West Kootenay/Boundary regions in southeastern B.C. The remainder of the ninety-nine new protected areas included several small coastal marine parks and private land purchases on southern Vancouver Island and in the Strait of Georgia. These represent significant additions to B.C.'s protected-areas system. Credit is due to a cooperative government and the many individuals and organizations who worked diligently to protect these spectacular areas. Determined campaign efforts by the Western Canada Wilderness Committee and the Sierra Club of Western Canada on Vancouver Island in the 1980s alerted the public to the urgent need to protect remaining ancient forests. This awareness grew into support for the protection of wild places across the province. More recent campaigns led by Tatshenshini Wild (now B.C. Spaces for Nature), the Friends of Clayoquot Sound, Greenpeace, the Canadian Parks and Wilderness Society, Ecotrust, the Valhalla Society, B.C. Wild, and numerous grass-roots groups, have helped maintain government support for and action on protected areas.

Pressure by environmentalists and other interest groups prompted the government to establish a formal planning process to address the complex and often conflict-ridden issues of land use. In July 1992, the government established the Commission on Resources and Environment (CORE), which embarked on what was arguably the most comprehensive land-use planning exercise in North America. CORE's mandate was challenging — to resolve land-use conflicts and valley-by-valley debates over protected areas by bringing together individuals representing diverse local interests to discuss, negotiate, and make recommendations on a land-use plan for their region. At the conclusion of this process, CORE would make recommendations to the government for new protected-area designations.

The government asked CORE commissioner Stephen Owen to tackle the three most complex land-use regions in the province — Vancouver Island, the Cariboo-Chilcotin, and the East and West Kootenay. Each one contains unique ecosystems and supports a range of commercial interests, including forestry, mining, agriculture, tourism, and back-country recreation. Newspapers printed mixed reviews from the environmental community, unions, and industry on how successful CORE was in fulfilling its mandate. In the end, however, the CORE process, combined with environmental campaigns subsequent to CORE's 1994 recommendations to government, resulted in many new protected-area designations. Government polls revealed a high level of public support for CORE and the land-use plans that resulted from its recommendations.

OPPOSITION TO PROTECTED AREAS

Resistance to the Endangered Spaces agenda in British Columbia became increasingly intense as the government began to make decisions on land-use plans and specific protected areas. Forest workers, ranchers, and miners were afraid that protected areas would mean an end to their jobs and way of life.

Share B.C. groups, based on U.S. wise-use movement groups and funded in part by forestry and mining corporations (see Chapter 4), formed to oppose CORE and protected areas. Share B.C. grew rapidly into a provincial network of locally organized groups united by the philosophy that there is little need for protected areas. Some people in this resistance movement engaged in confrontational activities, including hanging the CORE commissioner in effigy and erecting signs which read "To hell with the children, clearcut, slash and burn." During the spring of 1994, Share B.C. launched a "yellow ribbon" campaign on Vancouver Island. Fearing their jobs were at risk, 15,000 people wearing yellow ribbons gathered on the lawn of the provincial legislature in a mass rally to protest CORE's land-use plan for the Island.

In February 1992, as the Protected Areas Strategy and CORE gained momentum, sixteen B.C. forest companies established and funded a sophisticated public-relations organization, the Forest Alliance of B.C. After it hired the services of Burson-Marsteller, one of the largest public-relations firms in North America, the Forest Alliance assumed a high profile and aggressively promoted the importance of forestry to the B.C. economy. Many environmental groups believe the Forest Alliance was created to masquerade as a citizens' conservation group purporting to have an interest in maintaining B.C.'s forests and forest-based communities, while in fact pursuing an industry-oriented agenda to limit protected-area designations and defend status-quo forest practices such as extensive clear-cutting.

The need to complete a system of representative protected areas across Canada is supported by science and by those who feel it is essential for the survival of species. Attaining this goal has proven difficult in B.C., owing to lobbyists in the Share B.C. movement and the forest, mining, and ranching industries, who have negatively influenced government decisions regarding land-use plans and protected-area boundaries. The intention here is not to be unjustly critical of legitimate commercial interests. But too often protected-area proposals are whittled down, and sometimes eliminated, due to short-sighted economics. The result is a loss of options required to establish protected areas that truly represent natural ecosystems and that are large enough to maintain viable populations of indigenous plants and animals.

Our organization certainly can support the Wilderness Charter that you folks have drawn up (with considerable discussion and debate, I'm sure!). Your target for action seems quite optimistic. . . . Still, a target is essential to make things happen. Good luck.
DONALD L. WOODSTOCK, Comox Strathcona Natural History Society, Courtenay, 1989

THE CHALLENGES AHEAD

The B.C. government's commendable initiative to increase the area of protected land to 12 per cent has unfortunately created a mythical ceiling for protected areas. In order to really protect biodiversity, we all must focus on ecosystems rather than on a percentage target.

Many existing protected areas do not contain much mid- to low-elevation habitat. Alpine habitats are certainly worthy of protection, but most are less threatened than lower-elevation ones. The challenge in B.C. is to protect more of the latter. Sadly, in some cases, the option to protect large, intact, low-elevation areas that adequately represent an ecological region no longer exists. In these situations, the best we can hope for is protection of what remains, and the application of sensitive management in developed areas.

One of the positive results of CORE's land-use planning was the establishment of Special Management Zones, which are designed to provide buffers and habitat connectivity between protected areas. Resource extraction is allowed within these areas, provided it does not severely impact on ecological, scenic, and recreation values. These zones are where comprehensive forest management, small-scale forestry, and management plans to protect critical wildlife habitat will be the standard. The challenge now is to ensure that government and industry actually achieve the goals outlined in the management plans for these zones, so that the natural diversity of plants and animals is truly maintained across the landscape.

Another challenge for those working towards the Endangered Spaces goal is to work within the parameters dictated by the current public and political will regarding protected areas. With 12 per cent as the current political target, the most effective strategy may be to protect as much pristine, intact wilderness as we can, and as quickly as possible. While we have years to protect and rehabilitate partially developed areas, we have little time left to secure intact areas. However, some environmentalists disagree with this strategy, believing protection should be based exclusively on representation of ecosystem types. These two opposing views make it difficult to decide what in fact should be protected. For example, is it more important to save a valley-bottom old-growth forest or an entire watershed? Do we stop protecting areas because the ecosystem is already considered adequately preserved, when protecting more of it may be important for maintaining large carnivore populations? These are difficult questions to answer, but they must be considered.

Other impediments to meeting the Endangered Spaces goal include the fact that social considerations sometimes seem to outweigh the need to protect an area in an intact form. In addition, we often lack scientific information that proves we have not protected enough of an area to maintain its natural functions. WWF's gap analysis is helping to address this problem. Still, the compromises, the educated guesses, and sacrifices we make now will, in the end, determine whether or not we made enough correct decisions to conserve our natural ecosystems and spectacular wildlife heritage.

One thing is certain: It will be within our children's lifetimes that the last of B.C.'s unprotected wilderness will be impacted by roads and other development. What endures is up to us, so it is important to be clear about our vision. If our vision does not include healthy functioning ecosystems, the natural places and wild creatures they maintain will simply disappear.

WHAT'S LEFT TO DO

Despite recent protected-area designations in British Columbia, much remains to be done to meet the Endangered Spaces campaign goal. Continued public involvement and support for Endangered Spaces are essential if we hope to protect truly representative areas in all of our province's natural regions.

Candidate areas that should be a priority for protection are those that offer a combination of values, including ecosystem representation, wilderness, unique landscape features and critical wildlife habitats. Some of these areas in B.C. are:

Southern Chilcotin Mountains This area, located 125 kilometres southwest of Williams Lake, is one of the most outstanding unprotected wilderness areas in southern B.C. Spectacular landscapes and back-country trails have made it a popular wilderness recreation site for decades. A mosaic of old-growth forests and open meadows, arid grassland plateaus, streams, lakes, and striking multicoloured peaks is found within the South Chilcotin Mountains. This long-standing proposal-area, which is home to California bighorn sheep, mule deer, moose, grizzly and black bears, and mountain goats, is an essential component of a completed protected-areas system in B.C.

Stein Valley This proposed protected area of 109,000 hectares encompasses the largest undeveloped watershed in southwestern B.C. It is one of the last roadless watersheds flowing into the Fraser River. The Stein supports an important fishery, plus wildlife, forest, and cultural heritage values. It is an example of an ecoregion that is currently underrepresented in B.C.'s protected-areas network. Campaigns to protect this area have resulted in Forest Service Wilderness Area designations for the upper and lower portions of the valley. Under this designation, the area remains at risk of being crisscrossed with roads and logged. Ongoing campaigns by environmental groups and local aboriginal bands promote protection of the entire valley.

Pinecone/Burke Mountain This 38,000-hectare proposed wilderness area is literally in Vancouver's backyard. Its diverse habitats range from freshwater marshes in Widgeon Slough to ancient forest containing huge western red cedar and rare old growth–related species in the Boise Valley. After an extensive review of this area's natural, recreational, and cultural values by the Protected Areas Strategy process, which ranked the area as a priority for protection, public support for full protection was clear. Conservation groups in the Lower Mainland are encouraging the government to act quickly to protect the entire proposal area. (Protected since this chapter was written — Ed.)

Muskwa/Profit Northeastern B.C. contains the northern Rocky Mountains wilderness area, which has fifty intact watersheds greater than 5000 hectares in size. The largest, the Kechika, totals 2.2 million hectares and is the largest wilderness watershed in the province. If you can imagine Banff, Jasper, and Yoho national parks without townsites, railways, and highways you can imagine the northern Rockies! This is a truly wild place, where the grizzly bear, caribou, moose, mountain sheep, mountain goat, and wolverine roam free in large numbers. Located within this wilderness, the proposed Muskwa/Profit protected area covers 1,066,000 hectares of the east slopes of the mountains. It supports some of the largest and most concentrated populations of animals in northern B.C. This unique area is threatened by road development for mines, oil and gas drilling, and forest harvesting. Protection of this area is critical to the long-term survival of healthy large carnivore predator-prey systems in the region.

Randy Stoltmann Wilderness Only 200 kilometres from downtown Vancouver, you will find some of the best wilderness anywhere. The proposed 260,000-hectare Randy Stoltmann Wilderness includes roadless watersheds, ancient forests, and alpine meadows, which support populations of mountain goat, grizzly bear, wolverine, and moose. The area has important biological, recreational, and spiritual qualities, which are at immediate risk from development by logging interests. In addition to saving its wildlife, protecting this area will provide unique wilderness recreation opportunities and will help educate people about the value of wilderness. Time is running out for this area — road-building permits are being considered for approval.

Clayoquot Sound After years of campaigning by many environmental groups, the B.C. government agreed in 1993 to protect 33 per cent of the 260,000-hectare sound and promised to limit the size of clear-cuts on the remaining 67 per cent. To protest this decision, more than 12,000 people blocked a logging road in the summer of 1993 at the Kennedy bridge; more than 800 were arrested for civil disobedience. Most conservation groups, including WWF, agree that more of the ancient

W*e believe in wilderness. Please save the Tatshenshini and not lose another beautiful place to development. Please do all you can to save it.*
SHEENA, HEIDA, EMMA, ANDREW, AND ANITA, Folkstone Public School, 1993, in a letter to Premier Harcourt

forests of this scenic and biologically diverse area must be protected. Campaigns by local, national, and international organizations continue.

To fully protect these areas, and to guarantee completion of a B.C. protected-areas system over the next five years, the following actions must be taken:

- Increase the level of public awareness about the value of meeting the Endangered Spaces goal.
- Generate letters from the public and environmental organizations to convince the provincial government that it must honour its commitment to complete a system of protected areas representing all of B.C.'s natural regions.
- Encourage the government to legislate protected areas, address First Nations' concerns in protected areas, and ensure that legally designating protected areas does not prejudice aboriginal rights.
- Establish regional and subregional land-use planning processes for the Mainland Coast, the Southern Interior, the Lower Mainland, and the Northwest to review candidate areas and make recommendations for protected-area designations.
- Encourage the government to establish "Goal 2 Protected Areas" (areas smaller than 250 hectares) throughout the province to ensure protection of critical wildlife habitats, rare species, and unique landforms.
- Establish a cooperative arrangement between the federal and provincial governments to facilitate designation of marine protected areas on the B.C. coast (see Chapter 2).
- Actively monitor ongoing subregional land-use planning processes (Land and Resource Management Plans) to ensure protected-area recommendations are adequate to conserve remaining wilderness and represent the enduring features in all natural regions.
- Continually review protected-area designations to assess the degree of representation achieved and to ensure as high a level of protection as possible for all ecological regions.

The recipe for successfully completing a system of representative protected areas is relatively simple. Both public and corporate citizens must continue to support and donate money to environmental organizations. The public must continue to demand action from governments to ensure protected areas are designated in critical areas. Industry, unions, and local communities must embrace changes that accommodate conservation and sustainability of our ecosystems. We have only one chance to do it right. It can be done if we put our minds to it.

CONSIDER WHAT'S AT STAKE

The remaining wilderness on earth is precious, encompassing an astonishing genetic diversity of life. Wilderness contains the biological and ecological essentials for human survival. It is also a source of spiritual inspiration, scenic splendour, and recreational fulfilment. It is where wildlife — both predator and prey — thrive in primeval balance. It is the reminder that humans are part of something much larger, essential and full of mystery. Pristine wilderness areas are truly sacred places.

One of the best outcomes of the first five years of Endangered Spaces campaigning in B.C. is that we now know it can be done — "it" being the protection of wilderness and critical wildlife habitats. Completing the job, however, will require continued government commitment, propelled by persistent and strategic public pressure. To those of you already working to safeguard wilderness, keep up the good work. To those who feel you could be doing more, make a commitment to the Endangered Spaces goal. The earth and our children's children will be the beneficiaries. If you have not been to some of Canada's wild places, make the effort. Watch the wildlife and experience the air and the sounds that make nature so soothing to the human spirit. Without a sense of the land, it can be difficult to see the need to protect it. And if we fail to protect it, we all will have lost something which is critically important to the future well-being of our society.

8 / Alberta

DAWN MITCHELL AND DIANNE PACHAL

 It has been only sixty-five years since Ottawa gave the young province of Alberta control over the province's natural resources, lands, and waters. But, already, this province is left with just scattered remnants of its original wilderness landscapes. In fact, the end of Alberta's remaining wilderness lands and rivers is now painfully within sight, making us the last generation of Albertans who will have the choice to preserve sufficient examples of our wilderness heritage before development pressures forever foreclose that option. The time available for such decisions ranges from a few months for some areas to possibly ten years for others.

As the Endangered Spaces campaign hits its midpoint, Alberta has just approved a final version of its own policy, "Special Places 2000," in response to the campaign. The earlier 1992 draft version of "Special Places 2000" was the culmination of a highly charged, twenty-five-year-long political battle between preservation and development. It had reflected strong public support for protected areas. Unfortunately, the 1995 version was markedly changed, now resembling a multiple use policy, not a protected-area plan. How we got to this point and where we go from here are the focus of this chapter.

ALBERTA: MORE THAN THE ROCKY MOUNTAINS

From the flower-studded expanses of grassland and sky, to the shifting sands of a sea of dunes, to the deep evergreen forest home of the legendary Swan Hills grizzly, Alberta's remnant wilderness lands and rivers are dynamic and diverse. Alberta is often characterized as the province where the plains meet the Rocky Mountains, and most Canadians are familiar with the treasure trove of mountain landscapes protected in the Rocky Mountain national parks. However, Alberta actually has six major natural regions, each with its own characteristic tapestry of plants, animals, and landforms.

The province's large-scale natural regions are: Grassland, Parkland, Boreal Forest, Foothills, Rocky Mountain, and Canadian Shield. They, in turn, are broken down into twenty subregions, which form the scientific framework for representation upon which the Endangered Spaces campaign protected-areas network is based. Even though each of these subregions covers large tracts of land, opportunities to protect untrammelled pieces of the original landscape have become scarce. The chance to protect a sizeable tract of wilderness — at least the size of Alberta's larger cities (500 square kilometres) — has already been lost for seven subregions: three of the Grassland subregions, all three Parkland subregions, and one Rocky Mountain subregion. While 9.1 per cent of Alberta is already legally protected, almost all of this is accounted for in Banff, Jasper, Waterton Lakes, and Wood Buffalo national parks, which collectively represent only three of Alberta's twenty subregions.

Grassland Approximately 14 per cent of Alberta is Grassland, located in the southeast portion of the province. It is the warmest and driest natural region. More than 80 per cent of it has been turned into farmland, roads, and towns. Remnants of native grasslands are mostly found in areas that are not suitable for cultivation. Alberta is fortunate, however, to have the two largest wilderness grassland expanses left from Canada's once-vast native prairie: the Canadian Forces Base (CFB) Suffield, north of Medicine Hat, and the Milk River–Lost River area, in the extreme southeast.

The proposed Milk River–Lost River wildland is 285 square kilometres of native Dry Mixedgrass and Mixedgrass prairie. Of international significance, it includes extensive badlands, volcanic formations, varied coulees, rolling grassland vistas, the spectacular Milk River canyon, oases of plains-cottonwood forests along the meandering Milk River, and even yucca plants and horned lizards. Unfortunately, in 1984, the provincial government allowed the development of dugouts for cattle-watering within the last ungrazed portion of the 42-square-kilometre candidate Milk River Ecological Reserve. Only 66 square kilometres of the Milk River–Lost River area is currently protected; 11 square kilometres as an Ecological Reserve and 55 square kilometres as a less protected natural area.

Sweeping Dry Mixedgrass plains, a large complex of sand dunes and deeply gullied valleys, together with abundant pronghorns, numerous birds of prey, and fascinating archaeological sites, are some of the noted features within the 2600-square-kilometre CFB Suffield. The 420-square-kilometre Suffield National Wildlife Refuge Area has been designated along the base's eastern edge, adjacent to the South Saskatchewan River.

Parkland Between the Grassland in the south and the Boreal Forest in the north lies a belt of Central Parkland. It does not stand out as boldly to the eye as the massive Rocky Mountains or the expansive Grasslands and Boreal Forest regions do. Rather, it is a subtle, important mosaic of aspen woodlands, fescue grasslands, shrublands, and wetlands on a gently rolling landscape.

About 12 per cent of Alberta is Parkland. Development and farming have changed the vegetation considerably, particularly in the Central Parkland and Peace River Parkland. Consequently, only 5 per cent of the region is still in its natural state. Many native wildlife species were eliminated before they could even be documented. Today, the 180-square-kilometre Rumsey area north of Drumheller is the largest unit of Central Parkland in the world. About 19 per cent of Rumsey has been designated as an Ecological Reserve. The rest remains without legal protection, as a Crown Reservation for a future provincial park and a potential natural area. Oil and gas exploration and development, including road construction, continue within this last island of Central Parkland.

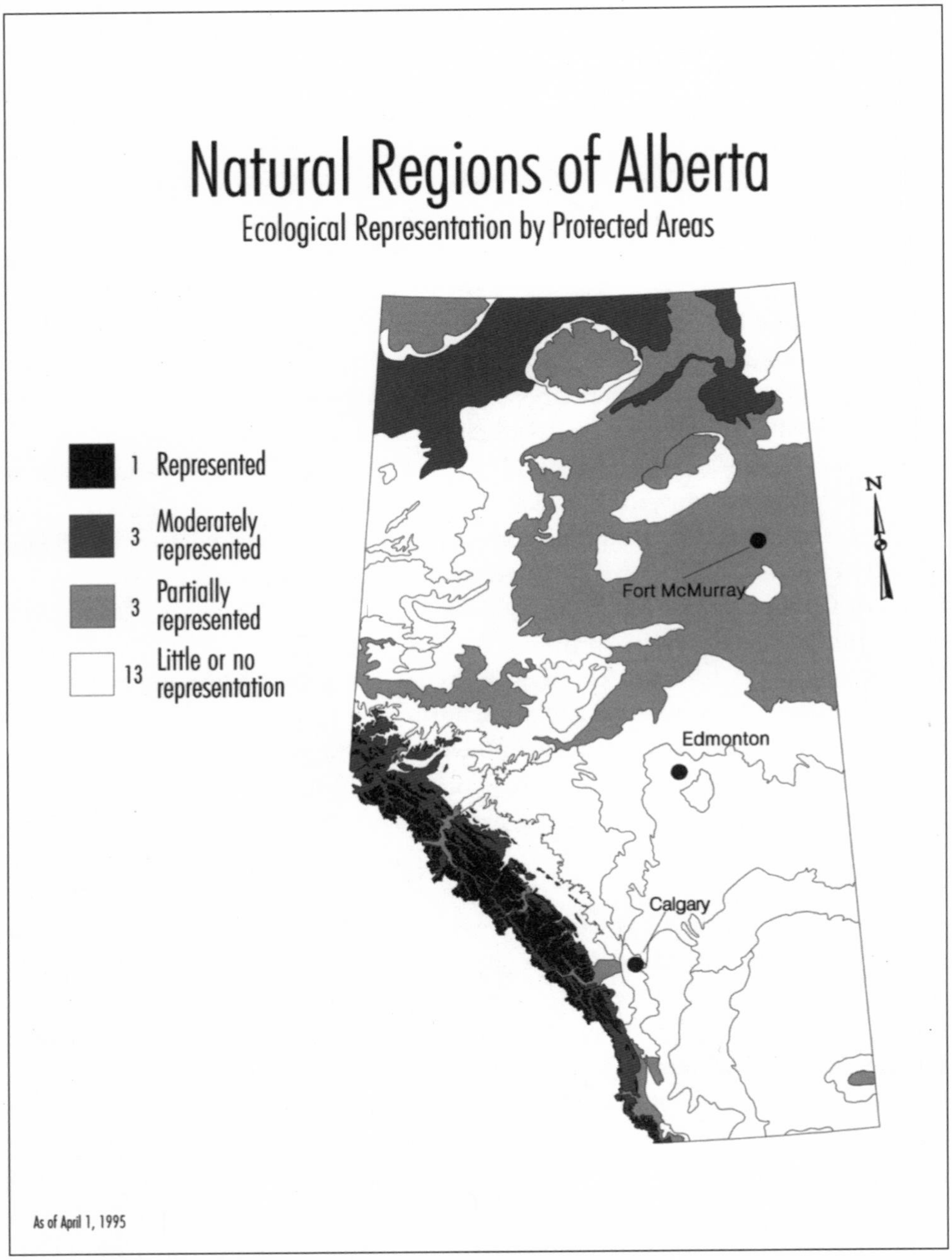

Natural Regions of Alberta

Ecological Representation by Protected Areas

■ 1 Represented

■ 3 Moderately represented

■ 3 Partially represented

□ 13 Little or no representation

Fort McMurray

Edmonton

Calgary

N

As of April 1, 1995

Boreal Forest   The Boreal Forest is Alberta's largest natural region, occupying 48 per cent of the province. In the largest sub-region — the Central Mixedwood — the land is almost completely covered by trees, with aspen and balsam poplar dominating the evergreens. Somewhat drier and warmer than the Central Mixedwood is the Dry Mixedwood, where evergreen forests are uncommon. Instead, aspen and balsam poplar occur, with mixed forests of aspen and white spruce occurring in the north of the subregion. Farther north, evergreens form a seemingly endless carpet, broken only by water in the form of fens, bogs, lakes, and rivers. In the north, four subtypes of Boreal Forest occur: the Peace River Lowlands, Wetland Mixedwood, Boreal Highlands, and Subarctic.

I wanted to help Canada's Endangered Spaces, so I organized an unusual Wilderness Crusade. I organized a veggie-a-thon where all my friends participated by going for 96 hours without any meat, fish or poultry. Money was raised by getting sponsors. It worked!
AMANDA FIELD,
Calgary, 1994

Until recently, the Boreal Forest was viewed as remote and removed from human development. Therefore, relatively little work has been done to identify and set aside wilderness lands and rivers there. Now, almost all of the region has been allocated for logging, so it is truly a landscape living on borrowed time. Lands known to be in need of protection include the Birch Mountains. This 5080-square-kilometre area, northwest of Fort McMurray, is a large plateau which supports unusual combinations of boreal, sub-arctic, and foothills plant communities, along with a variety of clearly visible physical features such as flutings, eskers, drumlins, and broken terrain. Lakes on the uplands are used by osprey, bald eagles, and white pelicans, among many other species.

Foothills   The Foothills natural region represents 16 per cent of Alberta. Most Albertans are familiar with the Upper and Lower Foothills region adjacent to the Rocky Mountains, which, together with the Rocky Mountains, are commonly referred to as the Eastern Slopes. However, the Foothills also cover a large area northwest of the town of Peace River, extending from the Eastern Slopes northeast to the Swan Hills.

Flat-topped hills which rise 300 to 600 metres above the surrounding lowlands distinguish the Swan Hills, home to the most inland race of grizzly bears in North America. The western Swan Hills were recommended for protection as a wilderness area in 1979 by public hearings on forestry operations. Sadly, no sizeable area has been protected, and now they have been largely lost to oil and gas development and to logging. The Clear Hills–Chinchaga in the Lower Foothills, and the Little Smokey in the Upper Foothills, the last large areas, are destined for the same fate if not protected soon.

Rocky Mountains   The Rocky Mountain natural region makes up about 8 per cent of Alberta and is generally well protected at the higher elevations. Canada's mountain national parks and Willmore Wilderness Park have made the Sub-Alpine and Alpine subregions familiar to people around the world. The low-elevation Montane, on the other hand, is the least protected and the most heavily developed subregion of the Rocky Mountains. Although the smallest by land area, it has the largest diversity and abundance of wildlife, functioning like an oasis in the mountain landscape of rock and ice. Found in limited areas along the main valleys of the southern Eastern Slopes, the vegetation of the Montane is strongly influenced by the mild Chinook-dominated climate, which keeps the area intermittently snow-free in winter.

Significant representative areas of the Montane subregion have yet to receive adequate legal protection. For example, the 236-square-kilometre Whaleback wildland west of Claresholm is Canada's last relatively undisturbed representative area of the Montane. The smooth, rounded hills of the Whaleback Ridge rise from the landscape like the vertebrae of a humpback whale. The grasslands of the Whaleback's southwest slopes give way to open stands of Douglas fir and wind-twisted limber pine. This wildland provides critical winter habitat for one of Alberta's two largest wintering herds of elk.

Canadian Shield Tucked away in the top northeast corner of Alberta is the Canadian Shield. The region's forest is low and stunted, and the landscape underlain with Precambrian bedrock. Thankfully, in this natural region, there are few signs of conflict between protection and industrial development. The majority of the region is in its natural state. North of Lake Athabasca is the Kazan Upland subregion, where outcroppings of the ancient Precambrian bedrock, especially granite, are common. The highest density of lakes in Alberta and extensive sand deposits, like those of the beautiful beaches of Lake Athabasca, characterize the Athabasca Plain subregion south of the lake. Within the Canadian Shield, the as yet unprotected 3491-square-kilometre Athabasca Sand Dunes–Richardson Lakeland is an outstanding wilderness area.

HISTORY OF WILDERNESS PROTECTION IN ALBERTA

The movement to protect Alberta's wilderness actually began before Alberta became a province in 1905. From 1885 to 1922, while the federal government still controlled the Crown lands and natural resources of the province, eight national parks were established. Unfortunately, three of them were "disestablished" to provide more livestock grazing lands and military reserves in two of our most threatened natural regions: the Parkland and Grassland. From 1930 to 1932, four provincial parks were established. However, most of the early provincial parks, as today, were small recreation areas. Of today's sixty-five provincial parks, only six could be considered to have protection as their primary focus, and only three are larger than 100 square kilometres.

Alberta's first designation of wilderness lands outside the national parks came in 1959 with the establishment of Willmore Wilderness Park. By 1961, there were three different pieces of legislation for four Wilderness Areas. There was also mounting public pressure for protection of wilderness, as well as broad concern for the environment in the face of rapid development of Alberta's Eastern Slopes. With the advent of the International Biological Program in the 1960s, it was clearly seen that Alberta needed to set aside and strictly protect samples of natural ecosystems as benchmarks against which to measure environmental change.

The public debate and hearings of the 1960s unfolded into the 1971 Wilderness Areas Act, which was understood to be a first step towards strictly protecting ecological benchmarks. However, specific actions to protect wildlands and rivers did not follow. In practice, and through further amendments to the act in 1981, decision makers addressed only one component of protected areas — small ecological reserves. They failed to provide for the preservation of large wilderness areas where non-motorized recreation would be permitted but development and vehicles would be prohibited.

Currently, the legislation and policy for the designation, protection, and management of natural landscapes in Alberta remain haphazard, with only Ecological Reserves and Wilderness Areas protected from industrial development. There are five types of legally protected areas: Ecological Reserves, Wilderness Areas, Wilderness Parks, Natural Areas, and Provincial Parks. They are covered under three pieces of legislation, the Provincial Parks Act (1980), the Willmore Wilderness Park Act (1980), and the Wilderness Areas, Ecological Reserves and Natural Areas Act (1981).

Although this legislation is workable, the political will to set aside natural areas and protect them from development has been generally lacking. The protected-areas system is far from complete, and is managed by chance rather than design, with no overall focus on completing a system of representative lands and

There is a sense of urgency in getting on with the task of completing a comprehensive network of protected areas. We must commit ourselves to our responsibility to past, present and future generations of Albertans to ensure the integrity of our natural heritage is protected. As the pace of human activity and resulting landscape change in the province quicken and intensify, new approaches and action are immediately needed to respond to the challenge of protected areas.
SPECIAL PLACES 2000,
November 1992

waters. This failing was acknowledged by the Alberta government in its 1992 draft policy *Special Places 2000: Alberta's Natural Heritage*, which firmly stated: "A systematic approach combined with immediate action is required if a comprehensive network of protected areas is to be passed on as a legacy to future generations."

So, Alberta entered the 1990s without a strong government commitment to completing a network of protected areas before it was too late. With political roadblocks to making progress on the ground, the Parks Service decided to put its resources into making progress on paper, refining what is perhaps still the best set of technical documents in Canada for a protected-areas system; complete with detailed natural-regions information and targets for strict protection.

Alberta conservation groups have a long history of wilderness advocacy. They signed on to WWF Canada's Endangered Spaces campaign in 1989, hoping the added national focus would finally bring about a protected-areas plan in their province. On March 11, 1992, at a joint news conference in Calgary, Premier Don Getty, Environmental Protection minister Ralph Klein, and Minister of Tourism, Parks and Recreation Don Sparrow, gave Prince Philip, International President of WWF, a commitment to prepare a provincial strategy for meeting the Endangered Spaces goal.

At the historic Tri-Council meeting of ministers in November 1992, Brian Evans, Minister of Environmental Protection, signed the Statement of Commitment, pledging to complete a protected areas system in Canada. The "Special Places 2000" *draft* policy was unveiled at that meeting.

The original document began with the statement: "The vision of Special Places 2000 is to complete a protected areas system that achieves the goals of protection, outdoor recreation, heritage appreciation and tourism." The Special Places 2000

On behalf of the executive and members of the Bow Valley Naturalists, I am pleased to inform you that we have endorsed the Canadian Wilderness Charter which serves as the mission statement for the Endangered Spaces campaign.
JON WHYTE, President,
Bow Valley Naturalists, 1989

strategy was based on a scientific framework that accounted for the ecological diversity of Alberta in the selection of candidate protected areas. Equally important, the document made a commitment to involving the public, including local communities, individuals, and groups, in the site-selection process.

In November 1993, a multistakeholder committee released its findings and report on the province-wide public review of the draft Special Places 2000. The advisory committee found that there was strong public support, to the point that Albertans wanted the protection goal to be the priority, and prompt action to protect areas. The committee not only recommended that the government proceed, but also provided specific recommendations on how to get the job done efficiently.

Reaction from hostile quarters to the advisory committee's report was swift. Albertans were wrongly told they would be completely shut out of the Eastern Slopes, so organizations representing outfitters and users of off-road vehicles wrote their MLAs, demanding that Special Places 2000 be killed. Rural Albertans were led to believe they would lose grazing lands, or that the lands would be expropriated. Therefore, the Alberta Cattle Commission lobbied hard against it too. The forest industry joined the mounting opposition because it was afraid that forest management agreements would not be honoured. And, after being incorrectly told that up to 30 per cent of the province would be "sterilized" or closed off to resource use, the powerful oil and gas industry also opposed the plan.

This combined lobbying effort presented Special Places 2000 with a major setback, and the government seemed temporarily to lose the political will to proceed — all this despite a June 1994 public-opinion poll of rural and urban Albertans which found that 93 per cent of them believed it was important to set aside wildland areas where there would be no industrial activity. Eighty per cent wanted the Alberta government to move immediately to implement Special Places 2000.

In July 1994, Environmental Protection minister Brian Evans succumbed to the pressure from the energy, forestry, and agriculture industries. He indicated that oil, gas, and other developments might be allowed to go ahead in new protected areas, and that the province might protect wilderness areas only where there was no potential conflict with any resource use.

Then the Whaleback happened (see also Chapter 6). On September 8, 1994, the Alberta Energy Resources Conservation Board denied Amoco Canada Limited approval to drill an exploratory sour gas well in the Whaleback wildland of southwestern Alberta. It concluded that "exploration drilling in this relatively undisturbed area of the province could jeopardize future provincial goals for the region" as it was a potential candidate for protection under Special Places 2000. This decision sent shockwaves through the oil and gas industry.

After considerable internal debate, the Canadian Association of Petroleum Producers (CAPP) announced their unanimous support for the Special Places 2000 initiative, and called on the government to move quickly. They believed the plan would provide "a rational, systematic procedure so that access to land is not frustrated by the inefficiency of the current hearing-by-hearing approach." In its news release, CAPP's chairman David O'Brien said, "CAPP recommends completing the review of certain protected core areas where no industrial activity occurs, including crude oil and natural gas exploration and development. . . ."

For the first time, a major force in Alberta's economic and political scene had come out publicly in support of a network of protected areas, and was willing to accept that there would be areas off limits to industrial development. Even more surprising was the fact that the oil and gas industry worked with conservation groups, including WWF, to get Special Places 2000 endorsed.

In January 1995, WWF met with Premier Ralph Klein, who personally assured the conservation community that the Endangered Spaces goal would be met in Alberta. Subsequently, the Minister of Environmental Protection, Ty Lund, said on a Calgary morning radio show that he was committed to having Special Places 2000 underway by April 1, 1995. First, there would be a process of site nominations by all Albertans, but Lund said his goal was to have the called-for network of protected areas completed by 1998. In an editorial, the *Calgary Herald* asserted that "there is little doubt that this step forward would not have been taken so readily by the province if the consensus between industrialists and environmentalists had not been achieved." Everything looked very promising.

. . . the private sector and the public at large must work cooperatively to establish a system of protected areas (including wilderness areas, ecological reserves, national parks, provincial parks, natural areas, wildlife refuges) to represent each of the natural regions of Alberta.

From a submission by the ALBERTA CHAMBER OF COMMERCE to the Government of Alberta, May 4, 1990

Unfortunately, the version of Special Places 2000 which was finally approved by Cabinet and announced on March 28, 1995, was seriously changed from the November 1992 draft that had garnered so much public support. The ecological-protection goal of the policy was downgraded, a veto was given to local committees (comprising representatives of all sectors) who might oppose specific sites, and the door was opened to a full spectrum of resource-development activities, including oil and gas development, which would effectively disqualify sites under the Endangered Spaces criteria. We can only assume that these changes were judged to be politically necessary to make Special Places more acceptable to a few concerned members of the legislature, to some cattle interests, and perhaps to all-terrain vehicle owners. In any case, they have seriously shaken the confidence of the conservation community in the new policy, and have raised questions about how effective a vehicle it can be for achieving the Endangered Spaces goal in Alberta.

WHAT NEXT?

For Alberta to move forward, we have to get beyond politics and actually protect areas! The void created by not having an effective protected-areas plan could mean that wilderness area-by-area battles will continue.

To prevent this, what has in effect been a moratorium on protected areas since 1977 needs to be visibly lifted by the immediate designation of the backlog of candidate protected areas which have already gone through studies, public hearings, and planning programs in the intervening eighteen years. Albertans faithfully gave their time and resources to participate in those processes. Seeing the areas actually protected could convincingly demonstrate that the now dubious Special Places 2000 implementation process (more meetings and advisory groups) can indeed result in the timely protection of Alberta's diverse wilderness heritage.

It will require "all hands on deck" to build an Alberta ark within the next three to five years. If immediate action is undertaken and the original intent of the Special Places 2000 policy is treated seriously, 75 per cent of the protected-areas network could be completed by the end of 1997, and at least 85 per cent completed by the end of 1998.

A well-informed public, with information in hand regarding areas needing protection and actions they can take in their local area, is needed to fuel the political will to nominate sites and then complete the job. The general public will be counting on Alberta's conservation groups to assist them in their communities. A provincial advisory body, comprising representatives committed to the establishment of protected areas, needs to be charged with overseeing nominations and designations, as well as filling in the ecological gaps if sufficient areas are not nominated by local communities.

There is no substitute for wilderness. Because of the rapid pace of development, the government must extend interim protection where the ecological integrity of an area may be impaired by development prior to a decision on its designation. Furthermore, such areas should be fast-tracked through the decision-making process. It's in everyone's best interest, industry and environmentalists alike, to complete this task sooner rather than later.

Assessments of environmentally significant areas in the whole of the Boreal Forest region and east-central Alberta need to be completed within two years. At the outset, priority must be placed on protecting a large wilderness area within each of the five major natural regions outside the Rocky Mountain natural region, plus an area within the Montane subregion in the Rocky Mountains. A further priority is nominating the largest remaining contiguous natural landscapes within each of the most threatened subregions. Finally, the government must prohibit resource exploration, industrial activity, and commercial development in existing protected areas, such as Willmore Wilderness Park, wildlife sanctuaries, natural areas, and those provincial parks that could contribute to the Endangered Spaces and Special Places 2000 protection goal.

The history of protected areas in Alberta has demonstrated a lack of political will on the part of its government, yet tenacious persistence on the part of Albertans. Today's provincial government is responsible for our last chance to protect Alberta's remaining wilderness lands and waters. Together we must make sure that, whether through Special Places 2000 or some other means, we preserve sufficient wilderness for this and future generations of people and wildlife alike.

Some of those who are most enthusiastic about the [Canadian Wilderness] Charter are visitors from Western Europe. They tell me that Europe has lost what we in Canada still have a chance to protect, and that they are looking to us for a future which includes wild places . . . Signing [the Charter] may seem only a small step, but is much more. It is an expression of their commitment and vision of the future.

Let's keep the ball rolling!
WARD HUGHSON, Interpreter, Jasper National Park, Alberta

9 / Saskatchewan

ALAN G. APPLEBY

 The Province of Saskatchewan was created through a land rush. Starting in the late 1800s, the "sod buster" era featured the granting of homesteads of Crown land to immigrants — people who came for a piece of this earth they could call their own, no matter the difficulties. While the stories of pioneer deprivation and hardship are legion across this province, they tend to focus on the settler experience. They are true and often heart-rending tales of human courage and ingenuity. But they are not the whole story. There have been few attempts to re-create the suffering of the land or its original inhabitants during this onslaught. And there have been few attempts to look honestly at what was lost.

Today, Saskatchewan is still largely a rural landscape. A land that, to the untrained or unknowing eye, presents a vision of vast tracts of wide-open spaces. You can travel many kilometres through the settled south without passing a farmstead or settlement. The province's towns and cities are small, even by Canadian standards. Half the people in Saskatchewan still live in rural areas, on farms or in small towns.

The north also seems largely undeveloped and uninhabited. In a province which has the highest per-capita length of paved road in Canada, no permanent all-weather road penetrates to the northern border, or even to within several hundred kilometres of it. Settlements are small and scattered. Significant natural-resource development on a widespread basis has only really begun in the last two decades.

So, can there be an endangered spaces problem, if so many open spaces remain? The truth, on closer inspection, reveals a different story of hardship in the settling of this land. This truth would talk about the eradication of the bison herds, and their replacement with enormous herds of cattle, grazing behind an increasing length of barbed wire, on more and more hectares of tame grass crops. This truth would speak to the elimination of the plains grizzly bear, and of the wolf, which once drew sustenance from the buffalo herds. And this truth would outline the systematic destruction of swift fox, prairie dog, and other wildlife populations on the prairie. Some might measure progress in the endless plough furrows that cut so deeply into the native soil and turned the natural prairie vegetation over to grain. But they should also look at what we lost in our rush to become "the breadbasket of the world."

In the book *Endangered Spaces*, David Gauthier and David Henry, authors of the chapter on the Prairies, said the following: "The Canadian prairies have become one of the most endangered natural habitats in Canada. Human efforts have been directed towards maximizing economic return. The natural productivity of the soil and precious water resources have been viewed as a bank in which the emphasis has been on withdrawals, not deposits."

The recounting of this change by Gauthier and Henry is perhaps one of the best we have today in a concise form. It is fitting that it served as the background against which the Endangered Spaces campaign was launched in 1989 for the prairie region and the Province of Saskatchewan.

TAKING STOCK: BEGINNING IN 1989

Where exactly were we in 1989? According to the Endangered Spaces Progress Report of 1990, 19,366 of Saskatchewan's 651,900 square kilometres were under some form of protective status in 1989. This was about 3 per cent of the total area of the province. More important, only about 1 per cent of this land was protected to Endangered Spaces standards: no mining, no logging, no hydro-electric development.

But this was a rough estimate. There was no actual inventory of all the areas that could be considered "protected" in one way or another, whether to Endangered Spaces standards or not. There was no accounting of how well or poorly these protected lands represented the biological diversity of the province. In fact, there was no agreed-upon map of ecological regions for the province!

Some Saskatchewan protected-areas programs were mired in a cycle of inactivity, or at least non-accomplishment. Although the Ecological Reserves Act had been proclaimed in 1982, only one area had been designated by 1989, despite the fact that dozens of background reports were sitting in government files.

The park system seemed to be in better shape, following the passage of a new Parks Act in 1986. Seventeen new parks had been created, including Saskatchewan's first wilderness park — the Clearwater River Wilderness Park. A parkland classification system provided for Protected Areas, and a Park Land Reserve category to bring new lands under protection.

During the early 1980s, wildlife programs had concentrated heavily on identifying "critical wildlife habitat," and during the latter half of the decade, had moved into the business of designating lands. All the remaining 9 million hectares of Crown land in the southern agricultural part of the province was analysed for its value to wildlife populations and more than a third was classified as "critical." This land represented the bulk of what was directly available to the province for protection in a highly changed area.

The Grasslands National Park, an idea whose time seemed to have almost come and gone, received a boost in 1988 with the signing of a new Federal-Provincial Amending Agreement to the Grasslands National Park Agreement. The original agreement, signed in 1981, had been plagued with problems. The new agreement acknowledged the province's ownership of the park's watercourses and associated riparian lands. That meant that the final park would be a patchwork of federal and provincial jurisdictions, arranged around gaps created by landowners unwilling to sell their land, and cemented by variable government relationships. But at least a Grasslands National Park seemed possible.

In the north, a mining boom had been under way for some years, leading to many new access roads and widespread exploration activities. Forest Management

Natural Regions of Saskatchewan
Ecological Representation by Protected Areas

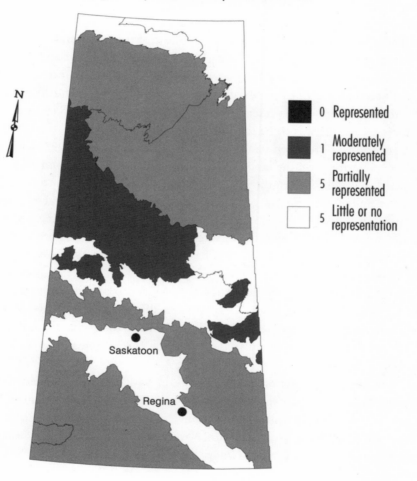

N

0	Represented
1	Moderately represented
5	Partially represented
5	Little or no representation

Saskatoon

Regina

As of April 1, 1995

Licence Agreements (FMLAs) were being negotiated and signed with large forest companies for extensive areas south of the Churchill River. Lands were also being selected by First Nations in fulfilment of the promises made in treaties to provide land for settlement and economic development.

During this period of northern development, there was no inventory of protected areas. Some areas had been set aside by Crown land-use policies, including 100 natural areas identified by the International Biological Programme (IBP) during 1969–74, and specific sites identified in local planning studies.

In most respects, Saskatchewan seemed to be right in the middle of the provincial pack in terms of progress among jurisdictions across Canada at the beginning of the Endangered Spaces campaign in 1989.

PROGRESS FROM 1989 TO 1995

There were some very promising beginnings during this early part of the campaign. The Parks System Plan, a comprehensive review of the needs and opportunities for the future development of the provincial-parks system, was announced in December 1990. This plan proposed twenty-seven new parkland designations, which would almost double the area of the existing parks system by the year 2000 and substantially reduce gaps in the representation of Saskatchewan's natural regions. An implementation schedule was to be released by late fall, 1991.

A government Protected Areas Strategy was under way by 1990. Its first project was an inventory of all the lands which government and others had designated and protected. Not all, or even the majority, of the lands identified in this study would meet the Endangered Spaces campaign standards. But at least there would be an inventory of what there was to deal with. An associated mapping project by Dr. David Gauthier of the University of Regina, begun in 1990, has produced a digital map of all land and water areas that have been identified as having some level of protection.

In 1991 efforts were renewed by the government to designate and manage more Critical Wildlife Habitat lands. Only about half the lands initially identified had been designated under the Critical Wildlife Habitat Protection Act during previous rounds, and much of what was left included the core of remaining prairie lands in the southwest.

On other fronts, environmental groups in Saskatchewan banded together to form the Wilderness Strategy Committee (WSC). The WSC is an alliance of government and non-government organizations, including the Canadian Parks and Wilderness Society, the Saskatchewan Natural History Society, the Saskatchewan Environmental Society, the Gaia Group, the University of Regina, and the University of Saskatchewan.

This committee was formed to provide a focus for public awareness and advocacy, and to work on specific contributory projects. One of their most important contributions to date has been the book *Saskatchewan's Endangered Spaces*, edited by Peter Jonker of the University of Saskatchewan. This book contains a compilation of information on natural areas, potential candidate sites, and strategies to achieve the goal of a network of representative protected areas.

Another project of the WSC, organized through the Endangered Species and

Barrenground grizzlies use this lone rock on the arctic
tundra as a scratching post. CHRIS O'BRIEN

Caribou tracks found on a Daring Lake
beach, N.W.T. CHRIS O'BRIEN

Protecting the Tombstone Mountains is a key
priority in the Yukon. KEN MADSEN

Additional protection is still needed for B.C.'s low-elevation forests.
ADRIAN DORST

Kluane National Park in the Yukon is a World Heritage Site.
KEN MADSEN

The Tatshenshini Wilderness Area, a one-million-hectare national treasure, is now safeguarded as a provincial park and World Heritage Site.
WWF

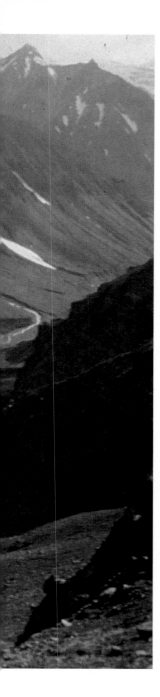

B.C.'s Khutzeymateen Valley is Canada's first grizzly
bear sanctuary. DUANE SEPT

A number of endangered grassland species live in the Okanagan Valley
of south-central B.C. ADRIAN DORST

Protection has now been secured for the lower half of Vancouver Island's Walbran Valley, an area where colossal west-coast red cedar grow. ADRIAN DORST

The recent creation of Juan de Fuca Park is a significant achievement for those who have worked tirelessly to extend Vancouver Island's West Coast Trail.
ADRIAN DORST

Marine protected areas are needed to preserve species ranging from this giant pink starfish to killer whales.
VALERIE J. WHETTER

The spectacular Kitlope watershed has been protected through the cooperative efforts of the Haisla First Nation, West Fraser Timber Company, and the B.C. government.
ADRIAN DORST

Spaces Committee of the Saskatchewan Natural History Society, was a Special Places map based on the natural regions of the province. The map is a product of the experience and expertise of many people in different walks of life, all considered in some respect as experts, and it indicates what areas they thought deserved protection.

A Saskatchewan Conservation Data Centre was set up in 1992 through efforts of the Nature Conservancy of Canada and the province, with the assistance of private donors. While the focus of this office is rare and endangered species, its mapping and information base will also be very useful in the overall effort to establish protected areas.

Political support was confirmed in 1991, when the new government of Premier Roy Romanow took office. Premier Romanow (and all of his caucus) had signed the Canadian Wilderness Charter while in Opposition. Two of his ministers were present for the signing of the historic Tri-Council commitment on protected areas in 1992.

In 1994, and again in 1995, a Private Member's Motion in support of the Endangered Spaces campaign was put forward by two Members of the Legislature (Mark Koenker and Lorne Scott). These motions each received over an hour's discussion, with positive comments from all three parties on both sides of the House. And in the fall of 1994, the province produced a first-class Ecoregions of Saskatchewan map, consolidating and replacing several different previous versions, so that everyone was working on the same basis for land protection for the first time.

It looked like Saskatchewan was making significant progress and, more important, providing itself with a variety of tools to help finish the job.

I move that this Assembly [the Saskatchewan Legislature] support the work of the Minister of Environment and Resources Management, his department, and conservation organizations in their efforts to achieve the goals of the World Wildlife Fund's action plan for Endangered Spaces.
LORNE SCOTT, MLA, Indian Head–Wolseley, 1994

THE REALITIES OF 1995

Nobody expected spectacular results. It takes time to put programs together, and to see the results begin to flow. By 1993, with the release of the fourth Endangered Spaces Progress Report, the area of Saskatchewan under protection had increased to 4.2 per cent, covering 27,322 square kilometres.

This was measurable progress; however, the province seemed to be falling behind other jurisdictions in the pace of activity. This was confirmed in 1995, when the fifth progress report was being put together. By February 1995, Saskatchewan's total area under protection had actually fallen to 20,684 square kilometres, as some lands had been removed because decisions on their use meant they no longer counted.

Many of the projects needed to maintain momentum were stalled, on hold, or inactive. The Parks System Plan Implementation Strategy, promised five years earlier, in 1990, had still not been issued, even in a draft version for public review. The Protected Areas Strategy had not been completed, and there was no estimate of when it might be done, if at all, although a useful inventory of protected lands did get completed.

Then there was the proverbial government reorganization. From 1993 to 1995, the lead responsibility for the protected-areas program bounced through four administrative units. During this time, minimal attention was focused on the program, and minimal activity ensued. In essence, it was two years of lost time, at a juncture when previous progress, combined with political and public support, could have accelerated the program to the extent needed to accomplish our goal.

At the halfway mark in the Endangered Spaces campaign, Saskatchewan has far less than half of its ecological regions represented by protected areas. Nevertheless, there does exist a basis for meeting the challenge and getting the task accomplished, including a solid background of inventory and analysis, as well as political and public support for the goals of the program. The question is not, *can* it be done, but *how* will it get done?

THE NEEDS FROM NOW TO 2000

What is needed, above all else, is one simple and straightforward document: a plan. A plan to show what needs to be done, how it will be done, and when the milestones must be reached; a plan to focus public attention and galvanize action. Recently, as this chapter was being written, the government did forward draft material which starts to outline the steps necessary to see the Endangered Spaces target reached. Those steps, combined with the recommendations of the Wilderness Strategy Committee, would see the following priorities endorsed:

- *Release a draft Strategic Plan for an ecologically representative protected-areas network for consultation with all conservation interests and land users in the province.* This is the one simple request that non-government groups, through the WSC, have been requesting over the past two years. This plan must be based on the Endangered Spaces principles of ecological representation and integrity. And the plan must be available for discussion with interested groups and individuals in the province.

- *Continue with the designation of existing candidate areas, as identified in the Parks System Plan and the Ecological Reserves Program.* Many studies have been completed both before and during the time of the Endangered Spaces campaign. Several of these have had some degree of public input, or are in a public forum now, including the Great Sand Hills, the Manito Sand Hills, Rice River Canyon, and the Wapawekka Hills. These studies should continue and be accelerated. Efforts should proceed to solicit public input regarding these candidate areas, and to make decisions on their designation as quickly as possible.

- *Conduct gap analysis to determine where additional representation of natural regions is required.* The candidate sites identified to date in Saskatchewan lack two essential elements required to achieve the goal of the Endangered Spaces campaign: some measure of ecological representation, and some confidence in their ecological integrity. Most of the designated areas, except perhaps those in the Parks System Plan, lack these essentials as well.

- *Continue analysis of Wildlife Habitat Protection Act lands to determine if protected-area candidate sites still exist on Crown agricultural lands that are in a relatively natural state.* One of the critical areas for consideration is the aspen parkland in the agricultural south of Saskatchewan. These are among the province's most highly modified lands, areas where only small remnants of the original prairie remain. Yet they are still under pressure for change and development. Any remaining large areas of contiguous Crown land in a near-natural state in this part of the province are essential components of a future protected-areas system.

- *Develop effective education programs and public involvement to ensure continued acceptance of protected areas.* The designations needed to complete the system in Saskatchewan will be made only with widespread public involvement. This will require public information and education to ensure that the goals and underlying principles of the campaign are understood and supported by a cross-section of society.

- *Encourage private land stewardship and protection of ecological integrity.* In the southern half of Saskatchewan, the majority of land is privately owned. In fact, the province has about 30 per cent of Canada's private land. Under these circumstances, there are many natural regions that obviously will not have adequate representation without the participation of private landowners. This calls for methods to involve landowners in the process; for example, innovative ways for retaining private ownership, and encouraging uses compatible with the objectives of a protected-areas system.

- *Protect the ecological integrity of the network in cooperation with land users such as the forestry and mining sectors.* Designating a system of natural areas will not be enough. Some of the setbacks in recent years have proven this. For instance, a gold mine was opened in Lac La Ronge Provincial Park in 1994. Plans and policies backed by principles enshrined in legislation are needed for the management of designated areas. The legislation must reflect the ecological principles upon which the system is built. And there must be safeguards against, and guarantees of protection from, arbitrary political changes.

- *Develop a working relationship with First Nations in the creation of a protected-areas system, and the designation and protection of land.* The first residents of this province have always had a special connection to the earth and its resources. About one-quarter of the Saskatchewan population will be of aboriginal descent by the year 2000. That proportion will increase as time goes on. Native peoples will continue to be important owners, users, and stewards of the land and its resources.

  The obligations of treaties signed with First Nations will need to be met. Those treaties guarantee access to resources, and access to and ownership of lands. According to the 1992 Treaty Land Entitlement Framework Agreement, outstanding treaty land entitlements in Saskatchewan involve twenty-six First Nations and amount to a total area of nearly 640,000 hectares. No system of protected areas in Saskatchewan will succeed without the active participation and involvement of First Nations.

THE NEED FOR A NEW LAND RUSH

Saskatchewan was opened up to settlement, and brought to its present state of development, by government policy. The homesteading era was a deliberate and well-advertised program of settlement, designed to further the economic interests of the country and to defend against the potential loss of territory through lack of

The Endangered Spaces campaign provides a perfect opportunity for concerned MLAs and MPs to address the issue of protecting representative regions of Canada. Some may act because of mounting evidence and sincere concern. Others may act because of public pressure. Their motives do not really matter. What matters is that they do act.
DOUG ANGUISH, MLA, North Battleford, 1990

development and use. Settlers were encouraged and assisted to come and "open up the prairies," with Red River cart, iron horse, and plough. This land rush resulted in the homesteading and subsequent sale of over a third of the area of the province.

What is required now is a new land rush, with many of the same features of the original, but some different objectives. This new land rush should be a quick and pointed effort to save the remaining natural areas of this province. It too should be carried out with the support of government policy and legislation. In this new land rush it should be government policy to save representative areas of this land in a natural state for all time.

The site candidates for this land rush should be sought as ardently and as widely as were the candidates for the original homestead grants of land. Surveys should be done to ensure that the boundaries of the land are known and the ownership is not in question. And laws should be enacted to ensure the sanctity of these protected areas, just as the homesteads of our ancestors are protected in law and title.

This new land rush will bring many of the same benefits of the original settlement. We will see new prosperity in our natural areas as they receive protection. We will see the residents flourish in a land where there is some certainty of continued existence. We will see protection for an ecological system that has been under constant change and threat for over a century. We will also see a rationalization and integration of the uses of our land, where sensitive areas will be safe from the harmful effects of uses on adjacent lands.

Stan Rowe, who was born and raised in the grasslands of southern Alberta, and who spent much of his working life in the parklands of Saskatchewan, sums it all up well in his contribution to *Saskatchewan's Endangered Spaces*: "I believe with Thoreau and Muir that humanity needs the wild. Just as we will not save the riverine forest without protecting the flood plain, or preserve the orchids without preserving the marshes, so our own fate is linked to the limits we set on domestication of the world around us, and to the offsetting effort we devote to maintaining the natural beauty and health of this one and only sustaining, enveloping Ecosphere."

10 / Manitoba

GAILE WHELAN-ENNS

 Visitors and native Manitobans alike marvel at the diverse natural beauty of our province. From tundra vistas and caribou herds numbering in the hundreds of thousands, to the remaining tall-grass prairie in southeastern Manitoba, this province has it all. Follow rivers untouched by hydro-electric development, where canoeists can be away from the paved world in a matter of hours. Or walk among land-locked sand dunes which visitors can barely believe exist — even after feeling the sand on their feet. And the lakes: the strongest sense of ocean inside a continent is the view from Delta Marsh or Elk Island across Lake Manitoba or Lake Winnipeg. These marvels make protection of Manitoba's natural-region features essential.

THE PROTECTION CAMPAIGN BEGINS

In 1989 Manitoba had one national park, at Riding Mountain. There were provincial parks located in most regions, but most of these permitted resource extraction of one kind or another. Only one wilderness park had been created — Atikaki, in 1985. Although existing laws provided for Ecological Reserves with relatively good protection standards, very few reserves had actually been established. None of the twelve natural regions in the province was fully represented.

When the Endangered Spaces campaign was launched in 1989, the Manitoba Naturalists Society began to plan how the campaign could be introduced in the province. Among other things, they aimed for an early commitment to the Endangered Spaces goal from the government, and they anticipated what should be in the first year's progress report.

In August 1990, at election time, Premier Gary Filmon was the first provincial government leader in Canada to make a commitment to the Endangered Spaces goal. This step was followed quickly by Ontario. So provincial government commitments across the country were begun by Manitoba! The premier personally circulated copies of the book *Endangered Spaces* to all members of the Manitoba legislature. And Manitoba citizens and community organizations began to sign the Canadian Wilderness Charter, indicating their support for the campaign.

By this time, the Manitoba Wilderness Caucus had been formed and was planning public education and lobbying activities. The caucus evolved from the Parks Committee of the Manitoba Naturalists Society and now includes conservation organizations and committed individuals from around the province who keep up-to-date on the campaign, lending their expertise to strategies identified for

Manitoba. An Endangered Spaces discussion map was produced, showing locations at greatest risk, and a curriculum package was made available to Manitoba schools.

In their planning sessions, the Manitoba Wilderness Caucus discussed a game plan for the Endangered Spaces campaign in their province. The challenge was to represent ecologically diverse natural regions, which include First Nations traditional and claimed lands, heavily farmed areas in the south, and various parks and other designated lands throughout the province. The potential for core reserves in the north was countered by the challenge of getting representation elsewhere in natural regions where there was little Crown land, few parks, and very changed habitat.

The caucus saw a need for a transition zone around Riding Mountain National Park, and two additional national parks — one along Hudson Bay in the Churchill area and the other in the "Interlake" area between the huge lakes in the Manitoba Lowlands. It began to monitor the existing national park and to lobby for a feasibility study, based on a federal-provincial memorandum of understanding, to assess sites in the Manitoba Lowlands. The caucus also began, with financial and technical support from WWF, to work with the Naturalists Society and other environmental organizations in the province to identify and secure tall-grass prairie. And they urged the provincial government to make better use of the Ecological Reserves Act to designate many sites which had already been identified.

It was clear that the level of protection in Manitoba's parks fell far short of the Endangered Spaces protection standards. In fact, the government policy permitting resource extraction in parks became a focus for efforts to identify the most endangered areas. In the agricultural south, designated lands (ecological reserves, wildlife management areas, parks, and provincial forests) offered the chief opportunities for natural-region representation, but management plans or regulations would have to be changed to upgrade their protection.

Several events provided signposts during the first half of the Manitoba campaign. After considerable lobbying in 1992, a Memorandum of Understanding was signed between Manitoba and the federal government to undertake a national-park feasibility study of three candidate areas for a park within the Manitoba Lowlands. Thus, the long process to achieve a national park in this region was pushed forward another step.

Although its contribution to ecological representation of natural regions has not yet been clearly defined, the designation of any river as a Heritage River draws public attention to its national significance and makes development along it that much more difficult. In 1985, Manitoba nominated the Bloodvein a Heritage River. This tamarack-lined wilderness river runs through Woodland Caribou Provincial Park in Ontario and through Atikaki Wilderness Park in Manitoba. Seven years later, Manitoba obtained Heritage River status for the Seal River, which flows into Hudson Bay. Its estuary forms summer habitat for beluga whales. Before the river's nomination, consultations were held with First Nations and local communities about possible designation and a river management plan. It's worth noting that veteran Minister of Natural Resources, Harry Enns, canoed and fished the Seal prior to its designation!

Manitoba is currently assessing more than twenty rivers for possible Heritage River status. First Nations have requested that the Hayes River be studied for nomination, and the Wilderness Caucus has suggested the Bell River and its canyon.

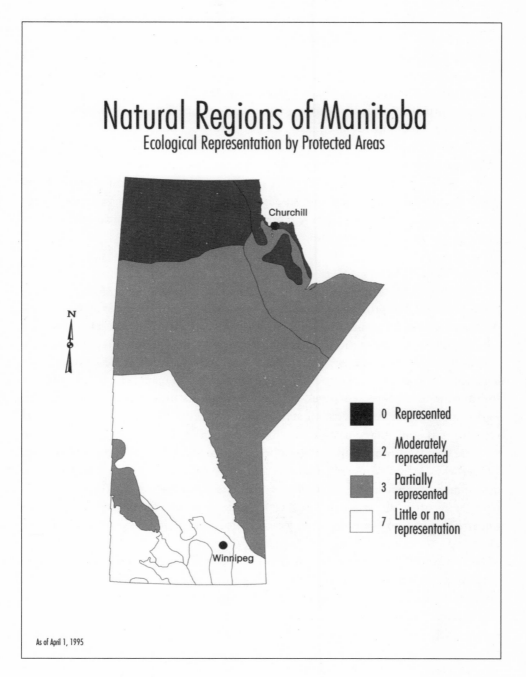

Natural Regions of Manitoba
Ecological Representation by Protected Areas

Churchill

N

■ 0	Represented
■ 2	Moderately represented
■ 3	Partially represented
□ 7	Little or no representation

Winnipeg

As of April 1, 1995

In June 1993, Manitoba reserved a portion of the Churchill Wildlife Management Area for Churchill National Park, which was being negotiated at that time by the federal and provincial governments, the local government of the District of Churchill, and First Nations represented by Manitoba Keewatinowi Okimakanak Inc. (MKO) on behalf of two of its member bands. This national park reserve was established using a special regulation under the provincial Wildlife Act. The regulation expressly disallowed logging, mining, and hydro-electric development in the area being withdrawn.

That same summer, the Manitoba government tabled new parks legislation, which was amended after extensive public hearings. The Parks Act's preamble confirms the province's commitment to the Endangered Spaces goal. However, this legislation also sanctions resource extraction in parks.

The provincial government had placed the responsibility for its Endangered Spaces commitment in the hands of the Sustainable Development Coordination Unit, which was attached to the Premier's Office. As a result, the Parks and Natural Areas Branch had little to do with Endangered Spaces actions. This changed in the spring of 1993, when the scientific representation piece of the campaign was set in motion.

REPRESENTATION SCIENCE

In 1993 and 1994, WWF worked with the Canadian Council on Ecological Areas to provide a tool for protected-areas decision making based on accessible common data and coarse filter analysis of landform features in each natural region (see Chapter 1). The first session presenting the draft WWF methodology was held in February 1994, at Winnipeg's International Institute for Sustainable Development. This seminar was attended by academics, scientists, parks managers, policy officials, foresters, industry representatives, and conservationists from across Manitoba. The Parks and Natural Areas Branch staff presented their first-stage work, and Parks Canada staff contributed case-studies for discussion.

That day, landforms representation became a priority in the Manitoba campaign. Wilderness Caucus members familiarized themselves with both WWF and provincial government methods, and responded to requests for more information that began to pour in after the seminar. Landscape students in the Faculty of Architecture undertook a gap-analysis project to assess protection possibilities in the Assiniboine Delta natural region.

By early 1995, the government had a review of natural-region boundaries underway, developed new biophysical inventories for its regions, and was beginning to apply technical criteria and exchange information with WWF regarding site selection and representation. Finally, an agreed-upon way to measure ecological representation in each Manitoba natural region was within reach.

SUSTAINABLE DEVELOPMENT

The province's Sustainable Development Coordination Unit continued to be the filter through which decisions and policy concerning the Endangered Spaces commitment passed. It published its "Action Plan for a Network of Special Places" in February 1994. Unfortunately, this plan combined various provincial commitments to protect biodiversity with a selection of candidate sites that were not based on representation or conservation science, but on "resource inventories." The province claimed that some of the natural regions were simply impossible to represent, and that any region with a large national park in it was considered to be already represented.

A further document, "Candidate Sites for the Endangered Spaces Campaign," was also released for review in the spring of 1994. Its incomplete land-use and natural-region information posed problems. At the same time, efforts to discuss resource extraction activities allowed in the province's parks continued with no positive results. Even the four parks identified by the province in its action plan for increased protection in 1994 — Whiteshell, Atikaki, Turtle Mountain, and Spruce Woods — languished with no decision. Meanwhile, the new Parks Act had still not been proclaimed, although there were repeated promises from government that each park would be reviewed and that possible improvements in protection standards could result.

Most recently, to address concerns regarding the protection of private lands, the Manitoba government has made a commitment to conservation-easement legislation, and it has started research on other jurisdictions' legislation. A period of consultation with all those affected will be essential to producing a successful conservation tool in this regard.

The Sustainable Development Coordination Unit brings a high public profile to the Endangered Spaces campaign in Manitoba, and potential support from the senior political level. As can be seen, however, it has not brought about significant improvement in the actual protection of the most endangered locations in the province. Intense public scrutiny resulted from the strong political commitment to the Endangered Spaces goal and to the work of the Sustainable Development Coordination Unit. However, development cannot run amok, or sustainable development is a sham. While there has been a move from 2.2 to 5.5 per cent of the province protected to Endangered Spaces standards, this has largely been based on the Churchill National Park reserve and the announcement, in February 1995, of four new northern parks. During the period between the protection of a reserve around Churchill and the designation of the four northern parks, resource extraction in protected and candidate areas and other designated lands in southern and central Manitoba increased.

Throughout the Sustainable Development public policy process, there has been consistent analysis from the Wilderness Caucus of actions taken that appear to be driven by short-term economic goals rather than the long-term integration of environmental, economic, and social considerations. For example, the potential for sustainable development and long-term protection does not appear to be fulfilled by granting forestry licences for large tracts without protected areas, or by a reluctance to withdraw protected lands from the Mines Registry. Failure to abide by the government's own Clean Environment Commission's recommendations to stop logging in Nopoming Provincial Park also serves to increase concern about the protection of biodiversity in Manitoba.

COMMUNITIES AND THE FUTURE
It is possible to fulfil the Endangered Spaces commitment by the year 2000 through a series of planned steps, making sure that every natural region is part of the plan.

Private landowners should be provided with the tools and incentives to protect their lands to Endangered Spaces standards. Manitobans should be able to see their parks, or portions of parks, likewise protected. First Nations should be full participants when considering new protected-area designations on their traditional lands. Partnerships should be formed across rural-urban lines. And both immediate issues and long-term goals regarding land use should be integrated at the community level.

The current focus on Manitoba's parks as potential sources of industrial resource development is short-sighted. Permanent legal protection to Endangered Spaces standards, on the other hand, can have many long-term benefits for our communities. We are only beginning to understand the positive consequences of maintaining biodiversity for future research and medical purposes. Conservationists point to that portion of our economy which is nature- and wildlife-based, and suggest that the potential for economic benefits from recreation and tourism are far from realized. In Manitoba, the move from one to three national parks in itself will have permanent and increasingly positive effects on the economy.

As of 1995, of Manitoba's twelve natural regions, two are moderately represented, three have partial representation, and seven have little or no representation. Most of our provincial parks still accommodate virtually any industrial use requested, including mineral exploration, logging, oil wells, and gravel pits.

The reserve for Churchill National Park, together with the four parks in northern Manitoba established early in 1995, increased representation in three natural regions in northern Manitoba. Riding Mountain National Park, located in the Western Uplands region, partially represents that region. Otherwise, a few small ecological reserves are the only other sites in Manitoba that currently reach Endangered Spaces protection standards.

There are many "natural" parks in the province's system of protected areas. There are also many areas in a state of protection approaching Endangered Spaces standards which present an opportunity for increased representation of natural regions. These include provincial parks and forests, wildlife management areas, and private land in conservation programs. However, current management practices would have to be changed or disallowed for these to qualify.

The most urgent step required to ensure that the goals of the Endangered Spaces campaign are met in Manitoba by the year 2000 is for the government to stop the irrevocable transfer of natural lands to resource companies before gap analysis is concluded and natural areas are identified for protection. For example, the province's forestry agreement with Louisiana–Pacific Canada Limited constitutes a serious setback for the campaign because it virtually eliminates important parts of four natural regions — none of which is fully represented — from the possibility of protection to Endangered Spaces standards. There is no plan to represent the natural regions involved in this agreement.

At the midway point in the campaign, the work that is left to accomplish the Endangered Spaces goal in Manitoba falls along a clear critical path:

- *Establish a plan for protecting enduring features in each forest management licence.* Exempt any protected areas or candidate sites from new agreements until their status is resolved. Identify areas for protection before signing new agreements. Make representation of the natural region a condition of forest management agreements. Continue this practice until the Endangered Spaces goal has been achieved in Manitoba.

- *Establish Churchill National Park.* Upon signing the agreement, federal and provincial governments, the local government of the District of Churchill, and MKO on behalf of Fox Lake and York Factory First Nations will establish a co-management board for Churchill National Park (1995). The board can then plan for the park. Lands need to be transferred, and training and staffing put in place (1996).

- *Establish the Manitoba Lowlands National Park.* Manitoba needs to complete representation of this natural region between 1995 and 1997. Change the mandate of the Lowlands Feasibility Study to allow the study team to consider all candidate sites for possible inclusion in the proposed park (1995). Ensure that final site selection is done primarily on ecological grounds and in full compliance with National Parks Policy (1996). Consult with local communities, other stakeholders, and First Nations concerning the establishment of the park. Impose a moratorium on development in the chosen site or sites (1996–97). Establish the park, withdraw the lands, and undertake development of a park management agreement and plan (1996–98).

- *Expand the tall-grass prairie preserve in southeast Manitoba to include all possible sites.* Continued work to identify tall-grass prairie remnants in southeast and southcentral Manitoba needs to be staffed and supported. Lands in the preserve, and Crown lands elsewhere with tall-grass prairie, require a moratorium on development, with lands withdrawn from the Mines Registry. All of the reserve and other remnant sites need to be protected to Endangered Spaces standards. A fully accessible information base of all remnant sites in the province needs to be established. Make sure that private landowners participating in protection of tall-grass prairie have information available to them about protecting sites to Endangered Spaces standards (completed by 1997, first steps in 1995).

- *Make better use of the Ecologically Significant Lands Program.* This program handles the establishment of ecological reserves on Crown lands. Coordinate inventory work in wildlife management areas, especially those already searched for tall-grass prairie remnants, and identify significant enduring features in natural regions so that these sites can be designated ecological reserves. Use this program to capture landscape features in regions in southern Manitoba that are difficult to protect (1995–97).

- *Review all sites designated on Crown land to determine their potential contribution to natural-region representation.* Zoning in Crown land sites could meet specific protection objectives. Wildlife management areas and provincial forests, in particular, hold important opportunities for representation of the Pre-Cambrian Forest, Manitoba Lowlands, and southern Manitoba natural regions (1995–97).

Our long-range goal reflects that of the World Wildlife Fund which is to ensure that a representative part of each of Manitoba's regions will be set aside and protected. This will help preserve wildlife in their natural environment for the enjoyment of future generations.
GARY FILMON, Premier of Manitoba, August 22, 1990

- *Increase protection in Manitoba's parks.* A public review of parks in the province is planned to commence in 1995 and to continue in 1996. During this process, public information regarding the potential for parks to protect biodiversity should be made available. With a clear statement in the preamble of the Parks Act regarding the Endangered Spaces goal, we assume that the government will suggest increasing representation through revised park management plans (1995–96). Such changes would allow Grassy River, Spruce Woods, and Atikaki, for example, to meet Endangered Spaces protection standards. Manitoba has the most permissive parks policy in Canada, with the result that none of the natural parks in Manitoba currently meets these standards. Difficult decisions regarding resource extraction in our parks will need to be made if this province is to protect its biodiversity.

- *Designate new protected areas to complete representation of all regions.* Thorough gap analysis of each natural region's enduring features is essential, so that all avenues for representation of natural regions can be explored. New protected areas that meet the Endangered Spaces standards will provide recreational, economic, scientific, and tourism benefits to Manitoba society (1996–99).

- *Provide private landowners with a conservation-easement tool.* This would allow a caveat to be placed on the title of lands, which would protect them for the long term to Endangered Spaces standards. Make full information available to landowners so they can determine how important their voluntary protection decisions will be. Establish, with the cooperation of non-government organizations and government programs, an ongoing registry of all private lands enrolled in various conservation programs (1996).

- *Build on existing conservation programs for private lands.* Determine locations in Manitoba's natural regions where private land can most contribute to representation, and provide incentives to landowners to upgrade protection. Changes in agricultural practices, the end of the grain transportation subsidy, potential changes in cropping, and the return of lands to non-cultivated status could all help increase protection on private lands (1995–99).

- *Ensure that the Parks and Natural Areas Branch has sufficient staff and resources.* This is necessary to complete the scientific work under way, including the review of the boundaries of Manitoba's natural regions, biophysical inventories, and full gap-analysis work to identify all unprotected landscape features. This information can be provided to government agencies, industry, and landowners as a basis for action to complete representation (1995–96).

- *Consult First Nations fully concerning any new land designation.* Where potential Crown land designations impact on treaty land entitlements, consultation on how protected areas can facilitate and ensure traditional uses is essential. Investigate co-management, training, and staffing opportunities for First Nation citizens when new designations are being discussed. Incorporate traditional knowledge into inventory or fieldwork on sites. Legal protection wording must identify First Nations activities which will be included, as well as development activities which will be excluded.

This will protect aboriginal rights to hunt, trap, gather, and travel in traditional lands. Confirm that existing treaties and agreements are being upheld, as well as provincial responsibilities for consultation and negotiation with First Nations. Identify any federal government involvement in lands under discussion. Confirm that the establishment of parks does not bar future land selection in a land claim. All Endangered Spaces partners in Manitoba need to provide support for decisions First Nations make regarding protection of their lands which could contribute towards natural-regions representation (1995–2000).

- *Make decisions that will assist in ensuring the long-term viability of Riding Mountain National Park.* Provide incentives and regulations that will increase, rather than decrease, protection around the park. Review Crown land classification, sale, and licensing policies as they affect national parks. Provide field staff with a mandate to work with national parks staff for the long-term viability of Manitoba's three national parks (1995–2000).

- *Find new ways to protect biodiversity in the agricultural areas of Manitoba.* In natural regions dominated by agricultural use, employ all of the available tools to achieve representation. Partnerships among producer organizations, conservation organizations, and local governments can help communicate the mutual benefits of protecting biodiversity. To find innovative solutions to conservation and protection problems, apply gap analysis, restoration techniques, co-management, conservation biology, and incentives to farmers and ranchers (1995–2000).

- *Complete the job of representation begun in northern Manitoba.* This means full consultation with First Nations concerning any future designations. These natural regions, where mining has not impacted on the landscape, present many opportunities for protection. It is essential to apply gap analysis and identify what still needs to be done to reach full representation of natural regions in the north (1996–98).

PROBLEMS AND OPPORTUNITIES

Inevitably, when the goals and standards of a national campaign are applied to each province, problems arise at the provincial level. And additional tensions and challenges appear at the local level. All parties who have signed on to the Endangered Spaces goal in Manitoba need to get their signals straight, exchange sometimes opposing views, and acknowledge both successes and failures. Hindsight clearly tells us, for example, that the four northern parks announced in February 1995 were chosen, not for their ecological potential, but for their lack of mineral potential. Also, First Nations feel they were not consulted adequately in advance, leaving questions about outstanding legal and fiduciary responsibilities on the part of government. Keeping ourselves focused on a common goal, and avoiding stepping off the critical path, are challenges for everyone who cares about protecting Manitoba's natural heritage.

What have we learned from the first half of the Endangered Spaces campaign in Manitoba? First, we need to do our homework together, sharing information closely as we go. Second, we need to be aware of and sensitive to local issues.

Maintaining the national goal and representation standards is the way to protect biodiversity in Canada. Identifying support and partners throughout Manitoba is the way to open doors to local success. Third, we need to work steadily with the government of the day, community organizations in the province, and all interested players from industry.

Achieving the Endangered Spaces goal in Manitoba *is* possible. All political parties in the legislature have indicated their support. What is required now is the will and cooperation to keep that goal in sight at all times. Fundamental change is needed to recognize and implement a conservation mandate for Manitoba's natural regions. This shift from short-term economic growth to a conservation mandate challenges all stakeholders to think long-term, to adjust attitudes that have reinforced short-term thinking, and to find new ways to reach the Endangered Spaces goal. We are halfway through the campaign decade. There is a great deal more to achieve in Manitoba. The remaining five years call for change and quick action to produce long-term results.

11 / Ontario

TIM GRAY AND JERRY VALEN DEMARCO

 Ontario is at a crucial point in its ecological history. Although development has consumed much of the provincial landscape, small remnants persist to remind us of what once was. Tiny pockets of Carolinian woodland, wetland, and prairie still harbour members of Canada's endangered southern natural communities. Scattered tall pines hark back to a much healthier Great Lakes–St. Lawrence forest. Tracts of relatively undisturbed boreal forest remain between dense strands of logging roads. And fortunately, the northern lowlands have thus far managed to avoid the most visible forms of environmental degradation.

These vestiges of wild nature bring to life the stories of aboriginal peoples and early settlers. Group of Seven canvasses are not yet entirely *historical* accounts of what preceded. But, without quick and concerted action, much of what is left will be lost. Our search for sustainability threatens to inch along, with less and less nature left to actually sustain. It is time to push forward the Ontario protected-areas agenda and maintain the province's ecological richness, while we struggle to redefine our relationship to the diverse landscapes we call home.

WHERE WE WERE

Ontario's protected-areas system began somewhat inauspiciously in 1893. In that year, Algonquin National Park, as it was then called, was established "as a public park and forest reservation, fish and game preserve, health resort and pleasure ground for the benefit, advantage and enjoyment of the people of the Province." The forests were being protected, at least in part, for the purpose of logging the tall pines. Park establishment continued on an *ad hoc* basis throughout the next eighty years, with a minor boom during the post–Second World War period, when the demand for recreation areas by an increasingly mobile public increased.

By the 1960s and early 1970s, the Ontario public was developing new attitudes towards uncontrolled development, uncoordinated land-use planning, and the corresponding loss of wilderness. People recognized that small recreation-focused parks were not protecting wildlife, watersheds, and wilderness. They voiced this concern through the media, and through membership in public advocacy groups. Together, these groups and individuals pressured the government to establish an ecologically based protected-areas system. The Ministry of Natural Resources responded to this challenge and developed a park planning and classification system.

Completed in 1978 and still in use today, the Ontario Provincial Park Planning and Management Policies ("The Blue Book") were rightly seen at the time as being among the most progressive in Canada. Based in part on an ecological framework, the system uses a matrix of life- and earth-science features to identify themes within each natural region. Representative examples of these themes are meant to be conserved within a system of protected areas. The system includes six classes of park, and is supported by other protected-area designations such as Conservation Reserves and Areas of Natural and Scientific Interest (ANSIs). While all areas within the park system and Conservation Reserves are protected from hydro-electric development, mining, and logging (except Algonquin), industrial uses are still possible within ANSIs, which keeps them from contributing to the Endangered Spaces goal.

A province-wide attempt at strategic land-use planning initiated in 1972, came to fruition in 1983. The establishment of 155 new parks was announced. This end-product of the planning process was somewhat disappointing because mining and hunting were permitted in many of the parks. However, in 1988, the provincial Cabinet released a revised parks policy. It required that most non-park uses be removed or phased out of the new parks. So, the spirit of the 1978 Blue Book had been reinstated after a brief hiatus.

Notwithstanding this evolution in terms of legislative and policy initiatives, as well as park creation, over the past 200 years Ontario's natural landscape has been changed on a scale greater than any other since glaciation. Southern Ontario has lost almost all of its wetlands, prairies, and forests to agricultural development and settlement. Canada's most diverse forests have quickly become monocultures of alien crops. Almost all of Ontario's tall pines have been cut. Large mammals have been pushed farther north and extirpated from great portions of their home ranges. The natural communities of the Great Lakes have been rapidly and irreversibly altered by pollution, habitat destruction, and alien-species introductions. Entire species have been extinguished.

WHERE WE ARE

A science-based protected-areas system plan, a newly approved Parks Policy, a long history of park establishment, and an upcoming Park Centenary placed Ontario in an enviable position to get an early start on meeting the goals of the Endangered Spaces campaign in 1989. On the political front, most initial signs were also encouraging. The Conservatives, Liberals, and NDP had all endorsed the Endangered Spaces goal prior to the 1990 provincial election. Surprisingly, the NDP won a majority and formed the government.

NDP leader Bob Rae had been arrested a year earlier for blocking the Red Squirrel Road extension, in a protest over the destruction of old-growth pine in Temagami, a rare unlogged forested area five hours north of Toronto. He and his party had clearly indicated by this and other actions that they supported environmental protection and land-use decision-making reform. Conservationists were therefore hopeful. Quick progress on the task of protecting wild Ontario seemed possible. Immediately after the election, discussions began with the new government to determine how it might best deliver on its Endangered Spaces commitments.

Initial responses were encouraging, if not overly ambitious. Only thirty-two of Ontario's sixty-five natural regions were considered to be represented in 1991.

Grasslands National Park encompasses one of the last vestiges of native prairie in Canada. LORI LABATT

The Great Sand Hills of southwestern Saskatchewan. DUANE SEPT

This mating ball of red-sided garter snakes was photographed in Manitoba's Interlake area. ROGER TURENNE

The Blind Lake Area is located in the Manitoba
lowlands, where a national park has been proposed.
ROGER TURENNE

The establishment of Churchill national park will help protect polar bear habitat in Manitoba. J.D. TAYLOR

Protection is being sought for Manitoba's Little Limestone Lake area. CELES DAVAR

A young grizzly lounges on a log, unaware of the threats to its wilderness home. DUANE SEPT

A recent decision of Alberta's Energy Resources Conservation Board spared the Whaleback montane area of southern Alberta from development, but it has yet to receive full protection. CHARLES TRUSCOTT

Is this a national park? Some conservationists maintain that Banff should no longer be considered one.
HARVEY LOCKE

A view of Moraine Lake in Banff National Park. CANADIAN PARKS AND WILDERNESS SOCIETY

Straddling the border of Alberta and the Northwest Territories, Wood Buffalo National Park provides a haven for many wildlife species, including the endangered whooping crane. WILF SCHURIG

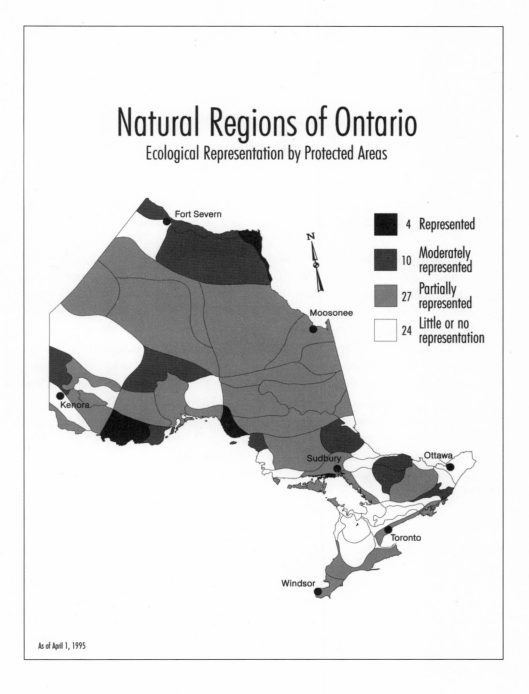

Natural Regions of Ontario
Ecological Representation by Protected Areas

Fort Severn

N

Moosonee

4 Represented

10 Moderately represented

27 Partially represented

24 Little or no representation

Kenora

Sudbury

Ottawa

Toronto

Windsor

As of April 1, 1995

On behalf of the students and staff of Seneca School, please accept this cheque for $82.50. Our students worked as Wilderness Crusaders and collected this money for the Endangered Spaces Program. We are happy in the knowledge that we have made an effort to help Canada's wilderness.

CAROL MOFFAT,
Seneca Public School,
Hamilton, 1993

Natural Resources minister Bud Wildman committed to fully representing an additional five by the end of 1993. In February 1992, a draft Natural Heritage Areas Strategy for Ontario indicated that the Endangered Spaces goal would be incorporated into a larger conservation agenda. Minor gains in the form of nature reserve additions in Algonquin, the removal of logging from Lake Superior Provincial Park, and progress towards protecting a portion of Toronto's Rouge River watershed instilled more hope.

Our cautious optimism was short-lived, however. By early 1993, the public was beginning to wonder what was up (or rather, what was not). The government had taken no action to fulfil its commitment. In May, it eliminated the Natural Heritage Areas Branch, which was responsible for protected areas, and incorporated it into a larger division of the Ministry of Natural Resources (MNR). The move transferred more parks planning and management decision-making power to the regional offices, but provided no mechanism to ensure that park objectives were met. The year 1993 was the provincial park's centennial, marking the establishment of Algonquin Park. This would have been a great time to rally the public behind the vision of finishing the park system. Instead, Ontarians were pacified with centennial posters and slick advertising campaigns, which completely ignored the challenges and commitments of the day.

A year-end surprise, delivered in December, saved the park centennial from being a complete bust. A 25,000-hectare wilderness zone, long-demanded by the Wildlands League, was established within the boundaries of Algonquin Park. It excluded logging and road-building activities, and encompassed approximately 40 per cent of the park's remaining old-growth red and white pine. The headway made in Algonquin was, of course, bittersweet, for it highlighted the fact that, by January 1994, more than three years into the government's term, our one significant gain was protection of a small area *within* a park that most people already thought of as protected!

The news was no better on the policy-development front. The draft Natural Heritage Areas Strategy had been virtually forgotten inside the Ministry of Natural Resources, and never reached a final form. Not a word had been heard about new parks legislation, ecological reserves, land-use planning, or a timetable for completion of the protected-areas system. Clearly something was off track inside the Ministry and the Cabinet Office. Protected-areas establishment was not a priority.

More disturbing than the silence surrounding the parks agenda were the noises emanating from the forestry section of MNR. Forest harvest across the province was to be increased by up to 50 per cent beyond current levels. This decision, which could only further constrain efforts to protect wilderness in the province, was announced by the new Minister of Natural Resources, Howard Hampton. It was based on recommendations made by a committee composed solely of representatives from the forest industry, labour, and government. The committee's final report was accepted by the government for implementation without a period of public review.

Expectations for wilderness protection were once again raised, then quashed, when the government unveiled its "Keep It Wild" campaign in early 1994. Billed as the government's mechanism for delivering on its commitment to the Endangered Spaces goal, it was largely a public-relations campaign and failed to deliver in any meaningful way. Seventeen new candidate protected-area sites were put forward for discussion, but they were mostly very small and had been chosen without regard to representation needs or consistent ecological criteria.

Despite the inadequacies of "Keep It Wild," the ecological values in some sites made modest contributions to the Endangered Spaces goal. Although small, many of the candidate old-growth forest sites announced under the program helped protect ecologically significant remnants of what once covered much of central Ontario. Their selection, if finalized by protection designation, will make a start towards representing this endangered habitat. Further work is necessary, however, in locations surrounding these sites to include areas containing a greater array of natural diversity and to make them large enough to accommodate natural disturbance processes. For example, in the boreal forest, many tree species depend on the renewing effects of wildfire to permit the germination of their seeds. Wildlife, in turn, depends on the existence of these young forests distributed across the landscape. In order to ensure the persistence of a natural forest in a protected area, it is important that fire be present and that the surrounding area be large enough to provide forests ranging in age from young to very old. This mosaic of tree species and forest ages provides food sources, breeding sites, and shelter for many different species at various stages in their life cycles.

The Company of Les Miserables, Toronto, would like to raise money for the Canadian Endangered Spaces campaign in the memory of a recently departed fellow cast member, Graeme Campbell.

On April 26th, the last day of Earth Week, we are going to embark on a 10K walk-a-thon throughout the streets of Toronto . . . We are all very excited to be able to assist in this manner and we hope our strength and size will result in a large contribution . . . I hope this will help in your very appreciated efforts with the Endangered Spaces campaign.
CHRISTY TAYLOR, Toronto, 1992

Two other sites also made modest contributions. The Jog Lake site in the Hudson and James Bay lowlands contained important representative features. The February 1995 announcement regarding the protection of the Obabika Forest in Temagami added another significant, but small, old-growth site.

Even for the more ecologically significant sites, however, the process of site selection was kept hidden from the public. MNR asked whether the public opposed or supported identified sites but gave people no sense of the context in which the sites were chosen or if there were better sites to fulfil representation goals. "Keep It Wild" announcements simply provided a forum for government lip-service to reforming the Provincial Parks Act and developing ecological-reserves legislation. Nothing of real substance resulted. In short, the "Keep It Wild" program has, to date, been grossly inadequate and disappointing. Its candidate sites, selected largely through flawed and hidden processes, were little more than tokens behind the fluff of a showy media campaign. The government claimed in the media, and in their own promotional literature featuring the premier with Prince Philip, that they had moved to meet their Endangered Spaces targets. In fact, they had done very little.

HOW TO GET TO 2000

As we enter the sixth year of the Endangered Spaces campaign and a new government, Ontario has hardly begun to ensure the basic building blocks of ecological survival. What was seen to be a desirable and finishable objective has become a waylaid agenda. Ontario started the 1990s with 5.5 per cent of its land mass in a protected designation, and managed to add approximately 0.2 per cent by the end of 1994. For a jurisdiction that was ahead of the pack in 1989, this situation is entirely unacceptable and profoundly disturbing.

In hindsight, we assumed that cooperating with a government that promised action would generate results. Obviously that has not been the case. Politeness and patience have not worked. Perhaps we have been foolishly duped into participating in government process and consultation. We entered each public-participation exercise with patience, good faith, and an open mind, then left with a bad taste in our mouths. Imprudently, we relived these experiences numerous times before realizing that the government had succeeded in keeping us all talking while projecting an appearance of doing something. In fact, the ecological-protection agenda was vacuous, and the conservation community simply lost valuable time and resources.

The response to this cynicism must be clear. All three political parties have endorsed the Endangered Spaces campaign. When elected, if they do not deliver, then they must be held accountable. Our response to their inaction must be swift, articulate, and unwavering, for we have little time left. The challenge is great, but not insurmountable. It is time to muster our strength and tell our government and industries that what they have been selling us to date is no longer acceptable. The following is a summary of the challenges facing the protected-areas agenda in Ontario and the steps that must be taken to overcome them:

1. *Protected-areas establishment and management must become a key component of what Ontario defines as "sustainable development."* The Ontario government has not yet shown that it sees protected-areas establishment as a cornerstone of its overall approach to resource use and stewardship. It has failed to make substantive progress towards meeting the Endangered Spaces goal, to establish mechanisms for sound land-use and protected-areas decision making in central and northern Ontario, and to revise and upgrade tools for designing boundaries of protected areas. Most troubling, the government has hampered future attempts to establish protected areas by dramatically increasing rates of resource extraction. Addressing all of these problems in an integrated manner is the only way that the Endangered Spaces targets will be met. The required process must have the following features:

   i. The Ministry of Natural Resources must implement a coordinated plan for establishing ecologically representative protected areas in all natural regions. Lands north of the St. Lawrence Lowlands are heavily forested and largely publicly owned. This places the responsibility for protection and planning clearly with the Ministry of Natural Resources. Planning must incorporate the principle that all natural regions *will* (not *may*) include representative protected areas, and not simply opportunistic sites of special character. In southern Ontario, there must be a similar commitment to ecological protection, but the approach required will have to be different (see point 4, below).

ii. Traditionally, Ontario has allowed the demand for timber and minerals to act as *de facto* land-use planning tools. According to this piecemeal approach, development occurred where there were resources to be "exploited." Areas that were inaccessible or had low mineral or timber potential were the only ones left wild. Only the vast size of Ontario has prevented this approach from extinguishing the wild throughout the province. To change this situation, we must reverse the order in which land-use decisions are made. Protected areas, tourism reserves, watershed buffers, and other non-extractive land uses must be determined *before* resource allocation begins. Where decisions can still be made, or when past allocations come up for review, candidate protected sites must be evaluated before development further precludes protection.

iii. In Ontario, the government signs guaranteed wood supply agreements with forest-products companies. Once signed, the contracts bind the government to providing an annual supply of wood to each mill. Decisions to enter into additional agreements of this sort are not open for public discussion or review. Increases in the amount of forest cut can make establishing protected areas that much more difficult.

Increased commitments of timber must be prohibited until land-use planning is complete. Since early 1994, over 2.5 million cubic metres of timber have been allocated by the government to four new and upgraded strandboard mills from Bancroft to Kenora. This is equivalent to the yearly volume of harvest from a triangular area stretching from North Bay to Arnprior and Bancroft and including all of Algonquin Park. Additional commitments are in the works. All of these moves have been made in the complete absence of public consultation and consideration of other commitments that the Ontario government has made in the past. Increasing extraction rates on an already overtaxed public forest must be halted, while we gather information on whether it can be realistically sustained over the long term and how it affects the establishment of protected areas.

iv. The selection of candidate protected areas in Ontario must be refined in light of the representation and ecological-integrity criteria that have been developed by the Canadian Council on Ecological Areas and World Wildlife Fund Canada. Despite being based on an ecological framework, the current government system has failed to adequately provide for two critical considerations: wildlife range requirements and natural disturbance. Large mammals, especially those with large home ranges and those that are migratory, such as woodland caribou, require substantial areas of suitable habitat for long-term survival. Furthermore, in vast areas of the province, large-scale fire is the major disturbance and

I whole-heartedly encourage the World Wildlife Fund to continue developing programs which preserve our wilderness areas from further exploitation.
LINCOLN M. ALEXANDER, Lieutenant-Governor of Ontario, 1989

After reviewing the information enclosed with your letter, and the book Endangered Spaces: The Future for Canada's Wilderness, *I am more than willing to support and sign the Canadian Wilderness Charter. The Liberal government is strongly committed to environment(al) concerns.*

JOHN B. FINLAY, MP, Oxford, 1994

renewal mechanism. As forestry, settlement, and other human activities intensify, it will become more and more difficult to ensure that the habitat needs of large mammals and the disturbance requirements of northern forests are met. To ensure the long-term survival of biological diversity, it is necessary to incorporate these factors into protected-areas establishment and land-use planning. (Since this chapter was written, Ontario did expand Wabakimi Provincial Park in the northwest to 900,000 hectares. This important accomplishment by government, industry, and conservation groups will help protect woodland caribou and maintain natural wildlife in a boreal forest ecosystem. — Ed.)

v. Land-use decisions must be made according to a clearly understandable decision-making process. One of the most frustrating aspects of land-use

planning in this province has been the hidden and technical nature of the decision-making process. Decisions are made via timber-management planning, rather than land-use planning, thereby excluding much of the public interested in broader concerns. A new process should make it clear what information will be used, how it will be weighed, and how decisions will be made. It should be as removed from political manipulation as possible.

vi. Quasi-protected areas such as ANSIs, Provincially Significant Wetlands, and Areas of Concern must be given legal protection from development. Past history has shown that these areas are often afforded varying and impermanent protection. The development of a long-promised ecological-reserves system that incorporates such significant areas could also be helpful.

vii. Protected areas must be included under a new provincial parks act that enshrines ecological integrity as the primary goal. At present, where management plans have been completed, parks are often carved up in an effort to satisfy every conceivable user. In this attempt to satisfy everyone, ecological considerations fall by the wayside. Equally disturbing is the fact that management planning itself is not seen as a priority. Many parks are still without plans. Waterway parks in particular have been designed and implemented as such narrow strips of land that their protection value is minimal.

The sequence of the steps described above is important. Action must be taken that recognizes that wilderness and nature are under more stress in certain parts of the province, generally those in the south. For this reason, land-use planning should proceed first in the southern site regions and must conclude by the end of 1997. All other site districts must be scheduled to be completed by the end of 2000, because no natural region has much time to spare.

2. *We must establish mechanisms to encourage the transition to an economy and society that recognizes the necessity of protected areas and ecological sustainability.*

i. Economic incentives for protecting natural areas must be established through the Forestry Futures Trust Fund. This new fund channels government revenue from forestry operations and general government revenue into forestry-related projects. There is an opportunity to provide for community economic development in areas where protected locales must be established. Funds should be used for such things as educational and scientific research facilities, tourism infrastructure support, park guide training, acquisition of ecologically significant lands, and restoration of degraded sites.

*P**lease keep up the good work. And thank you for providing us with an opportunity to feel like we can be a small part of the protection of our country through the Endangered Spaces campaign. We would like to believe that we can make a difference.*
LOIS FILION, The Environmental Club of Chippewa Secondary School, North Bay

ii. Revenues from administrative fines and legal penalties should be used for ecological protection. Fines levied for violations of forestry laws and regulations are currently paid into general government revenues. Revenues from these fines, and stumpage fees and operational area charges, should be used to encourage ecosystem protection. Diligent prosecution of violations under the Crown Forest Sustainability Act and the federal Fisheries Act would discourage repeat offences.

iii. Alternatives to degrading logging practices must be implemented. Large-scale clear-cutting and failed regeneration are the hallmarks of our current approach to forest harvest surrounding protected areas. Moves towards sustainability must include new harvest systems that more closely match the natural disturbance patterns of the forests in question and do not threaten their ability to regenerate.

3. *Aboriginal-claim negotiations must continue to move forward, and First Nations must be included in a system of comprehensive land-use planning.* It is the responsibility of the federal and provincial governments and First Nations to ensure that ecological protection is part of both aboriginal-claim processes and land-use planning. The wealth of information and historical land use of aboriginal people, combined with other scientific and non-scientific knowledge, must provide a basis for developing ecologically sound land-use decisions.

4. *Initiatives for natural-heritage protection and restoration in southern Ontario must be developed.* Loss of wetlands, forests, prairies, and their inhabitants across southern Ontario continues, despite greatly increased public support for protection. Existing protected areas are inadequate for long-term ecological survival. Given its predominantly agricultural and urban nature, southern Ontario requires special efforts by provincial and municipal governments and individual landowners to achieve protection goals:

i. Recent provincial land-use planning initiatives such as the Wetlands Policy, the Natural Heritage Policy, and the Environmental Protection and Hazard Policy, provide opportunities to protect what pieces of

The book [Endangered Spaces: The Future for Canada's Wilderness] is terrific and should be required reading for legislators at all levels of government.
CHARLES CACCIA, MP, Davenport, 1989

nature remain. Such policies will work, however, only if they assume that ecological protection is an imperative, not just an option.

ii. The province needs to combine efforts to restore degraded ecosystems with those that are seeking to protect remaining high-quality habitat in degraded areas. Areas such as Long Point–Haldimand–Norfolk and the Niagara Escarpment are excellent candidates for testing multifaceted approaches to expansion and rehabilitation of the southern wild. Funding must be provided to protect existing pockets of natural habitat, and to establish restoration programs.

iii. All southern Ontario conservation efforts are exceedingly difficult to carry out within the existing subsidy and tax system. Disincentives to protection still hamper private and public landowners from protecting natural areas. Uses that degrade the environment, such as agriculture and resource development, are often afforded tax exemptions and financial incentives. But activities that support ecological objectives are not.

5. *The federal parks system should be expanded.* The provincial government is not the only body capable of assisting in meeting the Endangered Spaces goal in Ontario. The federal parks system has a role to play, too. With the exception of Pukaskwa, all of the province's national parks are very small and subject to heavy use. Even Pukaskwa may not be large enough to sustain wide-ranging mammals such as woodland caribou. The federal parks system should be given a mandate and the funds to acquire any adjacent lands, especially in the south. These sites would stimulate an important new development in national parks management — namely, ecological restoration. In fact, rehabilitative work is already under way within Point Pelee National Park. Surrounding lands are equally suitable. The establishment of Bruce Peninsula National Park demonstrated that options for expanding the national parks system do indeed exist, even in the highly populated and degraded southern Ontario landscape.

6. *Individual and group action must complement government initiatives.* In these times of spending cuts and rationalization, more responsibility is being put on the shoulders of citizens, corporations, and non-governmental organizations. We all must lead by example and show that we are committed to protecting biological diversity. From practising environmental sustainability in the home to supporting nature advocacy groups, to writing letters to elected representatives, we all must show unequivocally that protecting nature is of utmost importance. Regardless of short-term economic realities, we cannot let the government off the hook in terms of preserving the province's natural communities.

ONE LAST PUSH

The year 2000 is not yet upon us, but widespread environmental degradation is. Wild nature is much of our environment, yet we proceed as if it is only a luxury to be enjoyed in times of plenty, or a resource to be exploited.

Protected areas alone cannot ensure that Ontario's natural diversity will be retained. In the long term they must be supported by people whose beliefs are based on a land ethic that is focused on ecological sustainability. Many positive signs indicate that we may well be on the road to realizing that goal. Would it not be a shame if we got there only to find there was little nature left to accompany us? By completing a protected-areas system, we can provide an insurance policy that ensures we do not leave nature behind.

12 / Québec

NATHALIE ZINGER

In addition to being the midpoint of the Endangered Spaces campaign, 1995 is a significant year for the Québec park system. This year its oldest park, Mont Tremblant, celebrates its centennial. Looking back at what has been done to conserve wilderness in Québec and ahead to upcoming challenges will give a good indication of what remains to be done to achieve a network of representative protected areas by the year 2000.

The picture of Québec's protected-areas system in 1989, when the Endangered Spaces campaign began, was rather grim. Headed by two different ministries, the two parallel networks of parks and ecological reserves actually protected very little of the province's biological diversity. With only 0.4 per cent of Québec legally protected to Endangered Spaces standards, there was an urgent need to identify additional candidate areas in the province's forty-three natural regions.

In 1986, a moratorium on the creation of new parks had been put in place by the government, which argued that the parks in the existing network had to be developed before the planning process resumed. In fact, with annual budget cuts, the parks system had entered a dark period that would last five years. The lateness of official and popular recognition of protected areas as a complement to development presented a significant additional hurdle.

CONSERVATION ACHIEVEMENTS, 1989–1995
Since the launch of the Endangered Spaces campaign, a number of important events that favour wilderness protection in Québec have taken place.

A Canada–Québec agreement was signed in April 1990 to establish and jointly manage a marine park at the confluence of the Saguenay and St. Lawrence rivers. Public hearings on the park boundaries and on the management plan were held in 1990 and 1993. However, legal establishment of the park has yet to be completed.

The moratorium on the establishment of new parks was lifted in late 1991, reactivating the parks-planning process. A year later, the Department of Recreation, Fish and Game released a five-year action plan, "La nature en héritage 1992–1997." It announced four candidate parks to be established in southern Québec, and the setting aside for park purposes of 57,000 square kilometres in eighteen ecological reserves north of the fiftieth parallel, four of which were to become parks by 1997.

In 1992, the Québec government announced its commitment to complete a network of representative protected areas by the year 2000, and to implement the

Biodiversity Convention of the 1992 Rio Conference on Environment and Development.

A government project to privatize Québec parks was stopped because of opposition from a dozen non-government organizations (NGOs) under the leadership of the Union québécoise pour la conservation de la nature, the Association des biologistes du Québec, and WWF. Delegating management of commercial activities within parks is still under study by government agencies.

In 1994, the two ministries in charge of protected areas merged and became the new Department of Environment and Wildlife (Ministère de l'Environnement et de la Faune/MEF). With this move, the potential for harmonizing the two parallel networks of protected areas and for developing a joint vision was strengthened.

In terms of actual on-the-ground protection, the Mont Megantic Conservation Park and twenty-nine new ecological reserves were established between 1989 and 1995. With the eighteen park reserves in the north and twenty-three proposed ecological reserves, the total area protected in Québec increased more than tenfold, from 6228 to 64,841 square kilometres, bringing the total percentage of protected area in Québec from 0.4 to 4.2 per cent.

These last figures represent a notable change in wilderness protection in Québec, but the fact remains that, of the forty-three natural regions defined for park planning, only two are adequately represented (Saguenay and Montérégiennes), three are moderately represented (Massif gaspésien, Massif Laurentides Nord, and North Shore Cuestas), and ten are partially represented (including Magdalene Islands, Sutton, and Laurentides boréales). Twenty-eight regions have little or no representation; two-thirds of these are to be found in northern Québec, although this will change once the representation of the eighteen park reserves has been evaluated.

SOME STRENGTHS AND WEAKNESSES

The Parti Québécois government has reconfirmed the commitment made in 1992 to establish a network of protected areas, and has restated the leadership role to be played by the network in conserving Québec's natural heritage.

Public support for the Endangered Spaces campaign has increased significantly. More than 50,000 Quebeckers have signed the Canadian Wilderness Charter. In a 1994 survey, Quebeckers expressed the strongest support in Canada for making sure their government respected its commitment to complete the job by the year 2000. More than forty NGOs have also endorsed the campaign. In fact, the active involvement of many of these organizations in land conservation has led to a number of initiatives to protect specific areas, thus contributing to the overall objective of the campaign. Among them, the Ruiter Valley Land Trust, the Province of Quebec Society for the Protection of Birds, the Parc d'environnement naturel de Sutton, the Mount Pinnacle Land Trust, the Association pour la protection du mont Rigaud, and the Fondation de la faune du Québec have played a meaningful role in conserving lands in southern Québec.

One significant tool for planning a network of protected areas has been developed by the MEF: its new ecological framework based on geology, relief, hydrology, geomorphology, and bioclimate will prove to be invaluable when applied to the evaluation of representation objectives in the protected-areas planning process.

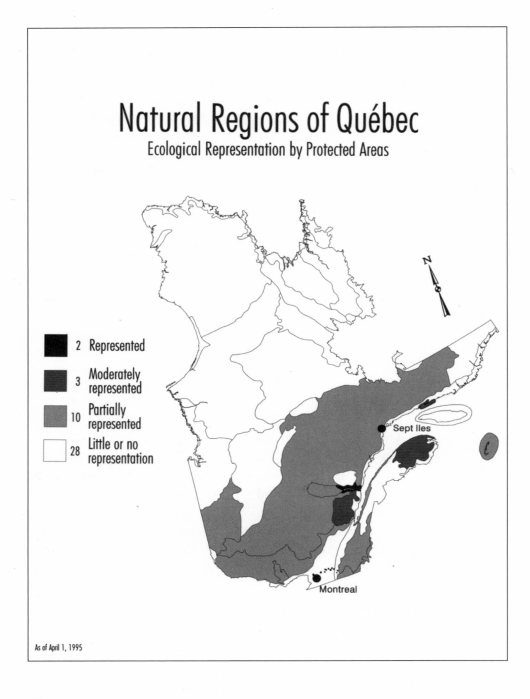

Natural Regions of Québec
Ecological Representation by Protected Areas

2 Represented

3 Moderately represented

10 Partially represented

28 Little or no representation

Sept Iles

Montreal

As of April 1, 1995

Even though their numbers have increased since the beginning of the Endangered Spaces campaign, protected areas in Québec remain small in size and are dispersed over a large territory. Only four parks are larger than 500 square kilometres — namely, Gaspésie, Jacques-Cartier, Mont Tremblant, and Mauricie National Park. Furthermore, the provincial action plan released in 1992 focuses solely on establishing parks on public lands, and does not target representative sites that may be fully or in part on private lands.

However, the biggest handicap in Québec is the absence of a systematic approach to protected-areas planning and the lack of an overall strategy to represent Québec's biodiversity through an integrated network of protected areas. The contribution of existing protected areas to natural-region representation needs to be evaluated, and potential candidate sites should be identified to fill gaps. Little effort has been invested in recent years in identifying new sites, which could become a major impediment as the year 2000 fast approaches. Another drawback has been the lack of timetables, including a timetable for completing the network.

WHAT IS AT STAKE FOR THE NEAR FUTURE?

Québec faces a tremendous challenge to complete its protected-areas network by the end of the decade, especially if the network is not integrated into an overall land-conservation strategy.

Nevertheless, many avenues exist in southern Québec for actually completing the system. For example, upgrading the protection status of areas such as wildlife reserves, which tend to be large, could contribute significantly to representation. However, special attention would have to be given to the management of these areas to make sure that activities held within and around them will not threaten their ecological integrity. Initiatives to protect private lands, such as setting up fiscal and legal incentives, along with promoting their contribution to the Endangered Spaces goal, are necessary. Most of southern Québec is under private ownership, so options to represent natural regions in this heavily developed part of the province will depend on private protection.

Fostering public support for protected areas and improving the public's understanding of the contribution made by these areas to a healthy economy are vital steps towards a shared objective. In 1992, over $2 billion was spent in the province on wildlife-related activities, contributing significantly to the provincial gross domestic product and supporting 28,000 jobs. Trips and outings accounted for 25 per cent of this spending. Yet, although 3 million people visit Québec parks every year, the urgent need to complete a protected-areas network remains unappreciated.

Strengthening the provincial government's leadership in planning and implementing a network and in ensuring the ecological integrity of the protected areas in it, should be complemented by increased participation from resource industries. The *municipalités régionales de comté* (MRCs) should also contribute to the overall protected-areas agenda by establishing protected areas with a conservation mandate. Unfortunately, recent amendments to the Municipal Code, by focusing on recreational development and multiple-use activities (including forest exploitation), have restricted the potential contribution of regional parks.

In northern Québec, it will be essential to harmonize First Nations' interests in protecting wildlife habitat with MEF proposals for future parks and ecological reserves, and Parks Canada proposals for candidate sites. Compliance with the James Bay and Northern Québec Agreement must also be ensured. Joint ventures to plan and manage northern protected areas have already begun in the Louis-Babel and Matamec ecological reserves; they will play an increasingly important role as more protected areas are established.

Most of all, tackling a number of persistent myths about wilderness protection will be vital to the success of the Endangered Spaces campaign in Québec. Large wildlife reserves, commonly known as "parks," do not qualify because logging is permitted in them. The presence of these areas as large green blocks on official road maps has led to serious public misconceptions about the extent of protected areas. This belief that large identified territories are still wild makes it difficult for the general public to understand the conservationist's sense of urgency about protecting endangered spaces. Furthermore, efforts should be made to counteract the underestimated contribution of protected areas to Québec's economy and regional development. These areas are not a handicap to development, and are not places where popular activities are unduly restricted.

In the end, moving beyond a restricted vision of protected areas and completing the task depends on the willingness of all involved parties to get the work done.

COMPLETING A REPRESENTATIVE NETWORK BY THE YEAR 2000

For Québec to achieve the objective it has set for itself, a number of major steps need to be taken:

1. *A Science-Based System Plan.* The most pressing step is to convince various government agencies to work together to devise a coordinated system plan for the completion of a network of representative protected areas. In addition to pinpointing representation gaps within the existing network, mapping of priority areas and identification of potential candidate sites on both public and private lands need to be integrated into the overall land-use planning process. Clearly identifying what needs to be done and how each agency, industry, municipality, and NGO can contribute will lead to dynamic solutions.

   The implementation of an ecological framework for the planning process should be given top priority. Then it will be necessary to communicate the results, along with proposed alternatives for securing adequate representation in some natural regions, especially in southern Québec. Different approaches should be developed for southern and northern Québec.

2. *Strategy for Southern Québec.* To ensure adequate representation of southern Québec's biodiversity will require a number of complementary approaches involving a large number of partners. These approaches must be based on a comprehensive system plan and clear representation targets. Coordinating the representation of natural regions through parks, ecological reserves, private sites, and upgraded wildlife reserves will be essential.

   The government's five-year action plan should see the establishment by 1997 of three new parks — Monts Valin, Vauréal, and Plaisance. These parks will help represent two natural regions, which contain no protected areas at the moment, and will upgrade the representation in another region, which contains one existing protected area. Through a 1991–94 program for ecological reserves, another eight reserves will be established in 1995, including the Muir old-growth forest, Pointe-Platon, and Grand-Lac-Salé.

Top priority should be given to natural regions where the strongest threats exist, where options are either less numerous or rapidly declining, and where few or no protected areas meet the Endangered Spaces standards for representation. Special attention should be given to southern natural regions, which include the Notre Dame Mountains, the Côte de Charlevoix, and the St. Lawrence Lowlands. In moderately and partially represented regions, areas such as the Hautes-Gorges of the Malbaie River, Mount Pinnacle, Mount Rigaud, and the Dune du Sud/les Sillons should be considered for protection.

Business creates wealth and wealth brings with it responsibility. WWF offers a superb opportunity to act on that responsibility. Contributors to WWF help in a very direct way to protect our natural heritage for the benefit of future generations. I commend WWF for their efforts in wildlife conservation and protection of wildspaces. I support them whole-heartedly.
DANIEL LANGLOIS, CEO
Softimage, 1994

Upgrading the protection status of wildlife reserves, whether in whole or in part, should be seriously considered for the Chics Chocs Mountains in the moderately represented Gaspésie region; La Vérendrye and Sept-Iles/Port-Cartier in the partially represented Laurentides boréales region; Port Daniel in Baie des Chaleurs; and Rimouski in the Notre Dame Mountains. Some national wildlife areas, such as Pointe-de-l'Est on the Magdalene Islands, should also be given priority.

The contribution, through land trusts or conservation easements, of private sites to the network must be evaluated and promoted. Private land owners and conservation organizations have already started to build support for protected areas and are actively conserving land. The creation of the Regroupement des organismes propriétaires de milieux naturels protégés du Québec, and recent workshops on private stewardship, are only two examples of the increased involvement of the private sector.

MRCs should also participate in protecting representative sites. The preliminary guidelines for regional parks developed by the Ministry of Municipal Affairs, the MEF, and the Ministry of Natural Resources highlight recreational development in a core area no larger than 10 square kilometres, with multiple-use management beyond the core. Those guidelines prevent regional parks from being considered as protected areas under Endangered Spaces rules. Furthermore, making candidate areas such as the Hautes-Gorges of the Malbaie River regional parks actually threatens the completion of an integrated network. Strengthening the protection mandate of the regional parks guidelines would allow a greater contribution from MRCs.

3. *Strategy for Northern Québec.* According to the government's 1992 action plan, four northern parks have been targeted for establishment by 1997: the Cratère du Nouveau Québec, the Torngat Mountains and the Koroc River, the Otish Mountains, and Albanel Lake and the Temiscamie River.

In addition, the Ministry of Natural Resources has been involved in developing, in consultation with First Nations, the first land-use plan for northern Québec. It will include both development projects and park and ecological reserve proposals. Native people have identified special interest areas and are preparing a master plan under the Loi sur les villages nordiques et l'Administration régionale Kativik. Potential boundaries for northern protected areas will, in all cases, need to be confirmed through a consultative process. Candidate areas must be identified for the James Bay Lowlands and Rupert Plateau, as no areas have been proposed yet for these natural regions. Finally, identifying to what degree the eighteen park reserves, the sixteen proposed ecological reserves, and the special interest areas represent northern natural regions must be assessed.

Parks Canada has candidate sites identified in northern Québec to complete the federal protected-areas agenda. Some of these — for example, the Lac Guillaume Delisle and Baie aux feuilles — have also been selected by the MEF. The harmonization of all proposed projects must take place to ensure full representation of northern natural regions.

4. *Marine Protected Areas*. Although Québec has the second-longest shoreline in Canada, planning for marine protected areas has focused mainly on one site — the Saguenay–St. Lawrence Marine Park.

Seven of Parks Canada's twenty-nine marine natural regions border Québec: six of them still need to be represented (James Bay, Hudson Bay, Davis and Hudson straits, North Gulf Shelf, Laurentian Trough, and Magdalene Banks). A scientific committee set up under the St. Lawrence Vision 2000 plan has subdivided the St. Lawrence estuary and gulf into twenty-one ecological regions, which could eventually be used for representing this great river's biodiversity.

5. *Park Management*. Another challenge for Québec is to ensure the ecological integrity of specific protected areas and the network as a whole. This concern was underscored by the recent effort of the MEF to delegate management of the provincial parks. Pressure from conservation organizations and from the public has been successful in moving the ministry away from its initial intention to privatize all on-site activities, to the more restricted delegation of commercial activities only. This type of delegation has been occurring since 1987, and has already resulted in a number of negative impacts; for example, overloading the carrying capacity of many habitats in and around camping sites. Other impacts include the degradation of park infrastructure and questionable intrusions, such as a municipal sewage-treatment plant in Oka Park. Within Mont Tremblant Park, education and maintenance services have been reduced, and non-compatible activities, such as snowmobile use in preservation zones, have grown.

There has also been an absence of open consultation on what constitutes a commercial activity, on how responsibilities should be shared between the government and its private partners, and on which control mechanisms are going to be put in place. Master plans are developed for each park, but no process guarantees their implementation, let alone an effective commitment to their conservation mandate. A public review of these issues is needed.

Cladonia lichen or "caribou moss" carpets an area of the newly expanded Wabakimi Provincial Park in Ontario. BRUCE PETERSEN

Less than 2 per cent of the wolf's range is legally protected in Canada. J.D. TAYLOR

Only small remnants of the original Carolinian forest of
southwestern Ontario remain. WWF

Carolinian Canada is home to a number of "southern" species, including the tulip tree.
DEBBIE FREEMAN

The Algoma Highlands
represent the largest remaining
unlogged area in the Great Lakes
region. GARY MCGUFFIN

Logging continues in 77 per cent
of Ontario's Algonquin Park.
DEBBIE FREEMAN

The final establishment of a marine park where the Saguenay River meets the
St. Lawrence is eagerly awaited. BRUCE LITTELJOHN

In the Gulf of St. Lawrence, the Magdalene Islands provide shelter and breeding habitat for many seabirds. BRUCE LITTELJOHN

Wild ginseng has been placed on Canada's List of Wildlife at Risk. DANIEL GAGNON

Blueberries and bunchberries brighten the forest floor. GARY MCGUFFIN

A white-tailed deer gazes out from its forest habitat on Anticosti Island, Québec.
BRUCE LITTELJOHN

This caribou herd relies on huge tracts of northern Québec for its survival. Yet none of this habitat has been protected from development.
SERGE COUTURIER

6. *Fiscal Reforms.* Fiscal reforms should be developed to promote conservation on private lands. Tax exemptions on capital gains for donors and exemptions from municipal taxes for owners of conservation lands should be further examined.

7. *Joint Ventures.* Joint ventures between the federal government and the government of Québec, such as the Saguenay–St. Lawrence Marine Park or the proposed northern sites, need to be directed towards the completion of a network of representative protected areas.

8. *Contribution from All Sectors.* The government of Québec must play a leadership role in achieving the year 2000 goal. But other players, including the forest industry, First Nations, MRCs and their municipalities, conservation organizations, and the general public, must also contribute to the process.

   Besides working within the principles of the National Forest Strategy, the forest industry should actively contribute to the integrity of the network by managing resources in a way that ensures buffer zones and corridors around protected areas on both private and public lands.

   In northern Québec, Native people will be able to contribute to wilderness protection, as candidate sites and special interest areas undergo review in each community. Beyond the selection and establishment of protected areas, the management of these areas must also be discussed. Co-management agreements such as the one signed between Québec and the Montagnais Council for the Louis-Babel and Matamec ecological reserves should be considered.

   Since many natural regions remain partially represented in southern Québec, MRCs and their municipalities should be given a clear mandate to upgrade the protection status of regional parks.

   Finally, support from non-government organizations is crucial. Increased public awareness and support of protected areas must portray these areas not only as playing a vital role in conserving biodiversity, but also as contributing to the local, regional, and national economies. Efforts by NGOs leading to on-the-ground protection must be recognized and encouraged as well.

9. *Setting Targets.* Representation targets must be set and met on an annual basis.

   By the end of 1995, representation of biodiversity through existing protected areas and candidate ecological reserves, and through southern and northern parks, must be determined. As well, an integrated system plan identifying potential candidate sites for representation should be developed, and the eight ecological reserves needed to complete the 1991–94 plan must be designated as protected areas.

   If the system is to be completed by the year 2000, the following schedule must be met:

   - One region moderately represented per year for 1996, 1997, and 1998, starting with the legal protection of the Hautes-Gorges of the Malbaie River.

- Two regions partially represented per year between 1996 and 2000, including the protection of Mount Pinnacle in the Sutton region, Plaisance and Mont Rigaud in the St. Lawrence Lowlands, and Dune du Sud/les Sillons on the Magdalene Islands.
- For regions currently with little or no representation, the Monts Valin Park must be established in 1995. In 1996, adequate representation must be reached in three unrepresented regions, including the establishment of the Vauréal Park, one northern site such as the Albanel Lake/Temiscamie River, and representation of another southern natural region. In 1997, four unrepresented regions must be represented, including the Cratère du Nouveau Québec, the Torngat Mountains, and the Otish Mountains, along with representation of one southern natural region. In 1998, six unrepresented natural regions should be represented, three in the north and three in the south. And the remaining fourteen unrepresented natural regions should be represented in 1999 and 2000 at the rate of seven per year.
- To these targets must be added the establishment of five ecological reserves per year between 1996 and 1999, and by 2000, the setting-aside, with interim protection, of another twenty sites for future designation.
- The Saguenay–St. Lawrence Marine Park must be established in 1995, and a plan to establish marine protected areas must be in place by 1998.

Canadians often think of the country as a land of limitless wilderness. But this is a myth! Our wilderness heritage is quickly disappearing. I'm determined to bring this sombre message to Canadians and show them that each of us can play a role in protecting our wildlife and wild places, through the Endangered Spaces campaign.
CHRISTOPHER GASCON, Montréal, at the launch of his cross-country in-line skating adventure for the Endangered Spaces campaign, May 1992

A number of additional steps must be taken to ensure the completion of a representative network. They include: applying ecological representation and integrity criteria to the selection of candidate sites, developing restoration objectives for degraded sites in southern Québec, providing interim protection for candidate sites on both private and public lands, setting the protected-areas agenda within a land-conservation strategy covering the entire territory, integrating land-use policies, refining regulatory tools and fiscal incentives to complement and support representation objectives, allocating adequate human and financial resources to achieve the goal, building stronger political support, involving industries more, and securing more aggressive support from organizations and the general public.

This is a daunting list, but a significant amount of groundwork has been done in the last five years. A solid set of tools, impressive expertise, and strong support should make it possible to establish a network of representative protected areas in Québec. Completing this network by 2000 would ensure the survival of Québec's natural heritage for future generations of Quebeckers.

13 / New Brunswick

ROBERTA CLOWATER

 New Brunswick is a maritime province with two very different coastlines: the cool, rocky cliffs and shores of the Bay of Fundy, and the warm, often sandy beaches of the Northumberland Strait/Bay of Chaleur. It is the most heavily forested province in Canada, with forests covering approximately 85 per cent of the land. Historic river watersheds and valleys, especially the St. John and Miramichi, dominate the inland landscape. New Brunswick is therefore perhaps best seen as a province of contrasts and transitions — with eastern hardwood forests giving way to mixed Acadian woodland; fresh water intermingling with salt; and forests yielding to coastal cliffs, dunes, and salt marshes.

As a result of these large-scale ecological transitions, we have a rich diversity of species, landscapes, and waters within the boundaries of our small province: from the northern right whales of the Bay of Fundy to the lynx and flying squirrels of our forests; from the Atlantic puffins on Machias Seal Island to the piping plovers along the eastern beaches. What is surprising is that so many species have been able to survive in a province that has been heavily influenced and altered by human settlement. Like the Micmac and Maliseet peoples who predated European settlers, most New Brunswickers continue to rely on natural resources for their livelihoods. For example, forestry is the largest industry in the province. Roughly 95 per cent of the forests are licensed to the forest industry or owned as private woodlots.

In the past, natural areas protected from resource extraction have often been considered non-profitable from a strictly economic perspective. However, it is now widely recognized that a comprehensive network of permanently protected natural areas is essential for the sustainability of a natural resources–based economy.

It is alarming, then, that only 1 per cent of New Brunswick's land base is designated as parks or other adequately protected areas. Considering how much of the province's land is being used for human consumption or settlement, it would seem to be common sense to set aside a larger area to be kept free from resource exploitation. This would help achieve a better balance between the management of land for fibre and timber production and its management for other reasons, including the maintenance of biodiversity.

THE STATE OF NEW BRUNSWICK'S PROTECTED AREAS IN 1989

In 1989, existing protected areas in New Brunswick that met World Wildlife Fund

Canada's Endangered Spaces criteria were mainly national parks, provincial parks, ecological reserves, and private nature preserves. With few exceptions, most of the qualifying protected natural areas were on Crown land, which constitutes 46 per cent of the provincial land base.

A significant part of the protected-areas network was, in fact, federally protected land — two national parks (Fundy and Kouchibouguac), two migratory-bird sanctuaries, and five national wildlife areas. Of these, the national parks were the largest protected areas in the province. No new national parks have been established here since 1969, and there are no plans to expand the terrestrial national parks system in New Brunswick.

The provincial parks system had been established mainly for recreational purposes, as is illustrated by their designations. The classes of parks included "recreation, picnic ground, beach, campground and resource." There was very little planning or policy consideration given to the conservation and protection function of the provincial parks, which range in size from 0.17 to 17,500 hectares. No new provincial parks have been added to the system since 1987.

Three ecological reserves had been established under the Ecological Reserves Act. These were small natural areas protected for the purposes of research, scientific study, and habitat for rare or endangered native species. No new ecological reserves had been established since 1985, even though fifty-one candidate sites were identified in the early 1970s.

The Nature Trust of New Brunswick, a non-profit, non-government organization, was established in 1988 to acquire and maintain nature preserves on private land and hold them in trust for the people of New Brunswick. This organization has also been working to identify and classify natural areas throughout the province, while fostering a sense of stewardship for our natural heritage. By 1989, the Nature Trust already had one 88-hectare preserve under its protection.

Environmental organizations, like the Conservation Council of New Brunswick, have been actively promoting new protected areas and new land-use and environmental policies over the past twenty-five years. Naturalists and scientists were instrumental in getting Mary's Point and Shepody Bay listed as Ramsar Wetlands of International Significance and Western Hemispheric Shorebird Reserves. In 1988, the New Horizons group researched and mapped 130 sensitive natural sites for its publication *Critical Natural Areas in New Brunswick*.

WHAT HAS HAPPENED SINCE 1989?

With the advent of the Endangered Spaces campaign in 1989, representatives from environmental non-government organizations (NGOs) began to work with government staff on an ecological land-classification and mapping system for New Brunswick's natural regions. This was to be the first step in establishing a revamped protected-areas network, which would include protected sites representing each natural region. The newly formed New Brunswick Protected Natural Areas Coalition also began lobbying the government to commit officially to the goal of the national Endangered Spaces campaign, and to update the protected-areas system.

A new Provincial Parks System Master Plan, written in 1990, recommended a change in emphasis from recreational to ecological values. It was proposed that the

Natural Regions of New Brunswick

Ecological Representation by Protected Areas

■ 0	Represented
■ 0	Moderately represented
■ 6	Partially represented
□ 29	Little or no representation

As of April 1, 1995

provincial parks be established and managed with conservation and ecological integrity as priorities, and that recreational uses be concentrated in smaller, more compact areas. These recommendations and policies were not immediately implemented because of a post-election ministry shuffle, which moved parks from the responsibility of the Department of Tourism, Recreation and Heritage (now Economic Development and Tourism) to the Department of Natural Resources and Energy (DNRE).

On behalf of the Province of New Brunswick, the Minister of Natural Resources and Energy, Alan Graham, finally endorsed the Endangered Spaces campaign in September 1992.

Two months later, the government's Executive-in-Council approved a new Protected Areas Policy. Policy objectives included protecting areas representative of major natural regions, as well as sites for critical wildlife habitat, recreation, and scenic values. New emphasis on ecosystem protection was reflected by a proposed reclassification of provincial parks. New categories being considered were "wilderness, natural environment, linear/waterway, recreation, day use, roadside rest areas, and park reserves." At long last, we had a springboard from which to dive in and protect natural areas!

Since 1989, ten more ecological reserves have been designated. Unfortunately, one of the steps needed for legal proclamation of ecological reserves is an official recommendation by the Environmental Council, an advisory committee of appointed volunteers that was disbanded in 1992 (apparently for financial reasons). Until the Ecological Reserves Act is amended to remove the need for recommendations by the non-existent council, new ecological reserves are being protected by the minister of DNRE under the Crown Lands and Forests Act.

In January 1994, the minister of DNRE announced the establishment of the Kennedy Lakes Wilderness Area, a 6880-hectare region in the north-central part of the province. As yet, we do not have any information on whether the area will be fully protected to Endangered Spaces standards, or how it will fit into the province's new protected-areas strategy and network.

The Kennedy Lakes announcement came in response to a coalition of environmental, aboriginal, wildlife, and angling organizations calling for protection of the Christmas Mountains, an area located some distance to the north of the Kennedy Lakes. The Christmas Mountains are 20,400 hectares of Crown Land, which contain what may well be the last large tracts of relatively unfragmented old forest in New Brunswick. They remain unprotected and are being actively logged.

The Nature Trust of New Brunswick now has five preserves under its stewardship, totalling 274 hectares. It is currently negotiating and cooperating with property owners and other groups to protect several other critical natural areas.

As yet, New Brunswick does not have any marine protected areas. A proposal to establish West Isles National Marine Park in the Bay of Fundy is being considered.

Much excellent, scientifically based research and planning have been done by DNRE staff in preparing the ecological land classification and a gap analysis of the existing system. With their recommendations from the gap analysis, a basis for the actual designation of new protected areas has been provided.

The New Brunswick Protected Natural Areas Coalition has a vision for the province's protected-areas system for the year 2000. That vision includes a completed network of areas representative of each natural region (called "eco-districts"), an established Private Stewardship Strategy for private land, and a completed gap analysis for marine areas.

CRITICAL PATH TO 2000

New Brunswick is far behind schedule if it intends to honour its Endangered Spaces commitment. For this reason, many of the milestones that need to be met must be reached as soon as possible. The following critical path reflects that fact, with most of the milestones coming sooner, rather than later. Nevertheless, it is recognized that many of the elements in the critical path are long-term processes that will be ongoing to the year 2000 and beyond.

1. *Completion and Public Announcement of Gap Analysis, Recommendations for Candidate Sites, and a Draft Natural Areas Strategy.* In 1995, the DNRE should release the results of its gap analysis plus any recommendations concerning potential natural areas that would contribute to the protected-areas system. Also, the draft Natural Areas Strategy outlining the process for protecting and managing natural areas on Crown and private lands, the different categories of protected areas, and the activities to be permitted in each, should be made public at that time.

    The New Brunswick Protected Natural Areas Coalition, with support from WWF Canada, has presented the provincial government with guidelines for the Natural Areas Strategy in a position paper entitled, "Toward a Protected Natural Areas System for New Brunswick."

2. *Public Education and Consultation.* In the interest of beginning public consultation on the areas intended for protection, a Protected Natural Areas Advisory Council should be established immediately. This council would involve representatives from environmental organizations, academia, scientists, industry and government departments. The minister of DNRE appears to be supportive of the formation of such an advisory council.

    Without public support, all the planning going on now behind the scenes could be wasted. Public education about the importance of protected natural areas is essential if we are to gain support for specific protected-areas proposals. This is one way the Protected Natural Areas Coalition can make a significant contribution to the Natural Areas Strategy.

3. *Protection of Representative Natural Areas.* Between now and 1997, at least half the ecodistricts that are still not represented must be fully represented with legally designated protected areas. The rest of the system should be completed between 1997 and 2000. The designated areas must be of adequate size to maintain ecological integrity. They cannot simply be small areas like our ecological reserves, although such areas are very important for the preservation of other natural-history values.

    Hot spots identified by the Protected Natural Areas Coalition as good candidates include:

    • *The Fundy coastal area, west of Fundy National Park.* Unlike the rest of southern New Brunswick, this coastal region has a distinctly boreal character, with spruce, pine, and fir forests; coastal bogs; and fens. Parts of this region are currently under license to the forest industry and are being cut.

- *The rich hardwood ridges and slopes of the St. John River watershed in western and southern New Brunswick.* The hardwood forests that cover these ridges and slopes are dominated by sugar maple and beech, and often contain stands of basswood and butternut, both of which are near the northern limit of their range. A number of plants, which are rare in the province, live within these upland hardwood groves. They include Goldie's fern, showy orchis, Sprengel's sedge, and cut-leaved toothwort (a member of the mustard family).

- *Riparian areas of the Restigouche River and northern portions of the St. John River.* On rocky shores and pebbled beaches there are many rare and interesting plants, including the endangered Furbish's louse-wort, northern painted cup, butterwort, and rare sedges. Because these habitats are maintained by seasonal flooding and ice scour, they, along with the habitats of the Atlantic salmon, would be destroyed by damming or other major developments.

- *The sand dunes and plains of the Acadian peninsula, in northeastern New Brunswick.* These dunes provide excellent habitat for shorebirds, including the piping plover, another endangered species. The sensitive dunes and beaches in this area are under immediate threat from development and illegal use of motorized vehicles.

4. *Research and Planning for Marine Protected Areas.* In 1995, the province, in conjunction with the federal government, should initiate research and planning on marine protected areas. This process should begin with ecological classification of marine ecoregions, a gap analysis, and the establishment of a Marine Protected Areas Advisory Council. Policies and protected zones for coastal areas must be integrated with those for open waters, as ecosystems in these areas are closely interrelated.

   Since the provincial government licenses aquaculture sites offshore, and has announced its intention to license the intertidal zone for rockweed harvesting, it has obviously accepted some responsibility for the marine environment around New Brunswick. Along with the privilege of harvesting from the ocean comes the responsibility to protect the environment from the deleterious effects of these activities, and to ensure the sustainability of marine ecosystems and life forms.

5. *Maintenance of Ecological Integrity.* In 1996, the provincial government should release the names of the current parks that will remain in the Provincial Parks System, how they will be classified under the new system, and the level of protection they will receive. Conservation plans should be established for current protected areas so that they will not become degraded by external or internal activities. The existing large parks in the province, both federal and provincial, should be expanded or modified to ensure the maintenance of their ecological integrity in the face of surrounding land uses.

To prevent our protected areas from becoming islands in a sea of development, attention should be given to corridors or linkages between them. Also, buffers around protected natural areas would help to safeguard them from certain external activities, while permitting others.

One example of a real threat is the development currently proposed for Kouchibouguac National Park. In an effort to boost the tourism potential of the park, and to help ensure "cost recovery," plans have been proposed to build a new campground, with a bridge leading to a sand dune that is now reasonably inaccessible. This dune is near a sensitive breeding area for the piping plover. The piping plover has become an endangered species in Canada, precisely because its breeding areas on sandy beaches are vulnerable to human disturbance. We cannot allow this kind of backsliding in natural areas that are already supposed to have protected status.

6. *Facilitating Protection of Private Properties.* By setting a good example on Crown lands, developing legislative tools, and forging new partnerships, the provincial government can facilitate the protection of private properties.

Provincial conservation easement legislation should be proclaimed no later than spring 1996. This legislation will provide incentives for private landowners to dedicate their lands for conservation purposes. Current proposals for amendments to the federal Capital Gains Tax are also under way to allow people to donate land for conservation purposes without being taxed for increases in the assessed value of the land. The province must support these amendments, and must also provide incentives to encourage property owners who reside outside Canada to help preserve our natural heritage.

These are crucial steps towards developing an overall Natural Areas Stewardship Program for protecting private land. Since over 50 per cent of New Brunswick is privately owned, stewardship agreements will be important in establishing a comprehensive protected-areas system that represents the biological diversity of the entire province. The Nature Trust of New Brunswick will no doubt help provide leadership and direction in the accomplishment of this task.

OTHER ACTIONS NEEDED TO HELP
ACCOMPLISH THE YEAR 2000 CRITICAL PATH

1. *Political Support.* One of the stumbling blocks to the establishment of protected natural areas in New Brunswick has been the lack of real political support for such initiatives. Politicians have traditionally been sceptical about the short-term benefits to their careers of removing areas from development. They have also been slow to accept the potential of both ecotourism and value-added manufacturing to revitalize our economy. It is often much easier for politicians to maintain the status quo and allow the management of natural resources to continue focusing on resource extraction.

One of the main tasks for New Brunswickers is to encourage our politicians to look past the next election, and make their decisions based on sustainability of the environment and economy, rather than short-term economic gain. The premier, other politicians, and their staff have been talking about sustainability in a variety of public documents, including the Premier's Round Table on the Environment and Economy. Now it is time for them to make specific decisions that will see us move in a healthy and sustainable fashion into the next century. One of the first things they can do to accomplish this is to be visionaries and promote the completion of a protected-areas network.

2. *Changes to Legislation.* The Provincial Parks Act needs to be amended to strengthen the objectives of ecological integrity and conservation within the provincial parks system. Currently, logging and mining are legally permitted within these parks, although there is a departmental policy that this will not occur. This policy needs to be entrenched in legislation to protect ecosystems within provincial parks from commercial resource extraction of any kind.

I am grateful for the opportunity of officially endorsing the World Wildlife Fund's initiative Endangered Spaces.

The haphazard destruction and misuse of our nation's wildlands is finally being recognized by a large sector of the general population. It is very encouraging to note that they are now making themselves heard and that steps are being taken to put a stop to this destruction.
GILBERT FINN,
Lieutenant-Governor of
New Brunswick, 1990

The Endangered Species Act needs to be updated to include legal protection for the habitat of endangered animals and plants. An advisory committee is currently working on revising this act. The habitats of endangered species may or may not fall within the network of representative areas, or they may be protected in ecological reserves.

3. *Altering the Profile of Natural Areas.* New Brunswick was built on the idea of using natural resources as commodities to be bought and sold, paving the way for European settlement of the "New Frontier" with its "endless" resource base. We know now, after hundreds of years of use and mismanagement of these resources, that the supply is not endless. Yet, we still cling to the outmoded idea that we can alter ecosystems to suit our boundless whims and wants, and scientifically predict exactly how ecosystems will respond.

This attitude has led to an overreliance on ecosystems to produce high yields of commercial products, whether trees, fish, or ducks. We can't see the forest for the trees, the ocean for the fish, or the wetland for the ducks.

It is time that New Brunswickers moved away from this antiquated view of nature and its place in our lives. The other life forms that share the forests and oceans with us have a right to their space. If we want to continue to use resources from ecosystems, we must also preserve extensive areas where there is no such use. Protected natural areas should be our way of recognizing that humans are not perfect. We don't know everything about the intricate ecosphere we inhabit, and we cannot ignore and blindly destroy the results of millions of years of evolution.

The New Brunswick Protected Natural Areas Coalition realizes that the task of establishing a comprehensive system of protected natural areas is an ambitious one. It is also a necessary task, for our survival and for the survival of the other living things that share our province. We also realize that our natural areas are being degraded as we speak (and plan and research). The goal of the Endangered Spaces campaign can be accomplished only if there is a cooperative effort among environmental non-government organizations, scientists, aboriginal people, industry, private-property owners, the general public, and the federal and provincial governments.

New Brunswickers are proud of our natural history. We enjoy nothing better than helping someone discover the best cove for watching the sunset off Grand Manan Island, the most scenic route for viewing autumn colours in the St. John River Valley, or the perfect spot for catching a glimpse of bald eagles or peregrine falcons. Our lives and our culture are enriched by such memorable moments. These are values well worth protecting — for now, and for generations to come.

14 / Nova Scotia

COLIN STEWART

People have been changing the nature of Nova Scotia for centuries. The Micmac arrived first, at least 10,500 years ago, but the land was little altered under their steward-ship. Europeans fished these waters, and presumably visit-ed these shores, for at least a hundred years before the French established Canada's first permanent European set-tlement, Port-Royal, in 1605. The French converted most of the Bay of Fundy's extensive salt marshes to farms. The heavy use of the forests, on the other hand, would wait for the British. The loss of the Thirteen Colonies increased Britain's dependence on Nova Scotia and its resources.

At Confederation, Nova Scotia was a "have" province, with fishing, shipbuild-ing, timber, and gold and other minerals as its economic mainstays. Farming was widespread, especially where fishing and other activities could be pursued. However, most of the province is poorly suited for agriculture, and today many for-mer farming areas have been abandoned. The tall trees were used up, many mines exhausted, and the economic centre of the country moved west. Economic renewal efforts of the 1950s and 1960s saw paper-making become the dominant use of Nova Scotia's forests.

Four centuries of heavy use of our natural resources have left little that is natural. Even the wolves and caribou have been replaced by coyotes and deer. Seventy-five per cent of the land is now in private hands. Most communities are coastal, and the road network reflects this. The few remaining roadless areas are mostly in the interior.

But all is not doom and gloom. Our forefathers did not reach every corner of the province; nor, because of the labour involved, were they quite as efficient at the removal of resources as we are today. Consequently, much of the original biological diversity has survived.

However, this is changing fast. Mechanization has increased the rapidity and thoroughness of change. The Endangered Spaces campaign's call to action in 1989 came none too soon for this part of the country.

PROTECTED AREAS

Nova Scotia's first wild protected area was the Waverley Game Sanctuary, near Halifax, created in 1926 at the request of the Boy Scouts to preserve wildlife-viewing opportunities near their camps. The prevailing opinion of the day was that prohibiting hunting in this area would ensure surplus game would move to adjacent areas. No other management of the area was needed. Much of this sanctuary has survived. Most of the other, and larger, game sanctuaries created in the early days have been extensively logged.

At the start of the Endangered Spaces campaign, virtually all of Nova Scotia's protected areas were in Cape Breton Highlands (CBH) and Kejimkujik National Parks. CBH, created in 1936, preserves 950 square kilometres of largely unaltered boreal plateau and adjacent rugged slopes. The inhabited coastal lowlands were, to a large degree, excluded from the park.

Kejimkujik, 360 square kilometres in central-southwestern Nova Scotia, was created in 1967. Although a centre for "sportsmen" for almost a century, most of the area had been selectively cut through the 1940s and 1950s. Recovery is progressing. In the 1980s, Kejimkujik acquired a seaside adjunct — 22 square kilometres of beach, bog, barachois, barren headland, and a bit of coastal forest.

The Fortress of Louisbourg National Historic Park includes 50 square kilometres of coastal hills, which were once largely denuded by the wood demands of the famous fortress and are now again covered by forest. The importance of this bit of nature has not yet been adequately recognized in the park's management plan.

Nova Scotia's provincial park system began with the Highways Department in the 1950s, with the objective of providing one picnic park for every 50 miles (80 kilometres) of trunk highway, and a campground in every county not serviced by the CBH National Park. In the 1960s and 1970s, an increasing interest in recreational areas led to the acquisition of several beaches and donations of significant private lands. In the 1980s, the vision included some large properties, still with recreational use in mind. However, in 1989, a revised Provincial Park Act included provision for zoning and conservation-based parks.

At the start of the Endangered Spaces campaign, the 230 parks and park reserves represented just 0.3 per cent of the province. Only twenty-seven of these sites contribute to the campaign's representation goals. Nova Scotia's starting-point in 1989 was rounded out by three Nature Reserves totalling less than one square kilometre, with Nature Conservancy of Canada and other private holdings adding a bit more. There were no marine protected areas.

At the halfway point in the campaign, the federal contribution is unchanged. Provincial parks have increased by a few, to add roughly 50 square kilometres (another 0.1 per cent). Nature reserves have more than doubled, to seven, and total about 20 square kilometres. The Nature Conservancy has added a few more parcels to their two holdings. And there are still no marine areas protected.

All in all, this represents a very small increase in the amount of land protected over the past five years.

There *is* hope, however. The proposed Systems Plan for Parks and Protected Areas in Nova Scotia was released in March 1994. If this proposal for thirty-one sites, totalling 287,000 hectares, goes forward unreduced, it will protect an additional 5.5 per cent of Nova Scotia, including the most significant remaining large natural areas. That would place Nova Scotia about halfway to the Endangered Spaces goal, and would see an improvement in representation of natural regions that few other jurisdictions could match.

Public comment and panel review of the new system plan concluded in February and May 1995. The government must now make its decision. The importance of

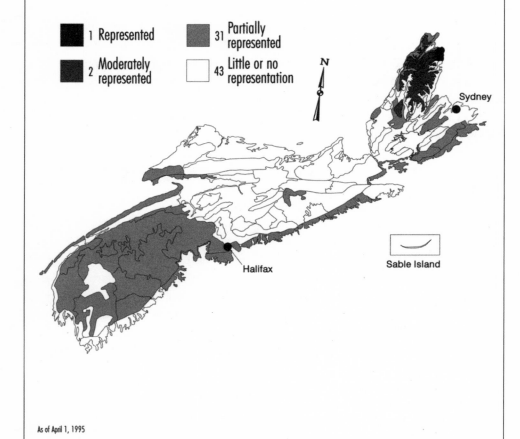

Natural Regions of Nova Scotia
Ecological Representation by Protected Areas

1 Represented

2 Moderately represented

31 Partially represented

43 Little or no representation

N

Sydney

Halifax

Sable Island

As of April 1, 1995

this cannot be overstated, for without the bulk of the proposal being approved, we are back at 1989, without much hope of recovering either the political will or the proposed sites while they still have ecological integrity.

With so much at stake, it is worth looking at how we got here, and what our failures and successes can teach us about reaching our goal by the year 2000.

LESSONS LEARNED

The Halifax part of the Endangered Spaces launch was sponsored by the Halifax Field Naturalists. Nova Scotia's Environment Minister at the time, John Leefe, heard some of the national coverage and phoned Monte Hummel to offer his personal support.

The government's first commitment was to a three-year system process of planning. This welcome announcement was made by the Lands and Forest minister, Dr. Chuck MacNeil, at the inaugural meeting of the Federation of Nova Scotia Naturalists in June 1990. Its significance was probably underestimated.

In 1992, John Leefe, by then Minister of Natural Resources, officially announced the government's support of the Endangered Spaces objectives. This had all-party support.

In June 1993, Nova Scotia changed governments. The crucial system plan was delayed for additional internal review by the new government. The completed plan was released for public consultation as a government proposal by the Minister of Natural Resources, Don Downe, and Premier John Savage at the end of March 1994. The merit of the proposal owes a great deal to the process used to prepare it. The first part of the process involved a review of the 1984 government publication *The Natural History of Nova Scotia*, which provided the technical base for determining the province's natural regions, and which had only ever been published as a draft. The review recognized that some weak areas in the study needed revision before the publication could be used as the basis for designing a protected-areas system. The Parks Division of Natural Resources and the Nova Scotia Museum, both major contributors to the original document, each initiated revision processes. The Museum's technical revisions to the document are now complete, but have not yet been published.

The Parks Division refined the theme (natural) region/district/unit component of the report. They developed this into a 77-unit "natural landscape" system. This system takes the natural-region concept a step farther, by identifying surficial features (such as a dominant ridge, drumlin field, or plain) which influence vegetation at a habitat level. Such an approach parallels, but is distinct from, the enduring-features approach of WWF's gap analysis, described in Chapter 1. It also means Nova Scotia is now using the finest resolution of any jurisdiction to ensure representation of its biodiversity.

While this framework to assess representation needs was under development, the Parks Division used 1:63,000 aerial photos to identify all "natural" areas over 200 hectares in size. Its definition of "natural area" was an area having no prepared roads or major disruptions. The next step was to select areas over 2000 hectares on Crown land, followed by rating and field checking. The primary criterion was representivity of landscapes and ecosystems, but unique or special features and wilderness recreation opportunities were also considered. This work resulted in recommendation for candidate protected areas totalling 330,000 hectares, which was reduced to 287,000 hectares through internal review, along with boundary adjustments, to minimize major resource conflicts. Although the government estimates this adds only nineteen new landscapes to the seven already judged well represented, they are generally in the largest natural regions; consequently, about half of the province's land mass is well represented under the proposal.

To prevent loss of ecological integrity, the candidate areas have been under interim protection since January 1993. The plan proposes a permanent level of protection consistent with Endangered Spaces criteria, and comparable to "wilderness" zones in national parks. Pre-existing mineral claims would remain valid. Specific details of use, including wilderness access, whether hunting will be permitted, the immediate fate of pre-existing cabins, and travel routes, have been left to the site-management planning process.

In March 1994, the plan was released for public comment. And in late fall, a five-member review panel was appointed to hear public comment, summarize it, and advise the government. It conducted thirteen public meetings in January and February 1995. This process is concluding as this chapter is being written. The results are critical to the future of natural representation efforts in Nova Scotia.

If the public isn't seen to support this level and amount of protection, the process will probably end with protection of some fraction of these sites. Conservationists making further arguments for major new protected areas would obviously face an uphill struggle; if the public didn't support the thirty-one original sites, why would they support new ones?

Fortunately, it seems clear that the public does want to retain the thirty-one proposed areas in their natural state. Most of the discussion has been about the process. Support seems to fall into three categories. Some people believe that protection can be achieved by simply leaving the sites alone. Others, primarily members of hunting groups but also including some motorized-vehicle users and "just local" people, do not trust the government. They fear that once approval in principle is given, management plans will close all existing camps, stop hunting and fishing, and keep all vehicles and people out. Therefore, while supporting the principle of retaining these areas in their present natural state, these people want to see the detailed management plans before confirming their support. A third large group of people are calling for implementation of the plans as proposed, and for the government to get on with filling the gaps it has identified.

The review panel and government must find their way through a labyrinth of public opinion. Many of the people who have suspicions are the same people who will be crucial to the long-term integrity of these sites. If, in the end, they believe that a fair process has produced the correct decisions and methods to protect these sites, they will treat them with respect, and support the implementation of management plans. If they feel railroaded, they may ignore many inconvenient regulations, knowing there is little chance of being caught, and they will certainly put little effort into monitoring the actions of others.

SPECIAL PLACES

The protection of Nova Scotia's biodiversity cannot rest on the new systems plan alone. One of the consequences of having so much land greatly altered and fragmented and under private ownership is that a lot of the diversity can be initially protected only in small packages, typically nature reserves. The Endangered Spaces campaign, among others, has repeatedly stressed the importance of nature reserves in Nova Scotia, but the results have been disappointing.

Since the identification of sixty-nine candidate sites in a report by the International Biological Programme (IBP) in 1974, government intentions have been good. A deputy minister of the day ordered that Crown land sites be reserved pending decisions, and requested that major companies do the same. And it was done.

However, it took until 1980 to create the Special Places Act, allowing the designation of nature reserves as well as palaeontological, geological and archaeological reserves. This was placed under the Nova Scotia Museum. In 1984, a staff position was authorized, by which time the number of candidate sites suggested had reached ninety. Under the legislation, archaeological and palaeontological reserves can be designated on discovery, but nature reserves require a management plan as part of the Cabinet designation process. This management planning process has drastically slowed designations.

By the start of the Endangered Spaces campaign, three nature reserves had been designated. McFarlane Woods, in southwestern Cape Breton, illustrates the act's potential by creating a nature reserve on private land with the owner's consent. "Natural history" support was willingly supplied by museum staff, and field and logistical support came from the Parks Division of Lands and Forests. However, there were other demands on the one staff person — mastodons in quarries, administration, and so on. The Special Places program was a small section of the museum's responsibilities, and the museum, in turn, a small section of the Department of Education. While all levels were supportive, or at least sympathetic, at budget time additional resources did not appear. Nor did candidate protected areas appear high on the list of presentations to Cabinet.

In 1993, a seventh reserve was created. Shortly thereafter, another government reorganization took place. Responsibility for the nature-reserve portion of the Special Places program was moved from the museum to Parks Division of Natural Resources. No new sites were designated in 1994, and in early 1995 the government indicated it was still identifying research needs.

The original IBP recommendations were made twenty years ago. Staff were first provided ten years ago. Seven sites have been protected. One hundred are waiting. This is a low-cost program which doesn't seem to be opposed by anyone. It has been worked on by concerned and dedicated individuals. The challenge seems to be to improve the efficiency of government.

OTHER EFFORTS

Through the Conservation Easement Act (1992), the provincial government has provided a major tool for the protection of natural sites on private property. This allows government or, significantly, "designated groups" to enter into agreements with landowners to protect property without the Common Law requirement of

We will soon be a country with no wilderness that isn't protected — just as in the lower forty-eight states where there's nothing left of wilderness that isn't protected. There's an overwhelming amount of industrial activity all over Canada's wilderness, and that's why it's so urgent to get on with protecting representative parts while we still have the opportunity.
HARVEY LOCKE,
President, Canadian Parks and Wilderness Society

owning adjacent land and demonstrating direct benefit. Both the Federation of Nova Scotia Naturalists and the Nova Scotia Nature Trust have been designated under the act.

In the past five years, non-government organizations (NGOs) have matured considerably. Several environmental NGOs, including Ecology Action Centre's Wilderness Committee, are active. The international Science and Management of Protected Areas Association (SAMPAA) was founded in Nova Scotia to foster scientific understanding about protected areas. It has also fostered greater academic presence and activity in achieving protection. The Federation of Nova Scotia Naturalists now hosts WWF's Nova Scotia Endangered Spaces Coordinator (me!). And the Nova Scotia Nature Trust, created in 1993, announced its first acquisition in May 1995.

Chapter 2 presents an overview of marine protected areas across Canada. While Parks Canada acknowledges a responsibility to establish representative Marine Conservation Areas, and some other protection measures exist, no federal or provincial agencies have seriously undertaken establishing a system of marine protected areas anywhere in the country.

The diversity and importance of Nova Scotia's marine environment can be appreciated through a brief description of the major areas. The Gulf of St. Lawrence has "the warmest water north of Florida," according to the Prince Edward Island tourism ads, but it freezes each winter. Only 40 kilometres away, the 13-metre tides of the Bay of Fundy prevent freezing, but the diurnal movement of this mass of water has year-round effects on weather and everything that lives in and around the Bay. The tides are smaller on the Atlantic side, though the waters don't freeze. Coastal bays, basins, and banks, including Sable Island, the continental slope and the influences of the Gulf Stream and the Labrador Current, all contribute to the rich marine diversity of the Atlantic side. Nova Scotia's other marine area is Cape Breton's Bras d'Or, surrounded by land but connected to the Atlantic by two deep channels.

The fisheries' collapse certainly cannot be described as a blessing, but it has brought home the importance of leaving some areas alone for spawning, restocking, and monitoring, and as a general insurance policy. A number of individuals and NGOs are beginning to work together to address the huge gap in Atlantic province marine representation.

THE WAY AHEAD

At the halfway point in the terrestrial campaign, most of the groundwork for reaching the representation target has been laid. If we are reading the public response correctly, and if the government does commit to the thirty-one proposed sites, then many of the most significant, large, intact sites should soon be secured. The key to completing the commitment to Endangered Spaces is working together, and moving forward.

The government's role is clear and quite challenging. At best, resources will remain at the current level, but they are more likely to be decreased. The Parks Division will soon have to deliver management plans for approved sites. If the government's past record of designing and implementing plans for provincial parks is a guide, then the quality will certainly be there, but the delivery will tend to be a lengthy process. To create and restore confidence, the process cannot be too lengthy.

It will also require working with local communities and a range of provincial interest groups.

The second major government task is to protect smaller intact areas and attempt to connect them. Many of these are on private land. NGOs will have to be involved here, because it is unlikely that government will provide sufficient resources to implement an adequate and timely private-landowner contact program. Furthermore, while many landowners would willingly discuss conserving their land with government, others would not. Even if distrust were not a problem, the price asked from government for land by private landowners often greatly exceeds what they would ask from charitable organizations. This provides another reason for NGOs to be involved.

The significance of the nature reserve program has not diminished. Many candidate sites are small and unique, or harbour endangered species. Many are also the last or best remnants of formerly widespread habitats. Private groups like the Nature Trust could use conservation easements or donations to protect a few such sites each year.

It should be clear from this that government and non-government organizations are going to have to work together to achieve completion of a protected-areas system in Nova Scotia. Government has the information to speed the identification of sites, and most of the responsibility and variety of means to secure protection. NGOs have credibility, and often local support. They will need to develop their skills in dealing fairly with local landowners.

In times of declining budgets and shrinking government, it is up to concerned citizens to ensure that the conservation of nature does not fall off the agenda. If those who are concerned about ensuring representation of Nova Scotia's natural diversity do not put in the effort, we will not get there. With so much to do, it is time for our concerns to be expressed through money and time contributed directly to efforts to preserve important landscapes. As a consequence of the fisheries' collapse, those of us living on the shore of "the sea without fish" now appreciate the need to help the ocean replenish itself. Have we learned the same lesson for the land?

15 / Prince Edward Island

DIANE GRIFFIN

 When World Wildlife Fund (WWF) Canada launched the Endangered Spaces campaign in 1989, the Land of Anne of Green Gables had already made some progress in terms of establishing protected areas. There was the Prince Edward Island National Park and a system of about twenty-five small, mostly recreational, provincial parks. As well, there were thirteen properties designated under the new Natural Areas Protection Act of 1988. There were also some substantial roadblocks preventing the protected-areas network from growing much larger.

On Prince Edward Island, 90 per cent of the land base is privately owned. Approximately 50 per cent is cultivated, the rest wooded. This woodland is either white spruce covering abandoned farmland, or woods that had been highgraded since the 1700s for shipbuilding, furniture-making, or sawmilling. In 1989 few truly natural habitats remained, and those that did were small fragments of untouched land.

Prince Edward Island is the most densely settled province in Canada. It is considered a "have-not" province, which means it could legitimately argue that it does not have the resources to develop and maintain a protected-areas system. So, yes, at the start of the Endangered Spaces campaign, the Garden of the Gulf faced some very real challenges. Should it even be expected to contribute much towards meeting the "at least 12 per cent" protected-areas objective for Canada?

WWF Canada wouldn't let us off the hook. If we couldn't protect 12 per cent, because all the remnants would not add up to that percentage, then what could we do?

In 1992, a target list of sites that were already protected or should be protected was drawn up by the provincial government. It amounted to about 7 per cent of the land base. Was it realistic to think we could even achieve this, given the amount of privately owned land in P.E.I., and the scarcity of available funds for land acquisition? It was decided that the Island Nature Trust (a private land conservancy) and the government would work together to make the most effective use of their limited resources.

First, the provincial government "signed on" to pursue the Endangered Spaces goal on December 19, 1991. Then it quickly developed processes for selecting candidate areas, and for completing management plans for the sites so that they could be designated under the Natural Areas Protection Act or other legislation. The Executive Council approved a Significant Environmental Areas Plan, which listed candidate areas, including privately owned sites.

The focus of this early effort was on terrestrial habitats, including wetlands; it did not include coastal cliffs or marine areas. These categories have since been added. Although some research has been done on coastal cliffs, everything is still needed to establish marine protected areas — research, an approved process for policy development, cultivation of community participation, methods for selecting candidate areas, development of management techniques, and so on. With the limited resources available, one could argue the advisability of sweeping the marine areas under the rug (or away with the tide) until completion of the terrestrial system. However, this province is surrounded by ocean, so it has become difficult to ignore the marine element, especially when it has always been a legitimate part of the Endangered Spaces campaign.

Once the Significant Environmental Areas Plan was approved, many sites were designated under the Natural Areas Protection Act. A number of these were sites on Crown land. Others were areas that were purchased by the Island Nature Trust. Yet others were, and still are, owned by a few private landowners who are interested in conservation. As a result, the total area now under various forms of protection is 12,800 hectares. This includes the national park, provincial parks that meet the Endangered Spaces criteria, designated natural areas, wildlife management areas, and additional Crown lands purchased for the national park — in total 2.2 per cent of the province, still some distance from our 7 per cent objective.

Much of the success so far has been an accumulation of small steps — the donation of a 12-hectare island with colonial nesting birds, the purchase of a 65-hectare property on the north shore with fine wetland habitat, the formal protection of the seventeen Crown-owned properties on the Morell River. A recent breakthrough, though, has added significantly to the quality and quantity of protected natural areas in P.E.I.

In April 1995, the province completed a land trade in the Greenwich area with an American developer. A magnificent sand dune and wetland habitat of 366 hectares is now the property of the Crown and has been designated for protection under the Natural Areas Protection Act. The area is home to several rare species and the nesting area for one endangered species, the piping plover. This took six years of negotiation, after an expensive and confrontational fight between conservationists and the developer during hearings before the Land Use Commission. As part of the Greenwich package deal, the Island Nature Trust purchased from the same owner the 25-hectare Gordon's Island, which is located in a five-island archipelago in Murray Harbour. Like the Greenwich dunes, the archipelago was recommended for protection in 1974 by the International Biological Programme — a major Canada-wide study of potential sites for protection.

Although it may not sound significant, one of the most important ingredients for ensuring the protection of natural areas has been a new spirit of cooperation among government departments, and between the government and the Island Nature Trust. Upon the release of the Maritime provinces section of the 1974 report by the International Biological Programme, there was a flurry of interest in setting up a system of protected natural sites. But leadership to direct this interest was missing. At least three government branches (Parks, Forestry, and Wildlife) had an obvious interest, but their efforts were halting and uncoordinated. As a result, in 1979,

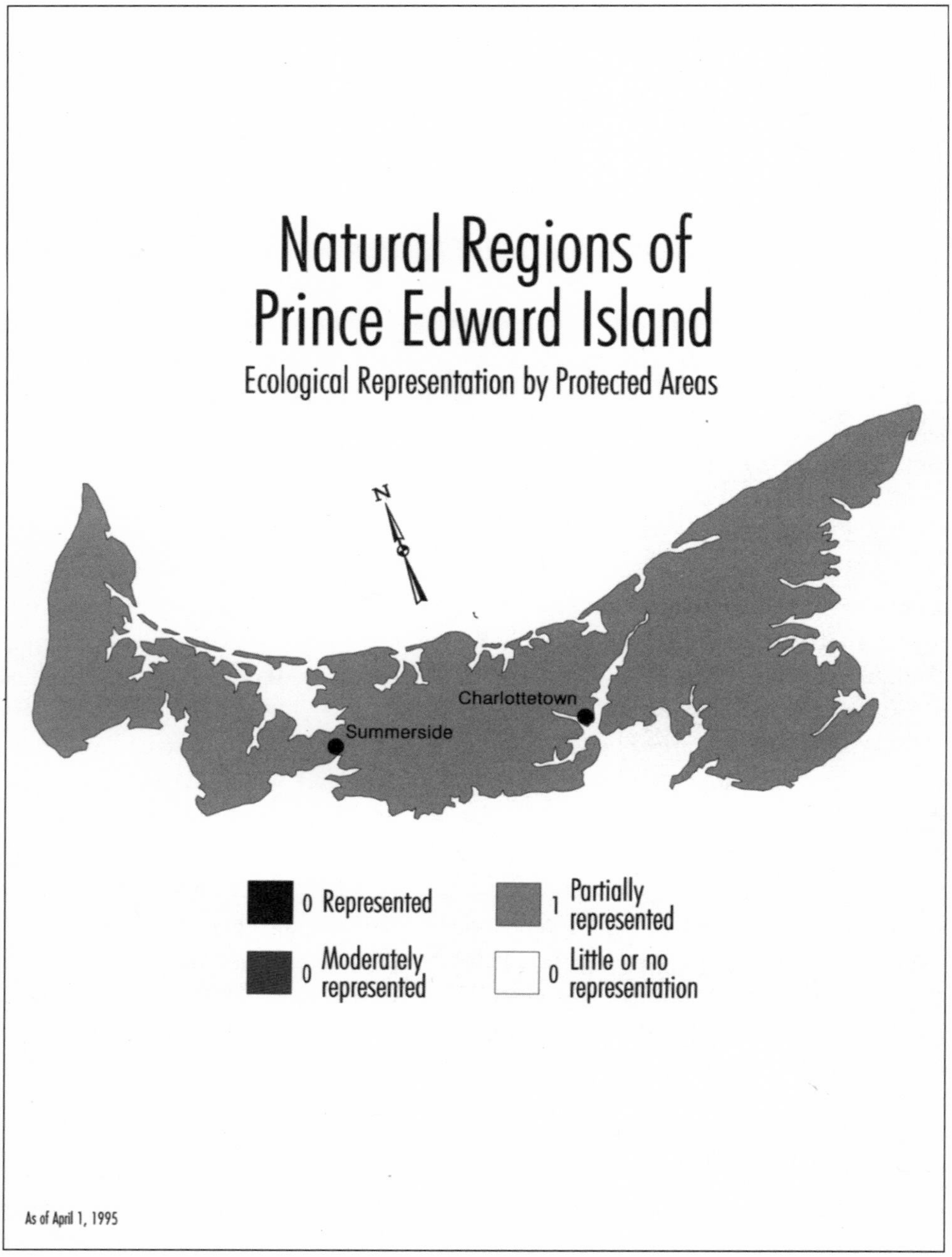

Natural Regions of Prince Edward Island

Ecological Representation by Protected Areas

N

Charlottetown

Summerside

■ 0 Represented

▦ 1 Partially represented

▨ 0 Moderately represented

☐ 0 Little or no representation

As of April 1, 1995

conservation-minded groups and individuals established the Island Nature Trust in an attempt to acquire land and to work with other landowners to encourage them to protect natural features on their properties. The Nature Trust also acted as an advocacy group for natural areas, and worked with the province to establish legislation, policy, and a system plan for the natural areas. Since 1988, there has been an active Natural Areas Protection Act Technical Advisory Committee comprising representatives of various government departments and the Nature Trust. This group administers the Significant Environmental Areas program, including preparation of site management plans.

As Governor General of Canada, I strongly endorse the Endangered Spaces campaign which is being launched by the World Wildlife Fund, and urge Canadians to work towards the conservation of our wilderness areas. JEANNE SAUVÉ, Governor General of Canada, 1989

Another major step forward was the emphasis placed by the Nature Trust on private stewardship. Rather than wringing our hands at the fact that the government owned so little land, it was time to look for opportunities to work with private landowners. As a non-government organization, the Island Nature Trust was in a good position to approach property owners. The government, for its part, offered property-tax relief to cooperating landowners who put restrictive covenants on their land. Designation of private land was made possible under the Natural Areas Protection Act, and a landowner-recognition program was put in place in 1990. Through cooperation . . . it was happening!

Now, for both terrestrial and marine protected areas, "service after sales" is going to be the long-term challenge. Obtaining legislative protection for a system of protected areas is actually only the start. The ongoing protection of these sites is equally important. Once again, the argument could be put forth that it is difficult to find the resources to do this properly. And once again, a counter-argument can be made that, while resources are indeed scarce, there are always ways to "do things smarter" with existing resources. This applies to natural-areas protection, just as it does to health care and the school system. Resources from the public and private sector can be pooled and used more efficiently. The provincial government and the Island Nature Trust have established a good working relationship that has been instrumental in encouraging volunteers to take part in various projects, including fundraising to procure more natural areas. Volunteer-based programs also help to monitor and manage natural areas. These include Conservation Guardians, Piping Plover Guardians, and the River Watch projects.

Because of the scarcity of wilderness areas in P.E.I., restoration has to be seriously considered on many sites. This would include some silvicultural work on woodlands to approximate their original condition. Restoration will take time — a long time — and a lot of money. However, this is viewed as a long-term commitment. Even small efforts at this stage will have a large cumulative benefit over time.

Legislative protection of areas is still seen as the number-one priority, as well it should be. Once areas are secured, management plans are developed and registered with the certificate of title for each property. It would be tempting to rest on our laurels once this is done. But "service after sales" will have to be pushed to the forefront, so that necessary management activities can be carried out.

Where do we want to be in 2000? It would be wonderful if Prince Edward Island could reach our 7 per cent objective by that time, followed by some marine protected areas by 2010. The Department of Environmental Resources has estimated that it will have achieved protection for close to 5 per cent of the province by the end of the Endangered Spaces campaign. Considering the land-ownership situation and the paucity of undisturbed natural sites, this is probably a realistic figure. In fact, it is not bad when one considers that 6.6 per cent of Spud Island is planted in the king of crops, the potato.

STEPS NEEDED TO PROTECT TERRESTRIAL NATURAL AREAS

1. *Ensure that adequate resources and a high priority are given to completion of the 7 per cent objective.* After a flurry of activity in the previous year, the pace to protect natural areas fell off in 1994. As in any jurisdiction, there is competition for attention. Many government staff have multiple responsibilities. Protected areas must be kept at the top of the government's agenda, and not be relegated to an inferior position.

2. *Designate and rank all Crown lands that meet the Endangered Spaces criteria as soon as they are identified through the Crown land review, scheduled for 1995.*

3. *Continue to encourage protection of private land, either by acquisition or by private stewardship.* While ownership by government or some other conservation agency is the surest form of long-term protection, substantial conservation gains also will depend on securing agreements that will protect private land.

4. *Put some emphasis on the new category of protected area — coastal cliffs.* The two most striking features of the Island are its pristine coastline and pastoral landscape. The coastline consists of sandy beaches and coastal cliffs. Sand dunes have long been a priority for protection, and good progress has been made. But the coastal cliffs also need protection because they provide nesting areas for colonial species such as the great cormorant and the bank swallow. As well, their outstanding aesthetic quality must be maintained.

STEPS NEEDED TO PROTECT MARINE NATURAL AREAS

1. *Get approval from the Executive Council of Cabinet to develop policy and promote community involvement regarding marine protected areas.* A steering committee should be appointed in 1995, consisting of government and non-government personnel, including conservationists and representatives from the fishing industry.

2. *Research the Island's marine environment to determine what the natural features are, and what sites need special management considerations.* Some of this information is no doubt already available through traditional knowledge, as well as through scattered ecological studies. It is time to pull all of this together to identify the information gaps and then fill them in.

3. *Find a community interested in working on a pilot project right away.* This would be useful in establishing a process for community participation, and in developing management recommendations for a specific marine protected

area. It would provide an opportunity for partnerships to form, which could result in strong community support for marine protected areas elsewhere on the Island.

4. *Ensure that suitable legislation and regulations are in place by 1996 to enable designation of marine protected areas by either the federal or the provincial government.*

5. *Ensure adequate financial and technical resources.*

6. *Demonstrate better intergovernmental cooperation.*

Most certainly, by the year 2000, Prince Edward Island will have achieved protection of the "easiest" terrestrial areas. Negotiations for other areas may well drag on for years after that, simply because landowners are unwilling either to sell these areas or to enter into private stewardship agreements with restrictive covenants. A high percentage of ownership by non-residents, especially along the shoreline, further adds to the challenge.

Like everyone else entering the field of marine protection, the Island has a quantum amount of work to do. However, if there were the same kind of interdepartmental cooperation for marine management as there has been for terrestrial management, plus local community cooperation, the results could be impressive.

Since the launch of the Endangered Spaces campaign in 1989, P.E.I. is one of the very few jurisdictions to have achieved an "A" grade for its accomplishments, which are evaluated by WWF through its annual progress reports. We're proud of this, especially given the limitations under which our small province has had to operate. Progress has been accomplished primarily through cooperation and partnership, rather than strident confrontation, and as such might even serve as a model for what could be done elsewhere. Nevertheless, there's much more to be done, and we look forward to reporting further successes by the turn of the century.

16 / Newfoundland and Labrador

LAURA JACKSON

For many years, dedicated Newfoundlanders and Labradorians have been working hard to protect our natural environment through parks and reserves.

The first provincial park was created in 1954; there are now forty-five. In 1980, the provincial Wilderness and Ecological Reserves Act was passed, and acclaimed as a model for conservation legislation. The Wilderness and Ecological Reserves Advisory Council (WERAC) was appointed in 1981. This official body, made up of government and non-government representatives, recommends sites for protection by the provincial government.

By the end of 1989 and the launch of the Endangered Spaces campaign, the province had two national parks, Terra Nova and Gros Morne; the 1070-square-kilometre provincial Avalon Wilderness Reserve; and six ecological reserves.

In the fall of 1989, after an inspiring visit by Monte Hummel, a group of conservationists led by Dr. Jon Lien formed the Protected Areas Association (PAA) of Newfoundland and Labrador. A non-profit organization, the PAA had and still has as its main purpose the pursuit of the goals of the Endangered Spaces campaign. The PAA began by commissioning a number of scientific studies, most notably *The Natural Regions of Newfoundland and Labrador*, to serve as background material in the preparation of a provincial protected-areas strategy.

In 1990, the magnificent Bay du Nord Wilderness Reserve was established. This 2895-square-kilometre area abounds in caribou habitat, salmon rivers, and lakes, and is a fine representative example of the Maritime Barrens natural region, the only ecoregion in the province considered to be adequately represented according to Endangered Spaces criteria. Two more small ecological reserves — Watt's Point and Table Point — were also established that year, protecting rare wildflowers and fossils.

In December 1991, Premier Clyde Wells committed the province to the goals of the Endangered Spaces campaign.

In the March 1992 Throne Speech, Wells's government promised to take part in feasibility studies for the establishment of national parks in the Torngat and Mealy Mountains areas of Labrador. By that summer the provincial government, Parks Canada, and the Labrador Inuit Association (LIA) had signed a preliminary Torngat agreement upon which negotiation could proceed. A Task Force on Parks and Reserves was also set up that summer to determine future directions for the province's protected areas.

By November 1992, the newly formed Department of Tourism and Culture had drawn up an action plan to carry out the Endangered Spaces commitment. It promised to define criteria for representation of natural regions by December 1993, and to target candidate areas for complete representation by the end of 1994.

In 1993, three more ecological reserves — Hawke Hill, Fortune Head, and West Brook — were designated. In the same year, the PAA finished its proposed system plan and sent it out for extensive review.

In April 1994, the provincial Department of the Environment brought out regulations restricting use of all-terrain vehicles (ATVs) to a list of designated areas. ATVs, in the hands of irresponsible drivers, had been wreaking havoc on sand dunes, stream beds, mossy ground, and wetlands. Although there are loopholes — for example, sand dunes are designated areas, as is any area once there is snow cover or frost in the ground — the regulations are a step in the right direction.

As of 1995, both the Main and Bay du Nord rivers have been nominated for Canadian Heritage River status. Baccalieu Island should be designated as a seabird ecological reserve by the fall of 1995. The King George IV Ecological Reserve awaits final designation; we applaud Noranda Minerals for giving up its mineral exploration rights in the area to protect this delta haven for migrating waterfowl.

One encouraging recent initiative from the Department of Natural Resources' Forestry Division involves designing a forest conservation plan. Each of its twenty-three districts is studying the PAA system plan and selecting an example of each forest ecosystem in their area for protection. These forest reserves could serve as control areas where natural ecological processes and ecosystem dynamics can be studied, to help foresters better manage their working forests.

People in Newfoundland and Labrador are beginning to discuss the potential of marine protected areas. Following the tragic collapse of our fisheries, we are looking for ways to rebuild. Taking an ecosystem-based approach would reduce the likelihood of our making the same mistakes again. Following the success of the Placentia Bay area lobster closure, other possible marine conservation areas have been suggested — Bonavista Bay, adjoining Terra Nova National Park, for one. Conservationists are recommending that the process of establishing reserves must be incorporated into the whole process of rationalization and reopening our fisheries.

WHAT ARE THE CHALLENGES?
We enter the second half of the decade with two national parks, two wilderness reserves, and thirteen smaller ecological reserves. But there are real challenges to meet before we can complete a network of protected areas.

Newfoundlanders and Labradorians treasure a long tradition of free use of our lands and waters and their resources. We have the highest percentage of Crown land — roughly 95 per cent — of any province. "The country" — unfenced and largely unguarded — has been regarded by many people as an extension of their own backyards. More than 60,000 Newfoundlanders cut their own firewood. Along with New Brunswick and the territories, we have the highest percentage of hunters in Canada. In the last decade, we have accumulated some 40,000 ATVs, which access the farthest reaches of the land.

The problem of garbage disposal has also become a serious one. The country is

Natural Regions of Newfoundland/Labrador

Ecological Representation by Protected Areas

0	Represented
2	Moderately represented
6	Partially represented
11	Little or no representation

N

St. John's

As of April 1, 1995

littered with refuse. And while families once had their own septic systems, today's community sewage systems generally flush their wastes, untreated, right into the sea.

When fishery moratorium compensation ends, there will be additional stresses on our natural lands, as people with more time and less income increase their hunting, trapping, wood-cutting, and other subsistence activities.

CRITICAL PATH — ACTION STEPS TO 2000

1. *Give full acceptance to a completed system plan before the end of 1995.* Newfoundland and Labrador does not yet use a system plan for the selection of natural areas for protection. Adoption of such a plan is a first requirement for rational conservation work in the province.

The province has accepted using the natural regions as its basis for selecting representative natural areas. WWF, PAA, and many planners within the provincial government see a system plan as the next major step in achieving a network of protected areas for the province. In the meantime, of course, designation of already targeted areas should continue.

With help from the province's Parks Division, the federal Department of the Environment, and WWF, PAA enlisted the help of scientists, academics, and conservationists around the province to produce a proposed system plan. Titled *Towards Sustainable Development: A Protected Natural Areas Strategy for Newfoundland and Labrador*, the plan has been completed and reviewed. It now has the support of a broad range of planners and scientists within government and the wider community.

The goal of the system plan is to protect the province's biodiversity through creation of a network of parks and reserves. This network has three components: large areas protecting the habitat of wide-ranging species such as caribou; medium to large areas protecting representative examples of each of the province's nineteen ecoregions; and special or unique sites — usually ecological reserves — protecting such features as rare species of trees and wildflowers, fossils, and seabird colonies.

Good news arrived in early March 1995 when the provincial government's Parks and Reserves Task Force, charged with determining the future direction of the province's protected areas, recommended that the PAA plan be reviewed and adapted for use by the province as its official protected areas system plan. Modifications would be accomplished by a multidisciplinary committee composed of members from both within and outside government, and the group would have a four-month deadline. As of late June, this committee was not yet in place, but preliminary work on making appointments was underway.

The provincial government should immediately give interim protection

Many of us have witnessed the destruction of our wilderness area and wildlife habitat. We have watched these areas die and ecosystems disappear . . . The Endangered Spaces campaign, sponsored by World Wildlife Fund, is an opportunity for us to demonstrate in a tangible way that we are committed to the long-term protection of some of our wilderness areas. I urge all Canadians and, in particular, the citizens of the province of Newfoundland to support the World Wildlife Fund in this most important undertaking.

JAMES A. McGRATH, former Lieutenant-Governor of Newfoundland and Labrador, 1989

to all areas proposed in the PAA plan. They should be red-flagged in the province's land-use atlas, and listed by both the Parks and Natural Areas Division and WERAC as areas under study.

As a general rule, areas should be given special priority if they meet the following criteria:

- They are located in ecoregions which so far have little or no protected-areas representation, (e.g., Labrador makes up three-quarters of the province, yet has almost no protection).
- They are fragile, under threat from development, or are already being degraded.

Only when the province has a framework for protection of individual sites will it be able to proceed with fulfilling its commitment to the Endangered Spaces goal. It is crucial that an official system plan be completed, adopted, and put into use as soon as possible.

2. *A commitment to protect the Torngat–Caribou House region of northern Labrador needs to be made by late 1995, with designation by 1997.* The ecological integrity of the study area for a Torngat Mountains National Park must be maintained. This is especially critical in light of recent demands that a large portion be removed from the proposed park to allow more mineral exploration and development.

In October 1994, Diamond Fields Resources announced discovery of a major nickel-cobalt-copper deposit at Voisey Bay, 35 kilometres southwest of Nain. Although located well south of the Torngat study area, the discovery has generated renewed interest in the mineral potential of other parts of Labrador.

The province's Mines Branch has identified a sequence of rocks known as "the Ramah Group" extending from Saglek Fiord to Nachvak — a large region within the Torngat study area — as having high potential for lead and zinc deposits. Those interested in mineral exploration would like this area to be excluded from a national park, which could mean moving the southern boundary of the park approximately 100 kilometres northward.

At the same time, conservationists want that same boundary moved farther south, to include the critical range of the George River herd, the world's largest caribou herd, estimated at between 700,000 and 800,000 animals. Labrador's three Native groups — the Inuit, Innu, and Métis — also have a strong interest in protecting this herd.

The Wilderness and Ecological Reserves Advisory Council has proposed a provincial wilderness reserve for the Torngat–Caribou House area, emphasizing the ecological importance of the southern area. Tempting as it must be for a province which has heard little but economic bad news for many years to jump on the development bandwagon, the integrity of this area must be preserved. The region, with its spectacular peaks and fjords, and its vast caribou herd, has immense adventure-tourism potential.

History has shown that the George River herd is not indestructible. Numbers have fluctuated greatly over the years, and wildlife biologists have been concerned about the deteriorating condition of animals in recent years.

Also, because of its traditional migratory route, there is a definite need for joint management of this herd with Québec.

The study-area boundary for the Torngat Mountains National Park should therefore be moved south, in consultation with the Labrador Inuit Association. Failing that, the province should establish its wilderness reserve as soon as possible. In the meantime, mineral exploration should proceed only under strict controls designed to protect the area's ecological integrity. All companies involved should be advised that their mineral rights will be withdrawn should the area become a national park or wilderness reserve.

3. *The province should sign the agreement to conduct a feasibility study for a Mealy Mountains National Park before the end of 1995.* The province should fulfil its promise to take part in a feasibility study to create a national park in the Mealy Mountains of southeastern Labrador. WERAC has long recognized the importance of this region, and has proposed a wilderness reserve encompassing portions of five ecoregions. It would also protect vital habitat of the Mealy Mountains caribou herd. However, the provincial wilderness-reserve proposal is waiting for the federal national-park process to proceed first.

While the government procrastinates, sorts out its differences with the Innu, and negotiates for a smaller study area, logging companies plan to clear-cut in the unique pristine forests of the area, and mining interests draw up exploration plans.

The province announced in March 1992 that it would be taking part in national park feasibility studies, and more than three years later still hasn't signed on. The other partners to the agreement are waiting.

4. *The Lac Joseph–Atikonak Wilderness Reserve could be designated by late 1996 or early 1997.* The proposed Lac Joseph–Atikonak Wilderness Reserve in southwestern Labrador could be the first major protected area in Labrador. The reserve should have provisional status and be well into its public-hearing process by the end of 1995. It will represent two ecoregions: the Mid Sub-arctic Forest and the Low Sub-arctic Forest.

With few current development pressures on the area, creation of this 17,000-square-kilometre reserve represents a real opportunity for the province, provided we move fast enough to take advantage of it. The area's varied wildlife, including the Lac Joseph caribou herd, and its many lakes and rivers will undoubtedly attract visitors.

Government must ensure that the Department of National Defence's low-level-flight training zone not be allowed to expand into the area close to the reserve; a buffer zone must be maintained if we want to protect natural wilderness values and encourage eco-tourism.

5. *Begin protecting the forests of the Cloud and Soufflets areas by early 1996,*

As emphasized in the past, the (Newfoundland and Labrador) provincial government's goal is to ensure that each of our ecoregions has adequate representation within a protected areas network. Therefore, we are committed to making every effort to complete a system of protected areas in the province by the year 2000. ROGER GRIMES, Minister of Tourism and Culture, Newfoundland and Labrador, 1994

with the goal of achieving provisional reserve status by early 1998. Wilderness reserves are needed to protect the forests of the Cloud and Soufflets rivers on the eastern coast of the Great Northern Peninsula. Flowing to White Bay through some of the peninsula's best pristine forest, these rivers have strong potential for wilderness tourism. The riparian vegetation in the Cloud area is unique, springing from unusual limestone soils. A large reserve encompassing these two areas and extending to the coast would provide representation for the Northern Peninsula Forest ecoregion, Beaver Brook subregion, Northern Coastal subregion, and Eastern Long Range subregion.

When Northern Peninsula tourism operators recently hired consultants to study this region, they were dismayed to learn that wood-cutting, cabins, garbage, and off-road vehicles had made large portions of the peninsula no longer suited for tourism.

Although threatened several times in recent years by logging roads that would open them up to heavy cutting, the Cloud and the Soufflets watersheds are two of the few remaining roadless areas on the Island portion of our province. They provide us with the opportunity to keep one area of northwestern Newfoundland as a natural repository of plants and animals, and a magnet for visitors.

The goal here should be one large reserve, including both areas. Failing that, there should be at least a corridor several kilometres wide connecting them. In creating reserves to represent the natural ecosystems of the Island, the Cloud and Soufflets regions should have high priority.

6. *By early 1996, create a reserve in the Little Grand Lake area adequate to protect both mature forest and the pine marten populations of the area.* It is vital to create as quickly as possible a permanent reserve to protect the threatened pine marten and old-growth forest of the Western and Central Newfoundland Forest ecoregions. Such a reserve has been studied and recommended since the early 1980s.

Meanwhile, there have been recurring demands by private loggers and pulp and paper companies to harvest in this area. Yet the official Recovery Plan for the pine marten clearly calls for a reserve, as has WERAC over the years.

A reserve here would appear to be highly "do-able," since much of the area falls within a Model Forest project area, and the Model Forest program supports forest reserves as part of an integrated resource management strategy. The reserve will be most effective in preserving marten populations

Our goal is the creation of a network of parks, ecological reserves and other protected areas to preserve the diversity of Canada's wildlife and wilderness for future generations. While progress in this project may not be as rapid as we may like, significant advances have been made.

As I noted last year, we cannot measure our concern for the environment solely by the creation of protected areas. It must be reflected in our stewardship of all our resources. Our best hope in protecting the environment and providing for sustainable development remains with the cooperation of governments, groups such as the World Wildlife Fund, the Protected Areas Association (of Newfoundland and Labrador), and the people of Canada.

CLYDE WELLS,
Premier of Newfoundland,
1994

Near Cape Enrage on the Bay of Fundy, a short distance north of Fundy National Park.
GREG STOTT

A coastal beach in New Brunswick's
Kouchibouguac National Park.
SCOTT LESLIE

Human disturbance of the piping plover's beach
nesting grounds is endangering this delicate bird.
MARK K. PECK

Sky waves of semi-palmated sandpipers at Mary's Point, New Brunswick, where they build up energy reserves for the long migratory flight ahead.
GREG STOTT

P.E.I.'s Greenwich Sand Dunes were officially protected in 1995.
DIANE GRIFFIN

The Mackinnon Bog in eastern P.E.I. was purchased by the Island Nature Trust. DOUG KELLY

Nova Scotia's Tobeatic wilderness area is the largest of thirty-one sites recommended for protection through the province's ambitious protected-areas plan. OLIVER MAAS

Cape Split in Nova Scotia is a significant natural area needing protection. OLIVER MAAS

A canoeist enjoys the peace of Nova Scotia's Kejimakujak National Park. MARK HOBSON

Marine protected areas will help replenish fish stocks for both puffins and people.
KATHLEEN BLANCHARD

Western Brook Pond in Newfoundland's Gros Morne National Park.
KARL SOMMERER

The Torngat Mountains of Labrador, where there are as yet no protected areas.
DENNIS MINTY

The coastal barrens of Canso, Nova Scotia. OLIVER MAAS

if natural corridors are provided to other forested areas.

7. *Work should begin on a reserve for the Gaff Topsails area in 1996.* A complete network of parks and reserves would include one to protect the calving ground of the Gaff Topsails caribou herd in the central area of the Island. Granite quarrying, including blasting, in the region threatens the ecological integrity of what is arguably the most important and sensitive natural area along the abandoned Newfoundland Railway railbed. This reserve would be especially valuable if it over-lapped the borders of the three ecoregions which meet in the area — the Buchans Plateau–Topsails subregion of the Long Range Barrens, and Central Newfoundland Forest's Northcentral and Red Indian subregions.

8. *Attain provisional status for the Serpentine Lake/Lewis Hills area in 1995, and designate status by 1997.* The provincial Cabinet is currently studying a report from WERAC recommending provisional status for a large wilderness reserve in the Serpentine Lake/Lewis Hills area of western Newfoundland. The highest hills on the island, a lovely unspoiled lake, pine marten, harlequin ducks, and at least thirty-five species of rare plants are some of the area's natural features. The reserve should protect a good portion of the Serpentine Range subre-gion of the Western Newfoundland Forest ecoregion.

There is fine canoeing on both the Serpentine River and Serpentine Lake, and one local entrepreneur even guides pack-trips on horseback over the spectacular windswept hills. The original study area has been amended to take into account local people's requests to avoid traditional wood-harvesting areas.

9. *Work on completing a system of ecological reserves should proceed in a planned fashion and at a faster pace, with priority given to those under threat.* These smaller reserves, which protect special and unique fea-tures such as fossil sites, bird colonies, rare trees, and wildflowers, are not generally as controversial as larger wilderness reserves. Most people can agree on the importance of protecting rare and unique features, and the smaller portions of land required are more will-ingly given up by resource extractors. In addition, there is considerable tourism potential in such sites, so presumably government will be motivat-ed to protect them.

The list of special sites, as delineated in the PAA system plan, provides protec-tion for sandy beaches, rare flora, grasslands, black ash, wave forests, white and red pine, and so on — forty-two sites on the Island and fourteen in Labrador.

The Protected Areas Association is dedicated to the conservation of natur-al areas in this Province. Working with the World Wildlife Fund Canada, they are the provincial sponsors of the Endangered Spaces campaign which has as its aim the establishment of parks, wilderness and ecolog-ical reserves across the coun-try. This is a most worth-while project and deserves our support. We owe it to our children and grandchil-dren to ensure that this Province and, indeed, Canada has sufficient wild spaces to ensure the viability of all species for generations to come.

As citizens of Newfoundland and Labrador, we must do our part to see that certain areas of our Province are designat-ed as protected areas and we must be cognizant of our responsibility for protecting our total environment.

FREDERICK W. RUSSELL, Lieutenant-Governor of Newfoundland and Labrador, 1994

Important ecological areas such as Sandy Point (Flat Island) and Cape Freels, Bonavista Bay, which have had heavy human use should be given interim protection as soon as possible.

10. *Raise public awareness.* There is a critical need for public-education work to influence people's attitudes towards our natural environment. The Department of the Environment, and the Parks, Wildlife, and Forestry divisions, should take a more proactive approach to educating us in ways to live sustainably. It is critical that people feel a sense of stewardship for their natural world.

The Department of Education should make their new Environmental Science course a core subject for all high school students. More importantly, environmental courses should be taught throughout school, starting in kindergarten.

We must not forget the role of NGOs in raising public awareness of issues. Conservation groups such as the PAA are often in a position to move more quickly than government, and therefore can complement and enhance government's public-education role.

I am glad to be a patron of the Protected Areas Association. Truly protected areas are absolutes against which we may always measure and compare our human values and achievements, from aesthetics to genetic engineering.

Not everything we do is bad, and not everything is good, but we lose much, maybe all of our capability to determine which is which if we lose these natural absolutes. Having compromised or lost our way, we will have no sure place to begin again.

CHRISTOPHER PRATT, Artist and Patron of the Protected Areas Association, Salmonier, 1994

POLICY AND PLANNING ISSUES

The Wilderness and Ecological Reserves Advisory Council needs more funding, a larger support staff, and freedom from undue political influence. WERAC's scientific staff is too small to accomplish the ambitious goals to which it is committed. Also, the whole reserve-establishment process has been painfully slow. This is necessary to some extent, since the strength of the act lies in its extensive public hearings and input. However, caught in the net of bureaucracy, the process is further complicated and slowed by the lack of an overall plan and clear priorities.

Another challenge for WERAC is the fact that community involvement must begin early on in the reserve-establishment process: there must be considerable local support for reserves, especially since public stewardship has to compensate for lack of enforcement resources.

WERAC can function properly only if it has a reasonable level of autonomy. To expedite its work, the council should advise cabinet through the minister responsible, have its own staff, and be able to proceed briskly at arm's length from government until its final recommendations are made to Cabinet.

There are at least eleven provincial parks which could contribute to ecoregion representation if specially protected conservation zones were created within them.

Some careful overall land-use planning should be done to create a network of Crown Land Reserves to stop the random spread of cabins. These reserves could also be used as buffer zones for places with special natural significance — ecological reserves, for example. There seems to be no planning behind the granting of permits to build. Whole developments appear to be permitted on an *ad hoc* basis, and more or less automatically, as long as there are no other resource-use demands. This points once again to Newfoundland and Labrador's crying need for an integrated land-use planning process.

Five years into the Endangered Spaces campaign, less than 2 per cent of Newfoundland and Labrador is protected in parks and reserves. Only one of our nineteen ecological regions is close to being adequately represented. So we have a long way to go. But fortunately the will to do it is growing.

As people realize that we have taken our natural world for granted, they are beginning to call for a more careful, rational approach. We have experienced with horror the disappearance of one of the planet's most abundant fish stocks, realizing that virtually any resource can be depleted.

In many parts of the province, citizens are now questioning proponents of forestry, mining, hydro, or other developments which are proposed without proper forethought. "Sustainable development" has become a buzzword, even among stakeholders who wouldn't have been caught dead in the environmental camp less than a decade ago. Reacting to years of haphazard, opportunistic development, people are now calling for integrated land-use management planning for the province.

The fishery collapse has provided a chilling warning to the people of Newfoundland and Labrador. We must not do to our lands what we have done to our waters. There is a growing commitment among us to use our natural resources wisely, while conserving portions of our natural world for the future. Let us advance this important work, and do it before it is too late!

17 / Northwest Territories

CHRIS O'BRIEN

 In the Northwest Territories, we have an opportunity to learn from the mistakes of southern Canada and the Yukon, and ensure that future generations of Northerners and other Canadians will always have an unspoiled North that befits the spiritual heartland of this country. There is strong scientific evidence that the best way to do this is to establish a network of representative protected areas by 2000. This will protect the pristine land and marine areas required for this system from degradation by industrial development.

However, the scientific credibility and importance of natural-regions representation must be proven to Northerners. They will not have the concept imposed on them. Success will be reached only if Northerners work together, and nothing will be achieved without the support of aboriginal people and local communities.

There are many interests and agencies involved in the creation of protected areas in the N.W.T. Besides several federal and territorial government departments, there are seven aboriginal groups who have already concluded land-claims settlements or are likely to do so within the next few years.

LAND-CLAIMS AGREEMENTS

In the N.W.T., aboriginal land claims are a primary factor in the establishment of parks and other protected areas. At the beginning of the Endangered Spaces campaign in 1989, only one aboriginal land claim had been settled in the N.W.T., that of the Inuvialuit in the western Arctic. One of the most interesting parts of the Inuvialuit Final Agreement (IFA), signed in 1984, was the creation of institutions for cooperative management of human use of land and wildlife within the Settlement Region. A provision for the creation of a national park in northern Yukon was included, as was further allowance for other parks to be designated in the N.W.T. after the agreement was signed.

The IFA set a useful precedent. It marked the beginning of a more positive attitude in the N.W.T. towards national parks and other protected areas, and towards the inclusion of aboriginal people in their management. Subsequent land-claims settlements — those of the Inuit, Gwich'in, and Sahtu Dene — have built on the Inuvialuit experience. They, too, have included provisions for the creation and cooperative management of national parks and other protected areas.

The role of land-claims settlements in the establishment of protected areas in the N.W.T. is closely related to the plans and actions of the federal and territorial governments.

PARKS CANADA

In 1989, Wood Buffalo was the only full-fledged national park in the N.W.T. There were also three national-park reserves (Auyuittuq, Nahanni, and Northern Ellesmere) and land that had been withdrawn for a proposed park on the East Arm of Great Slave Lake. At the time, Parks Canada thought that in order to represent all of the N.W.T.'s terrestrial regions, six additional parks would be required.

Although the federal government had ambitious plans to complete the national-park system and create more protected areas, it found its efforts slowed in a number of ways. Significant changes in the political scene — in particular, land-claims negotiations — meant that there were more stakeholders involved in the decision-making process, all with somewhat different agendas. Aboriginal groups had more pressing priorities than helping government establish protected areas. The mining industry voiced its disapproval of permanently prohibiting mineral and other industrial activity from what it considered to be unreasonably large areas of land.

The Government of the Northwest Territories (GNWT) and aboriginal groups were slow to accept that the creation of more national parks would be in the interest of Northerners. Even though hunting, trapping, and fishing by Native people would be allowed within national parks, some aboriginal organizations were concerned that parks might still be too restrictive; for example, in not allowing commercial activities. Many Northerners had little interest in preserving large areas of land for purposes other than the protection of wildlife populations that they could continue to *use*. The federal government's park priorities were seen to be insensitive to the conservation needs of aboriginal communities, and, in the early 1980s, the GNWT was neither sympathetic nor helpful towards the national parks agenda.

Since 1989, the climate has improved considerably thanks in large part to the land-claims settlements with the Inuit, Gwich'in, and Sahtu Dene. According to the terms of the Nunavut Land Claims Agreement, Inuit Impact and Benefits Agreements (IIBAS) for Auyuittuq and Ellesmere Island Park Reserves must be signed by July 1995, and legislation to establish these two parks must follow within one year. A similar arrangement has been worked out for the proposed national park on North Baffin Island. And three other parks are planned within the Nunavut Settlement Area.

In the Inuvialuit Settlement Region, two new parks are in the process of being established. Aulavik on the north end of Banks Island will be proclaimed as soon as legislation has been passed in Parliament, and land for Tuktut Nogait (Bluenose) to the east of the Inuvialuit community of Paulatuk will be formally withdrawn in 1995.

The Dene of Lutselk'e have long been concerned about the possible effects of a proposed park around the East Arm of Great Slave Lake on their traditional use of the area. But they have been assured by the federal government that a park will not be established without their agreement. Discussions about the park could resume in the context of future Treaty Number 8 Land Entitlement negotiations.

CANADIAN WILDLIFE SERVICE

In 1989, Environment Canada's Canadian Wildlife Service (CWS) managed sixteen migratory-bird sanctuaries and one national wildlife area (NWA) within the

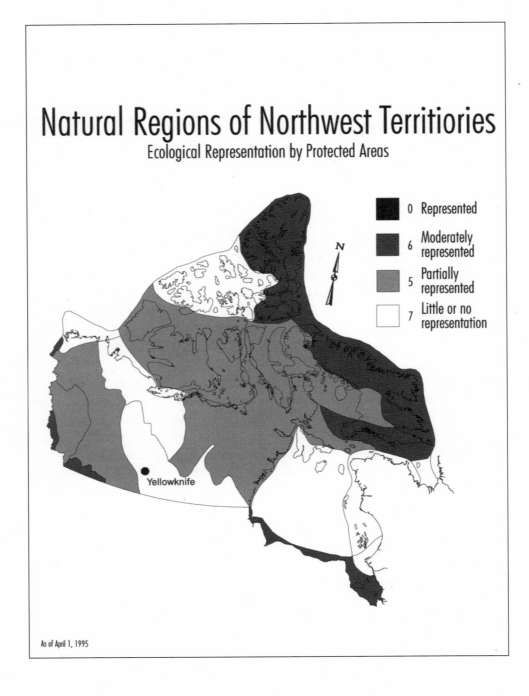

Natural Regions of Northwest Territiories

Ecological Representation by Protected Areas

0	Represented
6	Moderately represented
5	Partially represented
7	Little or no representation

N

Yellowknife

As of April 1, 1995

Northwest Territories, but none of these enjoyed the same level of protection as national parks.

Since then, one new bird sanctuary has been created, and the CWS is involved in a number of initiatives with communities to create more protected areas. For example, the people of Grise Fiord want to have Coburg Island designated as a national wildlife area, and the community of Clyde River is hoping to have an NWA created at Isabella Bay.

In a 1993 report, the CWS says that "the federal government is committed to setting aside 12 per cent of Canada's total territory as protected space" and that "a National Wildlife Habitat Network of protected areas will be established as one step toward [that] goal." Eighty Key Habitat Sites (important areas for breeding migratory birds) have been identified so far in the N.W.T., and twenty-two of them either already possess or are slated for some kind of protective status.

GNWT DEPARTMENT OF ECONOMIC DEVELOPMENT AND TOURISM

In 1989, existing legislation allowed the GNWT to create only recreational and historic parks. In any case, there was little interest in creating similar territorial parks to satisfy what were perceived to be southern conservation interests. Because of this, the GNWT had no plans to develop a parks-system plan based on any kind of biological criteria.

However, a milestone was reached in October 1991, when the GNWT's ministers of Renewable Resources (Titus Allooloo) and Economic Development and Tourism (Gordon Wray) wrote to WWF stating that the GNWT would support Parks Canada in completing its network of national parks in the territories. The two ministers also stated that the GNWT wished "to leave open the option of establishing a territorial system of representative protected areas, should that seem appropriate in future." They wished WWF's campaign well, and said they were "pleased to lend [their] support to it."

The impression of a new direction for territorial-park establishment was further reinforced in October 1992, when the GNWT's Minister of Renewable Resources signed the Tri-Council Statement of Commitment to Complete Canada's Networks of Protected Areas.

This increased interest in the conservation role of parks reflected changing political circumstances; for example, the introduction in 1990 of a Sustainable Development Policy by the GNWT. As well, there was an increasing awareness by the GNWT that, although territorial parks should continue to provide Northerners with economic and social benefits, the future of tourism in the N.W.T. (and, therefore, the success of the GNWT's parks system) would depend more and more on the continued existence of pristine land and water, healthy wildlife populations and intact ecosystems, as these became increasingly rare in other parts of the world.

The GNWT plans to release in May 1995 a public discussion paper on its parks policy, with the hope of getting approval for a new policy later in 1995. Once a new parks policy is in place, the next logical step would be to develop a strategy for identifying new park initiatives, an excellent opportunity to exercise "the option of establishing a territorial system of representative protected areas."

GNWT DEPARTMENT OF RENEWABLE RESOURCES

In 1989, as today, the Department of Renewable Resources (DRR) had jurisdiction over a handful of wildlife sanctuaries. In only one of them, the Thelon, was there any outright prohibition against industrial activity. This was not because of any power that the department itself possessed; rather it was because the land had been withdrawn years before by the federal government. However, the future of the Thelon is now being reviewed. Since the eastern half of the sanctuary lies within Nunavut and the western part lies within the territory of the Treaty 8 Dene, two management plans must be developed.

In 1993, Wildlife Habitat Canada, an independent agency based in Ottawa, provided the DRR with funding for a habitat-conservation program. The program's goals are to protect wildlife habitat from incompatible land uses and to ensure ecosystem integrity, biodiversity, and the maintenance of abundant and healthy wildlife populations. In order to achieve this goal, the DRR says it is concentrating on facilitating the establishment of a network of wildlife conservation areas, in consultation with government agencies, aboriginal organizations, co-management boards, communities, and other stakeholders. To this end, the DRR is involved in a number of initiatives, including:

- developing Critical Wildlife Areas Regulations under the N.W.T. Wildlife Act to protect wildlife and habitat within designated conservation areas;
- working on an agreement with the CWS to establish wildlife conservation areas;
- working on an agreement with the Department of Economic Development and Tourism to protect wildlife and habitat in territorial parks;
- encouraging Economic Development and Tourism's recent steps to enhance the conservation role of territorial parks;
- working with aboriginal co-management boards and communities to determine regional priorities for wildlife and habitat protection.

In an unpublished February 1995 background paper, the DRR stated that the identification of candidate wildlife conservation areas "will emphasize protection of habitats in ecosystems which are not represented adequately in existing conservation areas systems." This means that, although representation of natural regions is not the only selection criterion for candidate areas, the DRR will give priority to those areas containing habitat types of which little or none has so far been protected. The department also said that "the wildlife conservation areas network will be designed to complement existing conservation areas systems."

A REALISTIC ANALYSIS

In terms of the Endangered Spaces campaign, the great strengths of the Northwest Territories are its huge and still largely unspoiled land mass, and the fact that the majority of its inhabitants harbour very strong feelings about ensuring that the land is looked after.

However, while the pressures on the land may indeed be less than in most other parts of the country, there are some regions of the N.W.T. where the large areas required to complete a protected-areas network may be compromised. The area between Great Slave Lake and the Arctic coast, known as the Slave Geological

Province, is a good example. Since diamonds were discovered there in 1991, approximately 220,000 square kilometres have been staked for mineral exploration. A diamond mine proposed by the Australian mining giant BHP is now being assessed. In the excitement over diamonds and other minerals, the chance to protect a large part of the Central Barrenlands could be lost forever.

The Tundra Hills region is another good example. It was in this region that the land earmarked for the proposed Tuktut Nogait (Bluenose) National Park was encroached upon by prospecting permits issued by the federal Department of Indian Affairs and Northern Development (DIAND). If some quick work by the Paulatuk Park Committee and the Inuvialuit had not persuaded the company holding the permits to relinquish them, a significant area of the proposed park might have been lost.

There is a pressing need for DIAND to make changes to its regulations so that such a situation does not arise again. The problem seems to lie with their outdated free-entry system, which gives priority to the rights to prospect for minerals on Crown lands, to stake a claim, and to obtain a lease to develop a mine over other land uses.

From the perspective of the Endangered Spaces campaign, the main weakness of the N.W.T. is that, besides Parks Canada (whose objectives will not fulfil all of the campaign's goals), none of the government agencies in the N.W.T. that have the legislative power to create protected areas has as a clear conservation goal: the protection of areas that are representative of natural regions.

A closer look at individual components of the jurisdictional mix in the N.W.T. will give a better understanding of this situation.

ABORIGINAL LAND CLAIMS

The aboriginal people of the N.W.T. have long traditions of respect for the land. As a result, all of the settlement agreements have sections which allow for the creation of national parks and other protected areas, while assuring that traditional uses of the areas such as hunting, fishing, and trapping are not jeopardized. The agreements also have provisions guaranteeing that people in the settlement areas will be co-managers of any protected areas in their regions, thus ensuring that local people will exercise some control over what happens in these areas and derive some benefits from them.

The traditional affinity of aboriginal people for the land can work in favour of protected areas, but the support of Native people should not be taken for granted. Nor should it be assumed that their reasons for wanting to establish protected areas are the same as, for example, the objectives of the Endangered Spaces campaign. Perhaps too much emphasis has been put on trying to persuade government agencies to implement the objectives of the campaign. If aboriginal people can be persuaded that the Endangered Spaces campaign will help attain their own conservation goals, then they could have a very powerful influence on how the federal and territorial governments proceed.

THE GNWT

It is interesting that of the two GNWT departments concerned with the creation of protected areas, the one that actually has the power to do so is not Renewable Resources but Economic Development and Tourism (DED&T). Whether the DED&T's Parks Division will be able to make a contribution to the Endangered Spaces campaign depends on the GNWT being convinced that the campaign's objectives are in the interests of Northerners. So far, that does not really seem to be the case. There is a belief in the North that, when it comes to the protection of northern ecosystems, the priorities of Northerners lie much more in the protection of specific wildlife populations and their habitat than in the representation of natural regions.

It cannot be assumed that the GNWT ministers' letter to WWF in 1991 and the signing of the Tri-Council Statement of Commitment in 1992 were actual commitments by the GNWT to make its own direct contributions to achieving the Endangered Spaces objectives. The GNWT now says that the commitment was only to help Parks Canada complete its network of national parks. Nevertheless, the GNWT's own Parks Division certainly has more interest than it used to have in creating territorial parks with a conservation orientation. But, because representation of natural regions does not seem to be a criterion for creating these parks, they might well be established in locations that will simply not satisfy the selection criteria of the Endangered Spaces campaign.

The situation is similar at the DRR. As Derek Melton, director of the department's Wildlife Management Division, pointed out in a January 16, 1995, letter to the WWF, "Although the Wildlife Conservation Areas Program will undoubtedly help to conserve the NWT's biodiversity over the long term, the primary goal of the program is not to protect a representative sample of natural areas." In fact, new legislation would be required for the protection of areas specifically because they are ecologically representative.

PARKS CANADA

The National Parks Act is Canada's strongest conservation legislation, so national parks in the N.W.T. are likely to protect the land, wildlife, and habitat within their boundaries virtually in perpetuity. Although land-claims negotiations have slowed down the establishment of some parks, settlement agreements have also become an important factor in the creation of parks (see Chapter 3). There are now no major political hurdles standing in the way of Parks Canada completing the N.W.T.'s part of the national-park system within the next five or six years.

Another great advantage that the N.W.T. has over many other parts of the country is that, because of the sheer vastness of the territories, it is still possible to create the very large parks and protected areas necessary to ensure the protection of northern ecosystems. However, as pointed out in Chapter 1, one protected area in each region won't necessarily be enough to represent all of the regional elements, so even if Parks Canada does complete its agenda in the N.W.T., there will no doubt still be many gaps to fill.

CANADIAN WILDLIFE SERVICE

The CWS has done a lot of work over many years to identify and protect critical wildlife habitat. But, if its growing network of protected areas is to consist solely of national wildlife areas and migratory-bird sanctuaries, then, like the GNWT's parks program, representation of natural regions will not be a primary criterion for selection (although it is possible that some of the planned and existing protected areas might already satisfy representation criteria).

It is unlikely that the present protective status of areas established by the CWS will meet Endangered Spaces standards. Although the CWS considers the protection of wildlife and wildlife habitat as the primary use of its conservation areas, it is not the sole use. Industrial activities which do not interfere with wildlife habitat are allowed.

WHERE FROM HERE?

Many Northerners believe that the N.W.T. is different from the rest of the country, and that a different approach to conservation is required here. For this reason, there may be a problem persuading Northerners to go along with the Endangered Spaces agenda. Aboriginal people are going to play a very significant role in the establishment of protected areas, but they have quite a different approach to protecting the land. Derek Melton put it this way in his January 16 letter:

> Subsistence lifestyles based on wildlife harvesting, and other wildlife and wilderness-related activities (such as tourism, sport hunting and fishing, and commercial use of renewable resources), are essential to the survival of aboriginal cultures and small, remote communities in the North. As a result, residents of the N.W.T. are generally very supportive of measures for protecting the land and resources from incompatible land uses. . . . Private stewardship by aboriginal organizations, and co-management of natural resources with territorial and federal government agencies, are likely the primary means by which area protection will occur in the N.W.T. The Endangered Spaces campaign should maintain sufficient flexibility to be able to incorporate and encourage these types of initiatives.

The task, then, will be to identify where the gaps in representation are; to select candidate areas for each region; and to convince government agencies, aboriginal people, and other Northerners that there are not only sound, scientifically based reasons for protecting representative areas, but that doing so could also have economic, cultural, and social benefits. There is also a need to press for amendments or new legislation to allow appropriate jurisdictions to use representation of natural regions as a primary selection criterion for protected areas, and to give such areas adequate protection.

However, if Northerners remain unconvinced that a network of representative protected areas is essential, the best hope for achieving the Endangered Spaces campaign's objectives would be to persuade government agencies and aboriginal groups that, when they do establish protected areas, they do so in ways that will meet the campaign's criteria as closely as possible.

So there seem to be two possible critical paths, depending on whether or not Northerners accept representation as a criterion for the establishment of new protected areas in the N.W.T. In 1995 and 1996, WWF should:

- Arrange workshops on the objectives and the scientific basis of the Endangered Spaces campaign for all interested parties (government and aboriginal agencies, wildlife management boards, community conservation boards, members of the public, other stakeholders).
- Work with all parties to identify gaps in the protected-areas network that are not covered by proposed or existing national parks or other protected areas.

- Work with all parties to identify a number of possible candidate areas in each natural region.
- Seek final decisions from government, aboriginal agencies, and affected communities about whether or not they accept representation as a criterion for establishment of additional protected areas in each natural region of the N.W.T.

If they *do* accept, the steps in the following critical path should be taken:

- Ensure that all candidate protected areas receive some sort of interim protection from incompatible uses.
- Secure an agreement with all parties that they will work together to establish the required additional protected areas by the year 2000.
- Determine what roles government and aboriginal agencies, and people in communities can play in achieving Endangered Spaces objectives.
- Determine what, if any, changes might be required to federal and territorial policies and protected-areas legislation, and to aboriginal co-management mechanisms, in order to create and adequately protect representative areas that will satisfy Endangered Spaces objectives.
- Develop an action plan agreed to by all parties for the attainment of Endangered Spaces goals by 2000.

If they do *not* accept, the following steps should be taken:

- Determine which other mechanisms for the establishment of protected areas will most nearly satisfy Endangered Spaces objectives.
- Work with all parties to:
  - determine how the size and protective status of planned and existing protected areas can be modified to satisfy Endangered Spaces objectives;
  - determine whether there are equally viable alternative locations for planned protected areas that would better satisfy Endangered Spaces objectives;
  - develop an action plan agreed to by all parties for securing the above-mentioned changes and new protected areas by 2000.

From 1996 to 2000, we should work with all parties to get areas established with appropriate protection measures and cooperative-management arrangements in place.

Many people in the Northwest Territories are not yet convinced that northern conservation goals require the establishment of representative protected areas. But times are rapidly changing in the N.W.T., and if Northerners wait much longer, they will one day find that they have missed an opportunity that will never come again. The people of the N.W.T. must protect whatever areas are necessary to ensure the continued existence of ecological and evolutionary processes that are the heritage, not only of Northerners, but, ultimately, of all life on this planet.

18 / Yukon

JURI PEEPRE

Where the Rocky Mountains of British Columbia end, the Selwyn Mountains rise and stretch north for another 400 kilometres along the continental divide. These seemingly endless folds of sedimentary rock then curve west, turning grey and white like rows of bleached vertebrae from an ancient time. To the east, in the Northwest Territories, wild waters slice through sawtooth ridges to the great Mackenzie River and the polar seas. To the west is the Yukon, a vast and varied land, from the icy expanses of the St. Elias Mountains to the wetlands and arctic tundra of the north coast.

Every spring, giant spruce and cottonwood trees along the Liard River tumble into its flooding waters, spin along a thousand kilometres of the Mackenzie to the Beaufort Sea, then drift west to the Yukon's north shore. For millennia, coastal Native peoples have used these drift logs for shelter, transportation, tools, and firewood. Today, it is hard to imagine that rapacious logging of riparian spruce trees in the southeast Yukon is linked to driftwood shorebird habitat along the edges of the distant northern sea. This reveals the connectedness of Yukon ecosystems, still evolving, still emerging from the last great ice age.

Grizzly bears, wolves, moose, sheep, marmots, peregrine falcons, pileated woodpeckers, and hundreds of thousands of waterfowl, along with all the other native flora and fauna, depend on the Yukon's wildlands. It is here that the great migrations of caribou and salmon shaped the cultures of northern aboriginal peoples. It is a landscape still alive in most areas with fully functioning, healthy ecosystems.

Only two generations ago there were no highways in the Yukon. Now more than 5000 kilometres of roads and countless more vehicle-access routes have left a spaghetti pattern across the territory. Wildlife populations in parts of southern and central Yukon are already at risk, due mainly to overhunting from easy road access. Clear-cut logging of old-growth spruce in the southeast is eliminating the habitat of many forest songbird species. Although the Yukon is often perceived as untouched wilderness, the probing tentacles of industrial development have already left their mark.

Yukoners want to protect their natural and cultural heritage. Yet protected areas as an expression of this desire still have a tenuous hold on the consciousness of decision makers. The Yukon's laws and Euro-Canadian traditions governing the use of the land, at least since the Klondike Gold Rush, assume that wild nature is for the taking. Unless we learn to live within nature's ability to provide, our heritage will be whittled away, piece by piece, leaving us with remnant islands of nature like those now scattered across southern Canada.

Even though many Canadians imagine the North as a single faraway place, it is far from homogeneous. Protected areas must be understood in the context of a remarkable cultural diversity and differing approaches to what "protected" means. To many First Nations members, and more recently to environmentalists, it does not just mean protection of examples of nature. It means the care of complete ecosystems and entire traditional territories — all that is required to sustain wild nature.

YUKON PROTECTED AREAS IN 1989

For many years, Kluane National Park Reserve was the only protected area in the Yukon. Although the Kluane Game Sanctuary and other similar preserves were drawn in green on maps, they provided no safeguards against development. In 1984, the signing of the Inuvialuit Final Agreement (IFA) resulted in the establishment of Ivvavik National Park on the north coast, along with its satellite territorial park, Herschel Island. The IFA led to unprecedented co-management arrangements for protected areas and wildlife conservation in the western Arctic. However, although the IFA deals with conservation of marine mammals, marine protected areas were not included in the agreement.

Coal River Springs Ecological Reserve was created late in the 1980s, protecting a beautiful and fragile geothermal feature in southeastern Yukon. Unlike other protected areas, this reserve preceded land-claims agreements.

In 1989, at the beginning of the Endangered Spaces campaign, the Yukon did not have a park system plan based on representation of natural regions. A few candidate parks had been identified throughout the territory, some dating from the 1970s. These mainly contained special features of scenic and recreational interest. Although park planning was slow to evolve, other territorial initiatives demonstrated Yukoners' strong support for wildland protection. Land-claims provisions for protected areas and the Yukon Conservation Strategy prepared the way for completion of a protected-areas system.

Almost all protected areas in the Yukon are established through aboriginal land claims. Land claims allow for a wide range of protection options, including national or territorial parks, habitat protection areas, wildlife management areas, special management areas, and heritage rivers. Special management areas provide First Nations with an opportunity to tailor management arrangements to local needs. They may also be designated as parks or some other form of protected area.

THE SITUATION NOW

During the last five years, First Nations have led the way in Yukon protected-area achievements. Since 1989, they have negotiated three important protected areas through land claims. The Vuntut Gwitchin people were instrumental in creating Vuntut National Park and the surrounding special management area to the south in the Old Crow Flats. These safeguard part of the Porcupine Caribou Herd range, as well as wetland habitat critical to migrating waterfowl. The Vuntut Gwitchin also negotiated the Fishing Branch Ecological Reserve in northcentral Yukon. This reserve protects part of the region's grizzly bear and spawning salmon habitat. The Nisutlin Delta National Wildlife Management Area is in the Teslin Tlingit First Nation traditional territory. This is an important migratory-waterfowl habitat in

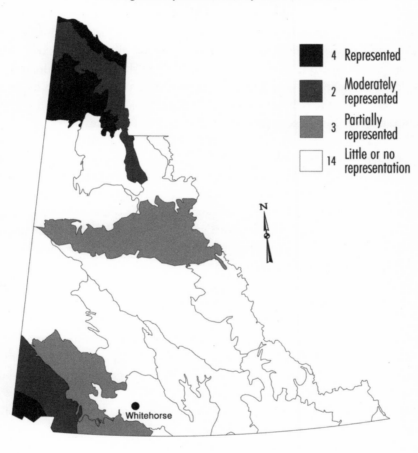

Natural Regions of Yukon Territory
Ecological Representation by Protected Areas

4 Represented

2 Moderately represented

3 Partially represented

14 Little or no representation

N

Whitehorse

As of April 1, 1995

southern Yukon. The Horseshoe Slough Special Management Area is a small wetland area in central Yukon, protected through the Nacho N'y'ak Dun land-claim agreement. Tatshenshini/Alsek Provincial Wilderness Park is in British Columbia, but it is culturally and ecologically connected to the Yukon and Alaska. It is in the Champagne and Aishihik First Nations traditional territory.

Since the start of the Endangered Spaces campaign, the Yukon government has produced a framework for a representative parks system, although most candidate areas have not yet been identified. The plan is consistent with the campaign's goals, but lacks a clear path for implementation. Protected-area potential has been assessed in about one-half of the Yukon's 23 natural regions. Government officials suggest that land claims are responsible for the slow progress, but the Parks Department could do much more to cooperate with First Nations and inform the public. In the absence of government initiative, most public education and research on the benefits of protected areas have been done by Yukon environmental organizations.

Using the Endangered Spaces standards, six of twenty-three ecoregions are represented or moderately represented by protected areas, all national parks. These parks are in the far North (Ivvavik and Vuntut), and in the southwest along the St. Elias Mountains (Kluane). Two natural regions are partially represented by smaller protected areas, while the remaining reserves, such as Coal River Springs Ecological Reserve, are tiny and not representative of their regions. The situation will change as First Nations settle land claims; however, as of 1995, the bulk of Yukon ecoregions still have little or no protection.

First Nations seek to establish new large protected areas, many in unrepresented natural regions. The Dawson First Nation is negotiating a territorial park at Tombstone Mountain, a well-known Yukon landmark. Most of the ecologically important land that the First Nation wishes to include lies north of the park boundary proposed by the government. Lands have been withdrawn from mineral claim staking, but the government proposal is too small to protect all the key wildlife habitat.

Other protected-area proposals are being discussed. They include the McArthur Range in central Yukon. The hot springs here are revered by Selkirk First Nation people. A relict stone sheep population, wetlands, and the Tintina Trench are other features worthy of protection. North of Kluane National Park reserve, the Kluane First Nation wants to protect the crucial life zone that wraps around the icefields. In addition to these two areas, several other specially managed areas may give some measure of protection. For example, the Thirty Mile Section of the Yukon River is a Canadian Heritage River, while the Bonnet Plume and the Yukon portion of the Tatshenshini River are in various stages of nomination or planning.

The Bonnet Plume River was nominated as a Heritage River through the Nacho N'y'ak Dun First Nation land claim. The First Nation supports both mining and Heritage River status. Environmental organizations respect the aspirations of the Nacho N'y'ak Dun to balance protection with economic development in the region. Still, the potential impacts of mining and new roads on the Bonnet Plume ecosystem have not been well considered. Mining here could threaten the ecological integrity of the entire Peel River watershed, as well as the merit of the Canadian Heritage River designation.

In the spring of 1994, the Canadian Parks and Wilderness Society sued the federal government over its interpretation of mining and environmental laws on mineral claims in the Bonnet Plume Heritage River area. The lawsuit challenged the government's environmental assessment of a winter access road and further questioned the view that mining exploration activities are exempt from environmental laws. The case will be heard in the fall of 1995. Some people saw this move as interference in local Native affairs. However, the way of life of the Tetl'it Gwich'in First Nation, landowners and downstream users of the watershed, depends on clean water and abundant fish and wildlife in the region. The Gwich'in people supported the lawsuit. This points to the challenges in resolving land-use issues where there are differing views on what constitutes protection.

The Vuntut Gwitchin of Old Crow, along with the entire Gwich'in Nation, continue to lobby for protection of the Porcupine Caribou calving grounds in the Alaska National Wildlife Refuge. The so-called 1002 lands on the U.S. side remain vulnerable to oil and gas development. Survival of the herd and the way of life of the Gwich'in people depend on protecting these calving grounds. Ivvavik and Vuntut National Parks, together with the Alaska National Wildlife Refuge, are among the most important protected areas in the entire Arctic, yet the integrity of these ecosystems is not assured.

As I travel the length and breadth of Canada, I am frequently awed by the variety of its natural regions and their intense beauty. I am gratified that World Wildlife Fund Canada has assumed a portion of the responsibility of not only informing people about the problems facing our endangered spaces but also initiating programs to resolve these issues.

As Governor General of Canada, I am pleased to support the Endangered Spaces program of World Wildlife Fund Canada.

RAMON J. HNATYSHYN, Governor General of Canada, 1994

THE NATURE OF OUR PROGRESS

Land claims force governments to deal with protected areas, and protected areas established through land claims are constitutionally secured. They cannot be altered by legislatures or eliminated by Cabinet orders-in-council. If all of the ten First Nations in the Yukon now negotiating land claims supported protected areas, then the majority of our ecoregions could end up with some form of protection. However, the national parks already created through land claims could make it difficult to negotiate additional large areas. Protected areas are not the focus of most land claims in the Yukon; support varies, and they are ancillary to the negotiations. Strong social and economic needs often take precedence.

Environmental organizations in the Yukon are shut out of discussions on candidate protected areas. In theory, the boundaries of special management areas are open to public review, but this has not been the practice. Although third-party discussions separate from land-claims negotiations may be cumbersome, they would ensure that public interest in protected areas is considered. Land-claims negotiators appear to act in the absence of adequate information on conservation biology and other protected-area concerns. Environmental organizations have tried to fill the information and public-education gaps by hosting conferences, carrying out research, and producing books and maps on protected areas and the conservation of biological diversity.

The possibility of creating more large protected areas in the post–land claims era is difficult to predict. Land-claims settlements will see about 10 per cent of Yukon lands in First Nations ownership, with the remaining Crown lands governed by various joint management boards. Once claims are settled, there is no legal reason why further protected areas could not be designated in cooperation with First Nations. Future public interest in protecting wildlands could help fill the representation gaps that land claims missed.

Natural regions are now the foundation of the Yukon park system plan, while the Fish and Wildlife Branch is concerned with protecting important wildlife habitat. Completion of an ecologically based protected-areas network will be hampered until the government acts on its own policy to designate at least one core representative protected area in each ecoregion.

A larger problem is the lack of a comprehensive protected-areas strategy that would marry the completion of a representative park system with ongoing efforts to protect wildlife habitat. The territorial parks system should be one part of a broader strategy to conserve biological diversity. As well, there are discrepancies between federal and territorial policies, legislation, and land-use regulations that hinder conservation efforts. For example, in 1992, the new territorial government announced a policy to allow mining in protected areas. This policy contrasts sharply with the 1994 recommendations of the Whitehorse Mining Initiative, a national multistakeholder forum, which concluded that mineral development should be prohibited in core protected areas.

The federal Department of Indian Affairs and Northern Development (DIAND) is a less visible, but a more imposing obstacle to completion of the Yukon protected-areas network. In the territories, the federal government is a permitting agency for the mining and forest industries. Most Yukon lands are owned by the federal government which appears reluctant to relinquish subsurface rights for protected areas. Antiquated mining and land-use laws from the turn of the century are being updated, but wildland protection and the conservation of biological diversity are not yet a meaningful part of the governmental vocabulary. There is, as yet, no regional federal voice for wilderness protection or the completion of a protected-areas system. Parks Canada Natural Region #7, which extends into the Yukon, is still unrepresented by a national park; most of the attention has been focused on areas in British Columbia. The three national parks already in the Yukon may make it difficult for Parks Canada to propose creating another.

MANAGING THE PROTECTED AREAS WE HAVE

Themes that were unique a decade ago are now common to Yukon protected areas established through land claims: co-management, merging traditional ecological knowledge with science, direct community participation, local economic benefits, and subsistence hunting and gathering. The notion of wilderness as "home," once new to non-Native people, is now widely acknowledged as an essential way of thinking about protected areas on Native lands. The debate continues over how much human use is appropriate in these areas, but the common desire to protect habitat helps bring differing views together.

To southern Canadians, northern protected areas were once exclusively valued for their wilderness, scenery or scientific worth. Now, the interpretation of Native place-names and stories passed on by a rich oral tradition reveal a cultural landscape previously hidden from visitors' eyes. Many aboriginal people have difficulty with the idea of protecting their traditional lands for someone else's use. Therefore, ensuring the continuity and use of local cultural and ecological knowledge is basic to successful protected-area management in the Yukon.

The new ethics of park management, and visitor appreciation for different cultural values, bode well for the acceptance of more protected areas in the Yukon. Yet protected-area designation does not necessarily lessen the challenge to save wild nature. In Kluane National Park Reserve, for example, motorized boat tours, air-craft landings, rafting, and roads, all in prime grizzly bear habitat along the Alsek River, threaten conservation efforts. This World Heritage Site faces other threats, as well.

In 1993, the Yukon government initiated a wolf kill near the boundary of the park, to speed the recovery of a caribou herd decimated by years of overhunting. Potential impacts of the five-year wolf kill on the greater Kluane ecosystem were not assessed and remain largely unknown. To Parks Canada's credit, they attempted to mitigate the effects of the kill by proposing a no-kill buffer zone around the park and by radio-collaring wolves in the park to track their movements. Of the approximately thirty-three wolves important to the park, eleven remained after the 1995 kill. There is no longer a full wolf pack residing in the park since the Sockeye Lake pack declined from eleven to four during the past year. The whereabouts of the alpha male are unknown.

Coal River Springs Ecological Reserve was set aside to protect a fragile tufa formation. The Yukon government installed a helicopter landing pad, picnic tables, trails, and toilets. Aside from the fact that few people other than new government ministers can afford to visit this remote site by helicopter, these developments seem peculiar in an ecological reserve of this nature. Without a clear definition of purpose for each type of protected area, park managers too often turn to inappropriate recreational development to show that the investment in protection has a tangible benefit.

THE NEXT FIVE YEARS

In the five years since the Endangered Spaces campaign was launched, the Yukon has inched closer to completing a territorial protected-areas system. We have the necessary promises, and most of the policies, plans, and land-claims arrangements that support the creation of more protected areas. We only need a government with a sincere interest in conserving northern wildlands, and the political courage to act.

Land-claims negotiations have schedules of their own, which are not related to the Endangered Spaces goals for the year 2000. Steady annual progress in the Yukon is not likely within the land-claims process. In spite of this, land claims will be the main tool for protection during the next half-decade. During the next two years, at least three more protected areas could be designated, with more by the turn of the century.

To fulfil protected-areas commitments by 2000, the territorial government must work more actively towards this goal in cooperation with the federal government, First Nations, communities, environmental non-government organizations (NGOs) and other stakeholders. Much of the needed work can advance simultaneously with land-claims negotiations.

First Nations and environmental NGOs could also cooperate more on many aspects of protected-areas work. This might include research on conservation biology or traditional ecological knowledge, economic studies, identification of potential protected areas, assistance with funding, or public education and training.

At this point in the Endangered Spaces campaign, the territorial government should:

- establish a special Protected Areas Unit to integrate ongoing protected-areas work and develop a Protected Areas Strategy; direct the unit to work cooperatively with First Nations and land-claims negotiators, carry out research on candidate protected areas, and prepare public-education programs;
- complete the territorial parks and ecological reserves system as part of an overall Protected Areas Strategy, which focuses on representation of the Yukon's diverse ecoregions and protection of special natural or cultural features;
- continue efforts to protect important wildlife habitat, wildlife migration routes, wetlands, and other biological values through the designation of habitat protection areas, wildlife management areas, and other means;
- continue to work primarily through the land-claims process to identify and establish territorial parks and other types of protected areas. Support First Nation efforts to establish special management areas;
- improve public awareness and support for completing the protected-areas system. Build alliances with stakeholders. Reframe the debate on protected areas from a defensive to proactive approach, focusing on the multiple benefits of protected areas;
- change government policy that now allows for industrial development in territorial parks. Prohibit industrial development such as mining, forestry, or hydro-electric projects in parks. Require orders-in-council, with full public review, prior to any zoning changes in parks;
- make park boundary designations and changes only through an act of the legislature;
- revise the Park Act to better reflect Yukoners' support for establishing a comprehensive protected-areas system. Change the Park Act to exclude industrial development from natural environment parks (a Yukon category of park) and ecological reserves.

The federal government should:

- support the completion of a territorial protected-areas network by withdrawing candidate protected areas from mineral claim staking. Transfer subsurface rights in protected areas to the territorial government;
- develop a wilderness policy to help guide land and water management on Crown lands. Assign staff to liaise with the territorial government and First Nations on wilderness-management and protected-areas work;
- support First Nation efforts to establish special management areas;
- move quickly to update mining laws.

Both governments should work together in cooperation with First Nations and other organizations on the following tasks:

By 1996:

- identify potential protected areas in the southeast Yukon, including the Liard Basin, Hyland Highland, and Muskwa Plateau. In particular, identify sites in old-growth forest riparian ecosystems in the Liard drainage basin. As a second priority, assess areas of interest in the northeast and central Yukon, in the Selwyn and Mackenzie Mountains ecoregions;

- support First Nation efforts to establish special management areas or other types of protected areas in the McArthur Wildlife Sanctuary, and the lands north of Kluane National Park Reserve. Withdraw these study areas from mineral claim staking;

- conduct research on the economic, environmental, and social benefits of protected areas. Select one or two proposed protected areas as case-studies;

- communicate the social, environmental, and economic benefits of completing a protected-areas system in the North;

- enlarge the boundaries of the proposed Tombstone Mountain Park to include important wildlife habitat and cultural features. Conclude negotiations with the Tr'ondek Hwech'in First Nation based on the expanded park boundary.

By 1997:

- identify areas of interest for representative protected areas in central Yukon, in the North and Central Yukon Plateau, and Klondike Plateau ecoregions. Assess protection options in the Whitehorse area;

- complete an inventory of potential ecological reserves in the Yukon. Allow for public identification and nomination of sites, and develop a roster of ecological reserve candidates;

- negotiate protected areas in the McArthur Wildlife Sanctuary, along with adjacent wetlands and a portion of the Tintina Trench. Designate a protected area north of Kluane National Park Reserve in the Ruby Ranges ecoregion, and another one farther east at Kusawa Lake in the Yukon Southern Lakes ecoregion;

- conclude protected-area assessments in the Eagle Plains and Peel River Plateau in north Yukon.

By 1998 and 1999:

- work with First Nations to identify, plan, and designate protected areas in remaining unrepresented ecoregions;

- designate protected areas in the Liard Basin ecoregion in the southeast, in the Selwyn Mountains, and in the Klondike Plateau;

- designate protected areas in the Eagle Plains ecoregion, at the Arctic Circle, and in the Peel River Plateau ecoregion.

By 2000:

- fill remaining gaps in the territorial parks and ecological reserves system as part of a Yukon Protected Areas Strategy.

WE STILL HAVE CHOICES

Yukoners, along with our northern neighbours in Alaska and the Northwest

Territories, will preside over the fate of much of the remaining intact wildlands on the planet. This is an enormous responsibility that we must embrace with vigour. The forces of change that affect wildlife and our own lives still come from far away, so we must also look to the South for help to protect northern wilderness. In light of the global destruction of wild nature, it is humbling to be living on the cusp of choices that could alter the North forever.

While governments have been evasive in implementing a protected-areas system in the Yukon, they are still accountable for their promises. Public support for protecting wildlife, habitat, and wilderness remains strong. Many First Nations have already demonstrated a clear commitment to protecting our natural landscape.

In the Yukon, we still have a chance to protect wildlands on a scale others can no longer even imagine. We don't have to allow the downward spiral of wildlife populations and ecosystems seen in so many other places. The Endangered Spaces campaign, linked with the aspirations of First Nations to protect their traditional territories, is one of the best tools we have to ensure that in 100 years all the wild species that now range across our lands and waters will still be here.

19 / The Federal Government: National Parks

KEVIN McNAMEE

 The Melville Hills area in the Northwest Territories is the calving grounds of the Bluenose caribou herd. It is also the northern homeland of the Inuvialuit of Paulatuk, a small community on the shores of the Amundsen Gulf whose members maintain a largely traditional way of life. In 1989, Paulatuk prepared a community conservation plan that identified the protection of these calving grounds as their top priority, and a national park as the best means to protect them. Six years later, prospects for a new national park called Tuktut Nogait, Inuit for "young caribou," are excellent.

To many Canadians, this is the northern frontier. Some see it as unspoiled wilderness. For Darnley Bay Resources Limited, a small Toronto-based mining company, the Melville Hills area held the promise of high mineral potential, profit, and jobs. But, in October 1994, its president, Leon LaPrairie, gave up his mineral-prospecting permits which covered 15 per cent of the proposed park (4200 square kilometres). He did so on his own accord, acknowledging the need to preserve the natural attributes of this unique landscape. Thus, a potential obstacle to Tuktut Nogait National Park was quietly removed, an unusual achievement, given the generally confrontational nature of wilderness politics.

The creation of new national parks requires both the initiative of communities such as Paulatuk and the support of individuals such as LaPrairie. But it also requires strong political leadership. When the Endangered Spaces campaign was launched in 1989, federal leadership came from Environment Minister Lucien Bouchard. At a meeting of national park superintendents in September 1989, Bouchard said: "I share the conviction of those who contend that Canada should, by the year 2000, complete the national park system." Citing the urgent need for Canada to protect its natural areas, he concluded that "we are among the last generations with an opportunity to preserve intact examples of our nation's threatened natural resources."

The federal government was indeed under pressure to seize that opportunity. In 1987, the federal Task Force on Park Establishment urged the government to complete the national-park system by the year 2000 when "the possibility of dedicating wilderness lands to conservation will have all but vanished." The Auditor General of Canada, Kenneth Dye, criticized Parks Canada in 1989 for not having a time-frame, warning: "There is a danger that opportunities to establish parks in some natural regions may disappear before the national park system is complete."

Several environmental coalitions representing almost one million Canadians pressed the government to complete the system by the year 2000. This support

When Parliament creates national parks, it speaks for the soul of Canada, and not for its pocket-book.
ANONYMOUS, 1957

enabled Bouchard to make the goal a major component of Canada's Green Plan, the Conservative government's environmental agenda that was released in December 1990. In it, the government committed to creating at least five new national parks by 1996, and to negotiate agreements by 2000 for the remaining thirteen parks required to complete the terrestrial system. The Green Plan was significant because it made completion of the system a government-wide responsibility, not just Parks Canada's responsibility.

The Endangered Spaces campaign succeeded in translating public support for new national parks into a federal target date for system completion. It is a commitment that withstood a national election and a change in government. When the Liberal party assumed power in November 1993, it did so pledging to maintain the commitment to complete the national-park system by 2000, and to accelerate the creation of new national parks to ten by 1997.

ON THE TRAIL FOR NEW NATIONAL PARKS

When the Endangered Spaces campaign was launched, just over 50 per cent of the national-park system had been completed, twenty-one of Parks Canada's thirty-nine natural regions were represented by thirty-four national parks covering 180,000 square kilometres (eight regions have more than one park). For the eighteen unrepresented regions, Parks Canada's task was clear: conclude negotiations on the four active national-park proposals: Vuntut, Banks Island, North Baffin Island, and Churchill; breathe life into the four inactive proposals: Torngat Mountains, Mealy Mountains, Wager Bay, and East Arm of Great Slave Lake; and confirm national park candidates for the remaining ten unrepresented natural regions.

Progress on new national parks clearly accelerated after the release of the Green Plan:

- Two new national parks were created in northern Canada, preserving almost 17,000 square kilometres of wilderness. Vuntut National Park (Yukon) protects the Old Crow Flats, an internationally significant wetland and important caribou habitat. Aulavik National Park on Banks Island (N.W.T.) protects some of the best muskoxen habitat in Canada.

- The federal government withdrew 22,200 square kilometres of land from industrial development on North Baffin Island, following a land-claim agreement with the Inuit to create a national park in the Nunavut Settlement Area. It also withdrew 28,800 square kilometres for the proposed Tuktut Nogait (Bluenose) National Park. (Land withdrawals are used to give candidate sites legal protection from possible development until a decision is made on whether or not to create a park.)

- The Manitoba government withdrew lands for the proposed Churchill National Park pending negotiation of a final agreement. This park will protect the world's largest polar bear denning habitat.

- Studies were initiated to examine the feasibility of new national parks in the Torngat Mountains of northern Labrador, on northern Bathurst Island in the western High Arctic, and in southern Manitoba on the western shores of Lake Winnipeg.

- Two additional areas, initially proposed as national parks, were protected

Parks Canada
Terrestrial Natural Regions

Presence of National Terrestrial Parks

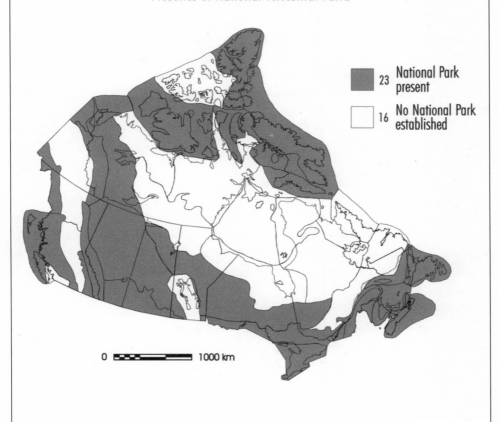

23 National Park present

16 No National Park established

0 ▮▬▬▬▬▬ 1000 km

As of April 1, 1995

by provincial governments. First suggested as a national park in 1922, the Lac Guillaume Delisle area on the eastern side of Hudson Bay was protected by the Québec government as a potential provincial park. The B.C. government established two protected areas in the Cariboo-Chilcotin region, protecting one-half of the proposed Churn Creek National Park. Both actions demonstrate that National Parks are not the only means of protecting nationally significant landscapes.

As with all campaigns, there are setbacks and missed opportunities. For example, despite strong local support for the proposed Hautes-Gorges National Park in southern Québec, the Charlevoix community was unable to motivate its Member of Parliament, Prime Minister Brian Mulroney, to pursue an agreement with the Québec government.

An opportunity to establish the long-proposed Wager Bay National Park, a candidate since 1978, was also missed. Negotiating on behalf of the Inuit, the Tungavik Federation of Nunavut sought a federal commitment to declare Wager Bay a national park within three years of ratifying their land-claim agreement. Parks Canada refused. It had not concluded its mineral assessments and community consultations. But it did promise other federal departments that, if a park was created, it would not prevent a transportation corridor from crossing it to allow industry access to potential mineral deposits to the west of the proposed park boundary. While the corridor would be subjected to an environmental assessment and public consultation, such roads are contrary to national-parks policy. Parks Canada is continuing its community consultations on the proposed park.

An opportunity to establish the East Arm of Great Slave Lake National Park disappeared with the collapse of the Dene/Métis land-claim agreement in 1990. The agreement included a section that outlined the terms under which a park would be created. A land-claim agreement is critical because the local community of Lutselk'e will consider the park only within a broader land-claim agreement. The rejection of the 1990 agreement by the Dene and Métis General Assembly meant East Arm remains inactive. Fortunately, because 7400 square kilometres of proposed parkland was withdrawn from development in 1970 by the federal government, the land remains off-limits to mineral staking and development and is still available for a future national park.

The B.C. government's Vancouver Island land-use plan did not protect the Quadra Island group in the Strait of Georgia, a proposed national park. Although the provincial and federal governments had identified the group as a very high priority for protection, the final plan ignored the area's conservation value. The Quadra Island Protected Areas Committee was then formed in 1994 to promote its protection.

Nevertheless, prospects for completing the national-park system have improved since 1989. It is now over 60 per cent complete, with twenty-three of thirty-nine natural regions represented. Candidate parks in four natural regions are now under interim-protection measures pending a final agreement. Feasibility studies are under way in three natural regions. And candidates have been confirmed for all but four natural regions.

CREATING NEW NATIONAL PARKS

Creating new national parks is a mixture of science and politics. In the late 1960s, the federal Cabinet made the political decision to increase the number of national parks. It fell to Parks Canada to select a guiding principle to translate this political mandate into the reality of new parks. They chose a science-based approach: to preserve samples of all of Canada's natural landscapes.

In 1971, Parks Canada divided the country into thirty-nine terrestrial regions, each with observable differences in physiography, vegetation, and environmental conditions. Their names readily define the kind of landscapes that Parks Canada wants to represent, such as: Prairie Grasslands, High Arctic Islands, Rocky Mountains, and Northern Labrador Mountains. The scientific task is to identify a contiguous, natural landscape within each region that best represents its diverse geological, physiographic, and biological themes. The political task is then to negotiate an agreement that protects such landscapes in a national park.

Once a park is established, federal parks legislation and policy prohibit logging, mining, recreational hunting, hydro-electric development, and the construction of new through roads. Legislation also directs Parks Canada to give priority to the protection of park ecosystems and natural resources over visitor use by maintaining most of the park in a wilderness condition.

There are five basic steps to creating a new national park in each unrepresented natural region: (1) identify several possible representative natural areas; (2) conduct fieldwork and other studies to select one as a potential national park; (3) launch a feasibility study to assess the practicality of a proposed park; (4) negotiate a park agreement that sets out the terms governing park establishment; (5) Parliament passes legislation protecting the area under the National Parks Act.

For all its simplicity on paper, it is a difficult process in real life. Provincial and territorial governments, aboriginal people, and local communities must consent to the creation of a new park. Provincial governments own the land, and must legally transfer it to the federal government. Aboriginal people continue to depend on the natural resources and wildlife that some national parks seek to protect. Many Native organizations have land claims, treaties, or other rights that cover proposed national parks. Local communities need to understand and prepare for both the impacts and the benefits of a new park in the area. Parks Canada must convince these parties to forgo industrial development in exchange for the ecological, economic, recreational, and educational benefits of preserving wilderness in a national park.

Federal political leadership is critical. However, federal ministers for national parks rarely visit candidate areas, or meet with local communities, aboriginal leaders, or their provincial and territorial colleagues to discuss their respective concerns or aspirations. Although most ministers want to announce a new park, they rarely roll up their sleeves, learn about the issues, and investigate solutions.

Nevertheless, many of our national parks exist because of the special interest and attention demonstrated by exceptional ministers. Jean Chrétien (1968–74) and Tom McMillan (1985–88) negotiated agreements for fourteen national parks, almost 40 per cent of the system. Others kick-started negotiations. For example, Hugh Faulkner announced public consultations on five candidate northern parks in 1978, and subsequent ministers, such as Charles Caccia, Jean Charest, and McMillan completed the task by each creating one of these parks during his term. As Secretary of State for the Environment, Pauline Browes convinced three provincial governments to begin discussions on at least four new national parks. She also orchestrated the 1992 Tri-Council Statement of Commitment which, in effect, obtained federal-provincial and territorial endorsement of the Endangered Spaces goal.

Still, the lack of sustained political interest is unfortunate. Park establishment is supported by a professional and experienced group of civil servants in Parks Canada. They have taken steps to better address the regional political and socio-economic issues that must be considered in park negotiations. Some new park planners and community consultation officers work outside Ottawa, in the provincial and territorial capitals of the jurisdictions where new national parks are required. This allows Parks Canada to better present its case for a new park to provincial politicians, aboriginal people, and local communities. Federal funding enables local communities to hire consultants to help them examine the potential impacts and benefits of a proposed park, and to participate in negotiations.

Relationships between Parks Canada and aboriginal organizations have improved because they have some shared objectives. Both acknowledge national parks as a means to conserve land and wildlife habitat, and to enhance and diversify the economy of local communities. Native people are more directly involved in park negotiations, are increasingly becoming co-managers of national parklands, and continue their traditional activities within park boundaries. This is a partnership that must continue for Parks Canada to have any hope of creating more national parks.

This shared purpose has produced results. The federal government and the Haida Nation agreed in January 1993 to jointly manage and safeguard Gwaii Haanas National Park Reserve "as one of the world's great natural and cultural treasures." First Nations supported the creation of Ivvavik, Vuntut, and North Baffin Island National Parks through the land-claims process. With governments prepared to discuss their land claim, the Labrador Inuit Association decided to support and participate in the Torngat Mountains feasibility study. Pond Inlet, N.W.T., rejected suggestions from the federal Department of Energy, Mines and Resources to reduce the boundaries of the North Baffin Island National Park by 10 per cent, in an area with high mineral potential. Increasingly, new national parks stand as testimony to the support of aboriginal people and local communities.

MAKING THE GRADE FOR NEW PARKS

Several actions are essential to complete the national-park system. Candidate sites for each unrepresented natural region should be publicly identified by early 1996. This will enable political negotiations to begin, and allow land-claim negotiators and land-use planners to incorporate national-park proposals into their work. Business interests will know what areas are closed to development and where not to invest. Local communities can begin assessing the potential impacts and benefits of new parks.

Once candidate sites are identified, Parks Canada should negotiate their withdrawal from industrial development, pending a decision on park establishment. This would ensure that the natural values of such sites are not compromised during negotiations. If industry does not have permits to develop in a proposed park, it will ensure lower overall compensation costs and reduce the likelihood of confrontation during park negotiations.

Advocates for new national parks must present their case to political and public leaders of the various parties involved in park negotiations, not just to the federal parks minister. Members of Parliament, representatives of other governments, Native organizations, and local communities should understand why Canadians support new national parks. In turn, park advocates must consider the needs and aspirations of provincial, aboriginal and community leaders, so that informed decisions can be made on creating new national parks.

Finally, the prime minister and the minister of national parks must play a more central and sustained role. Allocating land to wilderness conservation is a political decision, which demands the attention of those who direct government. The federal Cabinet should also ensure that other federal departments assist, rather than thwart, the creation of new national parks. As well, federal officials should stop reviewing each proposed park through the clouded prism of federal-provincial relations, which seem to be endlessly paralyzed over constitutional and economic issues.

Here are the milestones on the road to completing Canada's national park system:

- *By 1995:* Initiate a feasibility study for the proposed Mealy Mountains National Park in southeastern Labrador. Establish Churchill and the western portion of Tuktut Nogait National Park, which falls within the Inuvialuit settlement region and is currently the only part of the park that is the subject of political negotiations (the eastern and southern portions of the park are within other Native land-claim areas and negotiations for these portions have yet to begin). Withdraw from development the entire watershed of the proposed Wager Bay and northern Bathurst Island National Parks, and the site identified as a candidate park in the Manitoba Lowlands natural region.

- *By 1996:* Ensure that feasibility studies are under way for all candidate sites. Withdraw lands for the proposed Torngat Mountains National Park. Establish the North Baffin Island and Wager Bay National Parks in the Northwest Territories. Achieve representation of twenty-seven of the thirty-nine natural regions.

- *By 1997:* Negotiate land withdrawals for all candidate sites pending final agreements. Establish a national park in the Manitoba Lowlands, on northern Bathurst Island, and in the Torngat Mountains as Labrador's first national park.

- *By 1998:* Ensure all feasibility studies on candidate national parks are completed. Complete land-acquisition programs for Grasslands and Bruce Peninsula National Parks. Achieve representation for thirty-two of the thirty-nine natural regions.

- *By 1999:* Establish the Mealy Mountains National Park, and an additional two national parks, thereby representing thirty-five of the thirty-nine natural regions.

- *By the year 2000:* There should be a fully legislated National Park, or final agreements and land withdrawals, for each natural region of Canada.

OPPORTUNITIES AND CHALLENGES

National parks are a powerful country-wide force for conservation. Of the 520,000 square kilometres of Canada that is legally protected wilderness, the national parks make the greatest contribution by preserving over 40 per cent of this total from development. And they have many allies. For example, the governments of Newfoundland and Manitoba clearly welcome national parks as one means of contributing to their protected-areas goals. The Government of the Northwest Territories supports the completion of the national-parks system as its contribution to the goal of representing Canada's natural regions, and as a means to enhance local economies. According to a 1994 Environics poll, Canadians rate national parks as being as important as the Canadian flag, the national anthem, and the Charter of Rights and Freedoms as symbols of Canada.

In fairness, however, there are real, on-the-ground challenges to establishing new national parks. Time is of the essence in southern Canada, where no new national parks have been created since 1988. Here, two of the most developed natural regions in the country are still without national parks. Opportunities to protect dry coastal Douglas-fir ecosystems on the Gulf Islands in the Strait of Georgia continue to be lost to timber and urban development. Over 50 per cent of the Manitoba Lowlands natural region has been lost to forestry and agriculture. Land-acquisition programs for Grasslands and Bruce Peninsula National Parks are stalled, jeopardizing their ability to represent two of Parks Canada's natural regions.

Four of the sixteen unrepresented natural regions are in Québec, where prospects for creating new national parks under strong federal legislation are practically nonexistent. The province has a long-standing policy of not transferring provincial land to the federal government, a requirement under the National Parks Act. The two governments are more cooperative in protecting habitat when they focus on conservation objectives, and not legal, jurisdictional issues. Both are working to create a Saguenay marine park to protect the beluga whale, and both agree that the Lac Guillaume Delisle wilderness should be a park. Joint fieldwork to assess several other park proposals in northern Quebec is scheduled for 1995.

The allocation of potential national parklands for mineral development is one of the more prominent obstacles. The Bathurst Inlet area in the Northwest Territories was proposed as a national park in 1978, but was later shelved because of its high mineral potential. The federal department responsible for mining wants to reduce the proposed East Arm of Great Slave National Park by 50 per cent and release those lands to industry for exploration. The Manitoba government reduced the Little Limestone Lake study area, an area favoured by environmentalists for national-park status in the Manitoba Lowlands, by 60 per cent because of its very high mineral potential. These exemplify a double standard. Governments will quickly release land to mineral exploration and development with little consideration of its conservation values, and virtually no public consultation. Yet, they demand years of studies and consultation before any action is taken to protect land.

In 1993, a parliamentary committee recommended that the federal government work with the provinces and territories to identify the boundaries for candidate protected areas, so as to quickly remove the uncertainty for the mineral industry regarding the location of new parks. In September 1994, representatives of governments, industry, environmental groups, aboriginal organizations, and labour signed the Whitehorse Mining Initiative, an accord that, in part, supports creating protected areas which are free of mineral exploration and development, and which are required to represent Canada's natural regions by the year 2000. Some mining companies have made significant contributions to new national parks. For example, Petro-Canada, Noranda, and several others donated over 4000 square kilometres of mineral permits to the Nature Conservancy of Canada, thereby allowing Vuntut National Park to be created.

We have to do something fast for wild-places. We can't let these animals die for nothing. TIFFANY, St. Monica's School, 1993

Can we afford sixteen new national parks? In short, yes. There are several ways to reduce the cost of creating new national parks. Ensure candidate sites are quickly identified and given interim protection so that the government does not have to pay compensation to development interests. Once a national park is established, development of park facilities should be kept to an absolute minimum. Parks Canada is taking steps to strengthen its finances. To address a 25 per cent reduction in its budget over the next three years, it has developed a national business plan that places a priority on reducing expenditures on park facilities and generating revenue from park operations to help pay for new national parks. The money spent on new parks is a critical investment in the nation's ecological future.

On the flip-side of the budget coin is the question, can we afford *not* to protect some of Canada's premier wilderness areas? In 1885 some politicians objected to Parliament spending money on a new national park called Banff. What would have happened if they had won their argument? In 1895 civil servants said that the government could not afford to create a new national park called Waterton Lakes. If they had won their argument, would we be celebrating its centennial in 1995?

Finally, it is imperative that we build on community support for new national parks. Local people have supported national parks as a means of protecting valued landscapes and natural resources as far back as 1893, when ranchers advocated the creation of Waterton Lakes National Park. The challenge today is to recapture and broaden that support for the ecological, economic, educational, and recreational benefits of the land, and to help communities protect these values. It also requires working with them to develop transition strategies in preparation for the establishment of a new park, rather than dropping it on them like a bomb.

THE TASK AHEAD

Creating sixteen new national parks will make a significant contribution towards reaching the Endangered Spaces goal. But the federal responsibility does not stop there: it needs to work more closely with the provincial and territorial governments and First Nations to ensure that all of Canada's natural regions are represented. The federal Liberals sponsored a 1992 parliamentary resolution to this effect, and restated its commitment to this goal in its Red Book during the election. However, beyond creating new national parks, the Liberals have failed to articulate how they will reach their goal.

There are some practical things the federal government can do. Some of Parks Canada's natural regions are not adequately represented: for example, the four national parks in natural region 19 are so small that WWF considers the natural region to have little or no representation. Similarly, Pukaskwa National Park in Ontario cannot be judged to adequately represent the Central Boreal Uplands natural region, one of the largest regions, which stretches from Saskatchewan to

Québec. Parks Canada could work with other federal and provincial agencies to more adequately represent these natural regions by creating more protected areas, managing existing protected areas and adjacent lands on an ecosystem basis, and providing better incentives to private landowners to conserve representative landscapes. A proposed change to the Income Tax Act announced in the 1995 federal budget could assist private landowners, but further incentives are required.

Other federally administered protected areas such as national wildlife areas and migratory-bird sanctuaries do not currently contribute to the Endangered Spaces goal because they do not prohibit some forms of industrial development. However, these areas could make an important contribution to representing natural regions in northern Canada if mineral and oil and gas development were legally prohibited from occurring on them. Some of Canada's military bases contain significant natural areas that should be protected. The designation of part of the Canadian Forces Suffield military base in Alberta as a national wildlife area in 1992 was an important step in this direction. The base contains some of the last remnants of unbroken prairie.

National parks will survive only as islands of wilderness amidst a sea of development, particularly in southern Canada, if surrounding land uses are not compatible with park conservation objectives; thus, Parks Canada must act as a catalyst to get adjacent landowners to cooperate in the conservation of the broader landscape. Fortunately, with the creation of new protected areas by provincial governments on lands adjacent to national parks such as Pacific Rim in B.C., Waterton Lakes in Alberta, and Kejimkujik in Nova Scotia, these areas are better protected and contribute more effectively to the Endangered Spaces goal.

In 1969, when Jean Chrétien opened Kejimkujik National Park in Nova Scotia, he remarked: "Our national parks are part of the original face of Canada, inviolable spots which provide sanctuaries for man as well as nature. But it is man who must extend and preserve them. This is the task that lies ahead."

Now prime minister, Chrétien is both personally sympathetic and well placed to ensure that the task of completing the national-park system is met. In 1968, he wanted to create forty to sixty new national parks to represent the nation's landscapes. He urged that the task be completed by 1985 because of the rising costs and threats to natural areas. All of what Chrétien talked about in 1968 is central to the Endangered Spaces campaign today. As prime minister, he must make certain that his government remains dedicated to creating new national parks, and to protecting wilderness landscapes as an integral part of government decision making.

National parks speak to the heart of nation-building because they require a political consensus among Canadians on the need to preserve the wilderness landscapes that define us as a nation. They are also an important measure of our nation's commitment to conserving the earth's ecosystems. But there are no laws compelling politicians to create new national parks. Canadians must, therefore, speak for the "soul" of Canada and insist that the federal government honour its commitment to complete the national-park system by 2000.

Lessons Learned

20 / *Perspectives of a Target*

ADAM ZIMMERMAN

Fate conspired for me to have the job of chief operating officer of a major natural resource company at the same time the environmental movement ignited. Looking back on it, I'm glad I was there, and I take satisfaction from the constructive responses we were able to fashion as well as the gradual change in corporate culture.

If truth be known, I'd have to say that I was bound to react sympathetically to environmentalists. All my life I've enjoyed and adored the pristine nature of Ontario's Georgian Bay. I've also had the great satisfaction of reforesting some eroded land I own. But above all, my wife and four children are committed, and to some extent activist, environmental crusaders. They enlarged my knowledge and sharpened my arguments, but were never satisfied that I was doing enough!

That being said, I was and am, absolutely convinced that a well-placed corporate officer can make changes and improvements to the environment on a scale that can really mean something. However righteous that makes one feel, the fact is that it has been war out there. Indeed, part of what nourishes the environmental movement is the picture of corporate leaders as heartless, wanton despoilers of nature.

The argument between industry and environmentalists, if such it is, would be rationalized if society recognized that industry operates only with their consent. Fundamentally, industry operates everywhere with regulations that have been formulated by governments to protect the health and safety of workers, the consumer, and the environment within which it operates. It is true that at one time — back at the beginning, so to speak — industry did its thing and dumped its waste out of sight (for solids), into the air (for exhausts), and into a watercourse (for liquids). Very little thought was given to the immediate or cumulative effects of such behaviour. For a while, I suppose, this was tolerable, just as it was for householders to have a dump somewhere on their property. Snoop around any farm, or country property, or ditches on rural roads anywhere, and you'll find a dump. The cellars in most houses will inevitably collect garbage, too, which in certain circumstances could be damaging. But I digress. As the means of production enlarged and the volume of production expanded, and as the population increased and products multiplied and the convenience called "consumerism" became a religion, so the capacity of the receiving environment was first tested, then exceeded.

It was once believed that "the solution to pollution is dilution," and it also was once the case that people didn't really think much about the environment. Remember that most industries were familiar to the people living nearby. If you had lived in a mining community, you would have accepted the fact that a tailings pond contained the accumulated residue of the milling process — the ground-up rock from the mine after the metal had been removed. The fact that it had been treated with cyanide or acid, or contained heavy metals, would not have registered much, even if it had been known. Furthermore, the ability to test for deleterious elements and/or measure their long-term effects on the environment was likely rudimentary or inadequate. So naturally you might have believed that mining and milling, as it had always been done, was not a problem.

Had your life been in a forest-industry town, the sight of clear-cuts after logging would simply be part of the landscape to you. A beehive burner dealing with sawmill waste (i.e., half the log!) would seem perfectly ordinary, and the pulp mill odour would be passed off as the smell of money. Liquid wastes, of course, would have been dumped in the local watercourse — out of sight, out of mind.

I've written these vignettes of the mining and forest industries not to serve as an excuse, but to help get the reader's mind around the situation as the environmentalists found it in the 1960s. The causes addressed by various environmentalists at that time are now fairly well known, some being more valid than others in my view, using tactics from verbal harrassment to spiking trees, and some whose bona fides could be seriously questioned. Probably the toughest thing to deal with then, as today, was the unsupported statement — "Dioxin is the most deadly poison known to man" or "Secondary smoke is responsible for an elevated incidence of cancer." The combination of a settled resource community and the enthusiastic if not rabid ecologist was indeed the recipe for some pretty heated arguments.

As a corporate leader, I was always faced with the dilemma that might be described as *competitive reality*. On the one hand, I was ensuring that operations were on track within existing regulations. On the other hand, plant and process improvements had to be affordable, both financially and competitively. Frankly, it seemed foolish to try to get too far ahead of the competition, for fear that changing rules or technology might leave you hanging out to dry.

Then there was the business of validating the environmentalists' claims. For example, based on what we think is good scientific information, the pulp industry has thought all along that the significant cost of achieving new permitted levels of chlorinated compounds was being incurred to cure a non-problem (and now this is being publicly recognized). But the fact was that the scaremongers caught the headlines, while the "perpetrators" missed the bus.

Similarly, in the woodlands, the claims made by environmentalists about a tiny part of Canada and a minute fraction of its woodlands have been extrapolated to the point where Canadians are sometimes thought to be desertifying their country. The facts, as I understand them, indicate this is so far from the truth as to be laughable. Almost any observer who takes the trouble to examine what's really happening in Canadian forests comes away knowing that nobody practises the game any better than we do. Perceptions, as created by those I would perhaps call environmental "alarmists" (not "terrorists" — there are only a few of them) are regrettably often a long way from the reality practised by those I have chosen to call the "perpetrators." So what do you do?

The very first thing a corporate officer must do is try to understand the science

of the issue. While bias always exists, the first port of call beyond corporate technical staff is usually the industry's scientific establishments, both in Canada and elsewhere. Information so garnered can then be checked by independent "experts," be
they practising consultants or university-based scientists. After a time, a fairly clear
picture usually emerges, so that the ground on which you stand becomes firm and
well defined — strong enough to support you when the attacks come.

Meanwhile, back at the ranch, the company staff are trying to conduct business
as usual. Maybe they think the "crazies" are going to get them. They find their children coming home from school, and going so far as to accuse them of spoiling the
world. They may even see a split developing in the work force between those with
different views on the environment.

And what do their bosses think? Very often the immediate boss is a middle-aged
person who has been around a long time, has "seen it all" and "knows" that his or
her operation "ain't never hurt nobody." Their minds are going to be hard to
change. They will change their minds, but gradually, and only with good reasons.

The upper bosses have to cope with all of the above in some sort of coherent
way. The process usually starts with the preparation of what is called an "environmental code." This is intended to be a kind of apostolic confession of the faith to
which all employees can comfortably subscribe. It will facilitate their company's
defence of new ways of doing things or finding fault with the old ways. It will help
them maintain pride in what they are doing, and will be a useful benchmark for
comparing their operations with others'. It is all part of a "reasonable response." It
is also responsible. Corporate officers may well be bold, but as a group, they must
be reasonable as well. They must do the right thing and be seen to be doing it. They
must be able to articulate their position to an increasingly sceptical public.

Regrettably, terrible things do happen, like the explosion at the Westray Mine
and the sinking of the *Exxon Valdez*, where the lack of performance or wilful
neglect by the people concerned not only results in a tragedy, but also puts the whole
of executive management in doubt. Nevertheless, we soldier on, which is not hard
to do if one is fairly sure about being on the side of the angels. Of course, that may
be subjective, but if you've done your homework well and really believe it, then no
one can seriously embarrass you.

Real-life examples are doubtless more convincing than recollections, so here are
the kinds of exchanges that became the norm for me over hot issues:

Letter dated February 28, 1989, to Adam Zimmerman:
While I applaud your agreeing to appear recently on CHEK TV Daily Edition, I
must admit I was not so impressed with the way you represented yourself as an
environmentally sensitive industrialist.

In particular I refer to your stand that toxic emissions from pulp and paper
mills are not harming the environment. This is simply not credible, and you do
yourself and your company a disservice by making such a suggestion.

Humans who live near the mills (which are currently the world's worst
industrial polluters) are suffering health problems, including an increased rate
of cancer. The seafood and fishing industries in many areas near the mills have
had to be closed on account of contamination with highly dangerous dioxins,

furans, chlorophenols, and other poisonous substances. Heron eggs have failed to hatch, and the trees are dying.

The pulp kraft mills must start to clean up their act. This means keeping date deadlines for a significant reduction in the emission of toxic effluents, and the substitution of a chlorine-free oxygenation bleaching process for paper and/or the marketing of unbleached paper.

As regards the issue of over-cutting, sustainable yields, and the selective cutting alternative versus clear cutting, I would refer you back to the "round table" approach to forestry and other resource management as set forth by the Report of the National Task Force on Environment and Economy, of which you were yourself a member.

If Canada is to set a good example to "undeveloped" countries such as Brazil who are destroying their forests and endangering the whole planet, we must first set our own house in order. Perhaps you should take a leaf out of the book of your daughter in the Amazon!

Letter dated April 17, 1989, from Adam Zimmerman in reply to above letter:
Re your letter of February 28th, I felt I wanted to reply directly as well. I liked your half-compliment and didn't like your half-criticism, because I think that what apparently lies behind this is either an ignorance or prejudice with respect to the facts of the matter.

To our knowledge, no pulp mill in the world has ever done any lasting harm to anybody. There may be some minor harm done to some other living creatures, although the only two things I can think of are the fish that were deformed by mercuric slimicides used prior to 1975 in northern Ontario. The second was the recent evidence of dioxin in certain shellfish resident beneath the outfalls of three pulp mills in British Columbia. One of these has been completely cured, so to speak, and the other remains a little bit of a mystery. It does appear, however, that shellfish which hang around rather than swim around are more susceptible to toxic buildups in their systems.

Kraft pulp mills have indeed been cleaning up their act for quite a long time. Part of what worries you now are apparent threats from things which have only been measurable in very recent times and, at that, the levels measured are far below anything that does anyone any harm.

The forestry argument is a long and complicated one where anyone can prove anything by a particular instance. However, viewing the broad scene as I can and do, I'm satisfied that the Canadian forest is being increasingly well tended and that by the end of another decade we will be a model cited all over the world.

We would be happy to detail the facts by which we must live any time you wish. Thank you for your interest.

Letter dated September 19, 1989, to Adam Zimmerman:
Re: Sustainable Development. In the August 22, 1989, issue of the *Province*,

As trustees of a huge, magnificently endowed slice of the world's real estate, Canadians carry special responsibilities in planetary housekeeping. It is clear to WWF *workers that public sentiment is strongly on their side in its appreciation of the urgency and merit of making all parts of the planet more hospitable to its remarkably varied tenants.*

This is much more than a charitable gesture to wildlife. We could do ourselves an enormous favour.
GLOBE AND MAIL
EDITORIAL,
September 1990

you are quoted as saying: Sustainable development is possible and there is no great trick to achieving it.

I would appreciate knowing what you understand "sustainable development" to be, how it relates to forestry and why it is so easily attainable.

Letter dated October 3, 1989, from Adam Zimmerman in reply to above letter:
Your question is so brief that I may not be answering it properly. To be equally brief, however, let me say that all of the forests have theoretically been allocated on the basis of sustained yield. In other words, if one made the assumption that the growth cycle was a hundred years, then only 1 per cent would be logged in each of the 100 years. Experience has shown that this is partially a naïve concept and that nature has to be supplemented with hand planting. Some will argue that this creates a mono-culture, but again experience indicates that the species that grow best on a given site will in fact grow there and even if one plants only one species, others fill in.

The other part of sustainable development, which I think is more difficult, is the notion of whether industrial processes can be controlled so that they have no cumulative or long-term effect on the environment. It used to be said that the solution to pollution is dilution, however as the body of knowledge builds, it is known that some elements accumulate and some chemicals do not break down, except over intolerably long periods. So far as is known, this is not a major problem for the forest industry, but to the extent that it is a problem or there are problems out there, solutions are being found.

Obviously this is a huge subject which can't be dealt with in telegrams, but I hope I have given you some satisfaction.

Letter from Adam Zimmerman, dated June 7, 1990, to Michael Manolson of Greenpeace, in response to a Greenpeace circular accusing the forest industry of all manner of degradations:
It may surprise you that one of my family's larger annual donations is to Greenpeace. Thus I receive your mail and feel entitled to a hearing. Your recent letter concerning forests has elicited this response.

In the first place, your letter offers a confusion of statements and opinions which may be as a result of not knowing or else deliberate. My comments are based on thirty years in the industry which began with the [brand new] greenfield establishment of a major kraft mill in B.C. and has included the failure to repeat that success in Tasmania and the responsibilities of the chairman of Canada's largest forest grouping. I have seen and known about environmentally good things as well as bad things in that time, although by far the majority of the former. I am typical of industrial leadership today, which clearly places the environment at the top of every agenda.

You state that our concerns begin and end with making money and that is perfectly true. Without income, nothing survives, be it a business or a person. The income of a hunter or gatherer is meat and nuts, while your and my company's is simply goods and services expressed as money. The rate of income or profit is debatable. However, what I can say for sure is that forest industry income over the cycle is much less than bank interest and about half what is earned by some of our major customers, like publishers whom you manipulate so well. At the least, on the evidence, you simply have to acknowledge that our rate of profit is modest.

When it comes to allocation of forest lands, there are many different procedures in various jurisdictions. In the early days, they were just handed out to whoever asked. Beginning in the 1960s, it was usually by a public hearing process. After that, only the less commercially desirable tracts were left and really no one would risk them. With the advance of technology and the rise in demand occasioned by increasing population, these have gradually become economically viable as in the Prairie provinces. To my certain knowledge, the Alberta and Manitoba forests you allude to have been on offer for at least a decade and there were no takers and no objectors in all that period. As it happens, those particular forests have been at least partly utilized for lumbering since the turn of the century. A pulp operation will only make that more efficient in the sense of utilizing a lot of waste. The whole interior B.C. pulp economy was built on sawmill waste, previously burned.

You take issue with long-term tenure. I'd say two things of which the first is that billion-dollar commitments will not occur with uncertain tenure, if for no other reason than that they must compete with those who have secure tenure. Secondly, it is virtually a unanimously accepted perception that the world's best-cared-for forests are privately held: Sweden, Finland, Norway, the southern United States, Brazil, Chile, New Zealand, etc. Clearly no one has a greater interest in a healthy forest than those whose existence depends on it.

This then gets to the debate between the old-growth or virgin forest and the replanted new forest. There is a lot left to be discovered about what differences there may be and I would like to know the answers as much as anyone. Some claim that, after the harvest, the ecosystem is irreparably changed or destroyed. Others will claim that it restores itself fairly promptly, particularly if the opening is not too huge. Whatever the case, we seek the truth on this one; however, we do so on the basis that the forest industry is going to continue to exist. It will, however, as always, exist only with understanding and public consent.

At this point it is worth noting, and you must acknowledge, that as much forest is "clear-cut" annually by fire and disease as is taken by industry. And half the fires are man-made — which could be an excellent problem for you to help us cure. Even with that, Forestry Canada reports that not satisfactorily restocked areas are diminishing.

As to toxic discharges, as I said to Mr. Perks at our Annual Meeting, we believe the outcry has reached hysterical proportions. It's a neat way to "get" us, which it has, while causing the absorption of ridiculous amounts of capital and totally unjustified alarm in many circles. The response of this industry has

Commitment 1.8: All members of the forest community will work towards completing, by the year 2000, a network of protected areas representative of Canada's forests, to provide ecological benchmarks, protect areas of unique biological value and ensure wilderness experience.
CANADA FOREST ACCORD, 1992
(30 organizations signed on, including Ontario Ministry of Natural Resources, Council of Forest Industries, Canadian Pulp and Paper Association, Canadian Institute of Forestry, International Woodworkers Association–Canada)

been dedicated and successful, although it can only be hurried so much. For your part, you might define for us what is zero. In 1965, it was parts per billion, so then there was no dioxin; in 1985, it was parts per trillion, so then there were traces; and now it's parts per quadrillion, which can seem like a lot. Wouldn't you rather put some of that money into population control or Third World debt reduction, or development of tolerable energy sources?

I wouldn't have written this letter without some knowledge of and respect for Greenpeace. On the facts I have, your campaign is ill-founded and I would believe it could be redirected. Indeed, you could quite easily attain many worthwhile objectives and please your constituency by some mutually constructive actions where I believe we could be willing partners.

P.S. It would be interesting to see the response if you sent this with your next mailing.

The foregoing summarizes and epitomizes as nearly as I can what it has been like to be on the receiving end of claims made by environmental advocates. I hope it demonstrates that the apparent perpetrators of environmental destruction are basically surrogates for society as a whole. The response of people of goodwill and intelligence can only be positive. The world is a better place for the struggle between both sides of this debate.

Perhaps the most positive example to date is industrial support of some proposals by wilderness advocates. Assuming that the size of "set asides" can be agreed upon — and 12 per cent seems to be generally acceptable — industry has, for the most part, been agreeable to the notion. For example, it was not difficult for my companies, and indeed most of the forest industry, to support completion of the national parks, provincial parks, and ecological reserves system in British Columbia. To our companies, this was good business recognizing that all constituencies must be satisfied and that war is fruitless.

So, on reflection, it has been a fascinating struggle, for which we are all the better.

21 / Playing God in Endangered Spaces: Perspectives of a Donor

GLEN W. DAVIS

CRACK! A rifle shot shattered the stillness of a glorious late summer day. Three more shots followed in rapid succession.

My wife, Alice, and I were standing on the Alaska Highway, which marks the eastern boundary of Kluane Game Sanctuary, Yukon Territory. We had stopped to admire a pond, which provided a photogenic foreground between us and the newly snowcapped Kluane Range. An old pickup truck was parked just down the road.

What was going on? Were these shots fired by a poacher or by a Native person exercising his legal right to hunt? We didn't stick around to find out.

We were tourists, simply trying to enjoy what is advertised as a "game sanctuary." Perhaps the hunter was successful and his day made joyful. Our day was substantially ruined, and we wondered about the administration of this endangered space.

Two weeks later we returned. Summer was turning to fall, and the snow lay deeper on the mountains. The pond, the brilliant yellow aspens, and the mountains made an impressive picture. A number of birds rose and circled one end of the pond. I walked to a beaver house on the far shore. The works of the beaver family were everywhere — extensive dams, literally hundreds of downed aspen, and their lodge, which rose over two metres above the waterline. Continuing around the pond, I observed at least a dozen Yukon-sized ravens contesting territory with three even larger bald eagles. Unexpectedly, I was strafed by one of the eagles.

It was a wonderful day. Then, the cause of all the commotion became apparent. Lying hidden in dense brush were the remains of a moose and several beer cans, less than 100 metres from the highway.

No matter who the hunter was, it was obvious to me that several violations of the law had occurred. The shots were fired less than a kilometre from the highway, the carcass was abandoned near the roadside, the beer cans were litter. However, there is little law enforcement in this so-called protected area, and it is not clear that anyone cares much. Some game sanctuary!

ICON SPECIES — ICON PARKS

The grizzly bear is my icon species. Monte Hummel prefers the wolf. My personal interest is the creation of wilderness areas of at least 100,000 hectares and the protection of icon species, including the grizzly bear and the wolf, the cod and the salmon, the eagle and the loon. If we provide living spaces for these wild things, we will save a tremendous number of other species as well.

"Marian" was a female grizzly. She lived in Yellowstone National Park and was the heroine of Frank Craighead's *Track of the Grizzly*. The first radio-collared bear, Marian was studied for eight years. She was killed in Lake Campground by a park ranger acting in "self-defence." Her last litter of three cubs was born in 1968; all were dead by 1972, well short of adulthood.

"Foy's Lake female" was a wolf living in Algonquin Park. John Theberge tells her story in his essay in *Islands of Hope*. She made the fatal mistake of crossing the park boundary in search of food.

These two top predators symbolize the difficulties faced by their kind as they struggle to survive in nominal wilderness areas and in close proximity to people.

Yellowstone National Park, Waterton–Glacier International Peace Park, Canada's four Rocky Mountain national parks, and Kluane National Park Reserve are among North America's largest, most beautiful, and most famous parks. They are the icons of the system — that is, the biggest and the best, the model for all the others. Most people think of them as protected wilderness areas, but that is far from the truth.

The grizzly bear is under immense pressure. And counting grizzlies is difficult work. David Mattson, a researcher with the U.S. National Biological Service, states conservatively that there are a minimum of 360 grizzlies in the lower forty-eight states, with a minimum of 142 in Yellowstone and 175 in the North Continental Divide (Glacier) Ecosystem. Other experts give higher numbers. For example, Chris Servheen, of the U.S. Fish and Wildlife Service, estimates there are 700 to 900 grizzlies in the lower forty-eight states. In his 1985 book *Bear Attacks*, Steve Herrero estimated Alberta's grizzly population at 1200. Ten years later, Herrero's best guess is 800, with 200 to 215 of these in the national parks. He believes that Kluane's 300 to 400 bears may have the best sanctuary for the long haul.

It is hard to believe that the fate of the wolf in these parks is worse than the grizzly's, but it is. Wolves were eliminated from Yellowstone in the 1920s; there are only three packs, totalling 20-plus wolves near Waterton–Glacier; and there are an estimated 100 wolves in Banff and Jasper. The situation in Kluane is heart-breaking from a conservation point of view. As of February 1995, the Government of Yukon Territory is in the third year of a five-year authorized wolf control program in the 20,000-square-kilometre "Aishihik" area adjacent to Kluane. In 1993, it was estimated that twenty-four to forty-two wolves lived part of their lives in Kluane. Only one pack of seven or eight members lived entirely within the park. It is believed that the small number of wolves in Kluane has been cut sharply — but who knows? As in Yellowstone in the 1920s, wolves in Kluane today are being eliminated to protect ungulates, for the supposed benefit of tourists and hunters. Indeed, Man does play God.

WILDERNESS: WHAT IS IT?

We often hear that wilderness is an integral part of the Canadian psyche. So it should not be necessary to explain to Canadians what wilderness is. WRONG! Our performance in protecting wilderness indicates that most Canadians — bureaucrats, politicians, Native people, loggers, miners, farmers, ranchers, fishermen, businessmen, tourists, all of us — "just don't get it."

In 1972, the Wildlands League provided a definition of wilderness: Wilderness is an area where human activity is deliberately minimized, where non-human forces and forms of life remain virtually undisturbed by such activity. Wilderness is a place where neither the permanent addition of artificial objects, nor the removal of natural objects shall result from human use.

Wilderness is an ecological unit of a size sufficient to be essentially self-regulating. It should be large enough to ensure physical and psychological separation from the man-dominated environment.

As custodian of wilderness, man will exclude from such areas:

- roads
- permanent structures
- mechanized equipment and vehicles
- trapping and hunting
- natural resource extraction
- any form of commercial exploitation
- any other form of disturbance which is incompatible with wilderness and wilderness values.

Edward Abbey, the famed American conservationist, dealt with the same topic. Abbey was a vigorous opponent of what he called "industrial tourism." In *Desert Solitaire*, he wrote: "No more cars in our national parks. Let the people walk. Or ride horses, bicycles, mules, wild pigs — anything — but keep the automobiles and the motorcycles and all their motorized relatives out."

COMPARATIVE PARKS

There is an academic and practical interest in analysing the status of Canada's parks and other protected areas on a comparative basis. In *Parks and Protected Areas in Canada*, Hal Eidsvik concludes that Canada is probably second only to the United States in terms of the conservation effectiveness of our protected-areas system. Whether or not we are second-best in the world, our performance is totally inadequate when it comes to actually protecting our wilderness heritage.

One reason the United States provides better protection for its wildlife is better legislation. For example, the Wilderness Act of 1964 was enhanced by the Endangered Species Act of 1973. In 1975, the grizzly bear was declared a "threatened species," and the force of these acts has effectively helped the grizzly maintain its tenuous hold in the lower 48 states. Canada has no similar legislation. The Sierra Club, WWF, and many other conservation organizations place a high priority on such legislation, but some learned observers think the prospects are bleak because of Canada's jumbled jurisdictional interests.

When Canada's protected-areas system is studied, two important points are often overlooked. First, if and when our system is complete, only about 20 to 25 per cent of the total protected area will likely be in national parks. The rest will be under provincial or territorial jurisdiction. Second, the national parks system is covered by the most progressive legislation; provincial parks legislation leaves much to be desired. The provinces and territories face a huge task.

Algonquin Park, the fabled icon of Ontario's park system, is a case in point. At 7725 square kilometres, Algonquin is Ontario's most southerly opportunity to create a wilderness park, but most of it has been logged, and about 75 per cent of it is still zoned for logging. In addition, Native and non-Native hunting is permitted in some areas.

In 1993, Algonquin had its 100th birthday. In honour of that occasion, Kevin Kavanagh, president of the Wildlands League, called on the Government of Ontario to either fix Algonquin or stop calling it a park.

In *Algonquin Park at One Hundred*, Anne Bell approached the problem from a different perspective. She wondered how Ontario will ever achieve its Endangered Spaces goal of protecting representative areas totalling at least 12 per cent of the province if it cannot protect existing parks like Algonquin.

YELLOWSTONE

In *Playing God in Yellowstone: The Destruction of America's First National Park*, Alston Chase provides an often controversial look at the history and management of Yellowstone. It is a must-read for everyone concerned about issues of park management and the survival of top predators. *Playing God* and *Track of the Grizzly* describe the mismanagement of Yellowstone's wildlife, emphasizing the myriad of problems involved in the relationship between humans and grizzly bears:

- Chase summarizes his book this way: "Those visiting Yellowstone today will not see what Roosevelt saw (1900s). They may encounter elk, bison, and an occasional coyote, but they will see no thousands of antelope, no plentiful sheep or mule deer. They will be fortunate to see a grizzly and will find no black bears begging along the road. They will find no wolves or white-tail deer, and, in all possibility, no mountain lion, wolverine, lynx, bobcat or fisher. As a wildlife refuge, Yellowstone is dying."
- Yellowstone, at about 890,000 hectares, is the largest park in the lower forty-eight states. The Greater Yellowstone Ecosystem, the area where grizzly bears live, is about 2,225,000 hectares. Even the largest park is too small to do its job.
- The wolf was extirpated in Yellowstone in the 1920s. During the winter of 1995, after years of struggle, an attempt is being made by people, and by wolves without the help of people, to reintroduce the species.

I snowmobiled in Yellowstone — yes, controlled snowmobiling is legal in the park — during the winters of 1992 and 1994. The famous geyser basins, covered in mist and ice, and surrounded by elk and bison, are possibly more attractive in winter than in summer. It is easy to inadvertently manoeuvre your snowmobile into the middle of a herd of bison. I once did so, and sat with bison literally at arm's length on both sides for about ten minutes. It was also exciting to stand on the shore of the Madison River at −30°C, while rare trumpeter swans flew almost into my camera lens. Yellowstone can give you the feeling of wilderness. As bad as the management may be, it is still a wonderful place.

WATERTON–GLACIER

Waterton–Glacier International Peace Park is a wilderness gem, a back-packer's paradise. The park provides countless scenic vistas and opportunities for short hikes for those tourists who enjoy parks without straying far from their vehicles. I have visited this area about twenty times, and had my only "up close and personal" encounter with grizzlies while walking along a creek in Waterton. Unwittingly, I had passed two cubs frolicking in the creek, and then was alerted by their playful growls. Where was Mother? It turned out that Mother was in dense brush behind the cubs, and thankfully she permitted me to proceed slowly and quietly on my way.

Waterton–Glacier is the home of the largest grizzly population in the lower forty-eight states. Montana's Glacier, at 410,000 hectares, is not particularly large for this purpose; however, it is buffered by adjacent large wilderness areas such as the Bob Marshall Wilderness at 950,000 hectares. Alberta's Waterton was once 1095 square kilometres, but it was reduced to its present 505 square kilometres in 1921. Waterton is totally inadequate for the purpose of protecting grizzly bears and other wildlife. It has long been my opinion that Canada has not played its proper role in protecting this international wilderness.

Nevertheless, there is real hope. For decades a few isolated voices have cried out for the restoration of Waterton. More recently, the political struggle has been waged by the "Crown of the Continent" coalition and groups such as the Alberta Wilderness Association and the Canadian Parks and Wilderness Society (CPAWS).

Today, there is a good possibility that British Columbia will act to protect the 22,000-hectare Akamina Kishinena Valley, immediately to the north of Glacier and adjacent to Waterton. The valley has been logged, and there is considerable pressure from hunters. In time, the forest will rejuvenate itself, but the hunting problem remains.

West Castle Valley is part of the old Waterton Park. Vacation Alberta Corporation has applied to construct recreation and tourist facilities in the valley. The developers requested $20 million of public money to construct two hotels, two golf courses, 288 condominium units and an expanded ski resort. In December 1994, the Alberta government approved the building applications, but declined financial assistance. Most important, the government ruled that construction could not begin unless a Wildland Protection Area of 739 square kilometres is created.

Canada has an important opportunity to improve its record in the Waterton–Glacier area by effectively increasing the size of Waterton from 505 to about 1465 square kilometres. This improvement will require a concerted effort on the part of the governments of Alberta, British Columbia, and Canada. The major obstacle may well be the hunting issue. Nevertheless, if wildlife is to be safeguarded in an area defined as a protected wilderness, then in my view hunting must be eliminated.

BANFF

Banff, Jasper, Kootenay, and Yoho are Canada's four Rocky Mountain national parks. At more than 20,000 square kilometres, the parks are approximately the size of the Greater Yellowstone Ecosystem. In addition, the four parks are located next to several large provincial parks and wilderness areas in Alberta and British Columbia. There is tremendous potential for the establishment of a world-class protected area. However, Banff itself has become some kind of a black hole, or wildlife "mortality sink," and some of the adjacent provincial parks and wilderness areas still permit hunting and mining.

For historical reasons, management of the Rocky Mountain parks is difficult.

In 1900, the town [Banff] was an island of civilization amidst a seemingly unlimited wilderness. In 1950, the town was a community serving the park. In 1990, in the eyes of many, the park exists simply to attract people to the town.

R.W. SANDFORD
The Book of Banff, 1994

They are plagued by two national railways, two national highways, airports, several townsites (Banff, Lake Louise, Field, Jasper), and three world-class ski resorts and golf courses.

If Alston Chase thinks Yellowstone has been mismanaged, he should come to Banff. A sign in CPAWS's Calgary office states: "All the development in Yellowstone, Grand Canyon, Yosemite and Great Smoky Mountains National Parks does not add up to as much development as Banff contains." And new development plans are everywhere.

For the first time in a half-dozen years, I visited Banff in December 1994. Pictures did not prepare me for the event. It was shocking and ironic to stand at the corner of Bear and Wolf streets, and have the view obliterated by one of Banff's new shopping malls. Just west of Banff, the Trans-Canada Highway used to be a restricted speed zone. Today, the speed limit has been raised, and ugly but necessary fences have been installed to protect wildlife. At 100 kilometres per hour, I was unable to keep up with a loaded logging truck. I looked for the herd of mountain sheep above Vermilion Lakes, a tourist favourite for decades, only to learn later that the herd was extinct.

In Banff, Greg McKnight, executive director of the Banff–Lake Louise Tourism Bureau, says, "To remain competitive with the Whistlers and Vails of the world, we have to keep up." Pardon me? Has Parks Canada, or anyone else, asked why it is necessary for a wilderness park to be compared with, much less "keep up" with, world-class convention, golf, tennis, and ski resorts? Dave Day, a former superintendent of Banff National Park and now executive director of the pro-development Association for Mountain Parks Protection and Enjoyment, doubts that Banff's environment is as compromised as environmentalists say it is.

He should consider how Man plays God in Banff:

- From the perspective of wilderness protection, the Banff townsite cuts the park almost in quarters, that is, from east to west and from north to south.
- A town of 3500 in 1975, Banff has grown to 7500, and plans to grow to 10,000 plus in the short term.
- Construction in Banff National Park was worth $19,768,000 in 1980 and $105,692,000 in 1990.
- Elk, it is said, are too numerous near Banff townsite, and some may have to be removed. In the Bow River Valley the elk population is in decline. An average of 139 elk were *reported* killed each year from 1985 to 1992 by road and rail traffic.
- Moose, never plentiful but thought to number sixty in the 1950s, may now number just four. There are plans to reintroduce ten more.
- Black and grizzly bears are under extreme pressure in the Bow River Valley. It is thought that, unless conditions change, the black bear may be extirpated by 2010.

Banff National Park is an awful mess. Paul Paquet, a carnivore biologist at the University of Calgary, writes that "the Bow River Valley in Banff National Park, which comprises about 50 per cent of all usable habitat for large carnivores in the park, has been reduced to 10 per cent of its original effectiveness for wolves and grizzly bears because of development."

I have concentrated on development in the Bow River Valley and the Banff townsite. However, the broader question is the future of the four Rocky Mountain parks in the face of the current unprecedented invasion by humans. In addition to Banff, there are townsites at Jasper, Lake Louise, and Field. And the other river valleys in the four parks area have also been significantly compromised, including the headwaters of the Kootenay, Kicking Horse, North Saskatchewan, Athabasca, and Fraser rivers.

In our search for ways to mitigate the degradation of the four Rocky Mountain parks, we recognize that the current townsites are unlikely to shrink significantly and the international ski resorts are equally unlikely to disappear. Nevertheless, there are some partial solutions to the problem:

- Declare a complete moratorium on growth. Let's be clear, this means having a no-growth or a negative-growth economy for all time.
- Improve the wilderness quality of the Bow River Valley, and the other river valleys, by decommissioning a number of non-conforming man-made artifacts (roads, airports, etc.).
- Bring the surrounding provincial parks and wilderness areas up to the highest conservation standards.

KLUANE

The good news is that Kluane National Park Reserve is part of the largest international protected area in the world. Alaska's Glacier Bay National Park and Wrangell–St. Elias National Park combine with Kluane and British Columbia's Tatshenshini–Alsek Provincial Park to form a protected area of almost 10 million hectares. In addition, areas such as the Kluane Game Sanctuary serve to buffer these parks.

The bad news is that much of this huge area is scenic rock and ice. Part of the Kluane story is told by a sign in the park headquarters: "In Kluane, we are particularly interested in grizzly bear movements and home ranges as they relate to jurisdictional boundaries. Since only a small portion (18 per cent) of the park is suitable bear habitat and it is distributed as a long, narrow band along the park's eastern boundary, many bears frequent lands managed under different political jurisdictions. The impacts that management regimes surrounding the park are having on the park's grizzly population are currently unclear."

I visited the Kluane area in 1992 and 1994, taking spectacular raft trips on the Tatshenshini and Alsek rivers. I also spent several days driving around the park and found that, while there are a few roads and trails, they are primitive compared with those in Yellowstone, Waterton–Glacier, and Banff.

Kluane is part of a great wilderness. However, the park is in deep trouble even if park managers, territorial and federal politicians, and bureaucrats don't know it. The disease is Industrial Tourism and its signs are everywhere.

Haines Junction, the key town, is growing like a weed. There are demands and plans for better roads and tourist facilities. Each year there are more raft trips, airplane flights, helicopter flights, and greater use of snowmobiles. There are demands

Enter Glacier National Park and you enter the homeland of the grizzly bear. We are uninvited guests here, intruders, the bear our reluctant host. If he chooses, now and then, to chase somebody up a tree, or all the way to the hospital, that is the bear's prerogative. Those who prefer, quite reasonably, not to take such chances should stick to Disneyland in all its many forms and guises.
EDWARD ABBEY,
The Great Bear

for jet boats on the rivers — right in the heart of grizzly country.

Wildlife is already feeling the effect of this human onslaught. The grizzly bear is suffering, a reminder of the Yellowstone situation. Steve Herrero reports that "during 1990, 12 garbage-conditioned 'problem' grizzly bears were destroyed at the Haines Junction Dump. One grizzly bear was destroyed during 1991 in a 'control' action, and three grizzlies were shot illegally and died. . . . During the 1980s in the Slims River Valley there was a decrease in grizzly bear avoidance behaviour and an increase in neutral and approach behaviours, including 'serious' incidents. Management actions resulted in the death of five grizzly bears; five translocations, and area closures."

It is accepted as fact that the precipitous decline of moose and caribou populations in Kluane Game Sanctuary and the adjacent Aishihik area has been caused by road access and over-hunting by Native, non-Native, and tourist hunters alike. The decline in moose and caribou populations near Kluane has had two direct effects. First, there is the "wolf control" program. Second, some local people believe that the lack of game may be driving Native people to hunt not only in Kluane Game Sanctuary, but also in Kluane National Park Reserve. As for poaching, no one knows for sure what is going on!

The wolf control program is designed to kill 80 per cent of the wolves in Aishihik. It is believed that in the first two years of the program, 100 wolves were killed, at a cost of $1 million. CPAWS and WWF have opposed this program with all of their verbal and written strength. In my opinion, the Yukon government may be acting more to exterminate the wolf than to control it.

The governments involved have discovered the mother-lode of tourist dollars in Kluane, and they are promoting the same policies for it that have destroyed so much of Banff. Do Canadians have the will to save this wilderness area, or is it already too late?

I am one of several major donors to WWF's Endangered Spaces campaign. Among other projects, I have supported the publication of *Endangered Spaces*, *Islands of Hope*, and this book. While supporting the Endangered Spaces campaign across Canada, I have been particularly active in supporting projects in Alberta and British Columbia.

My chapter has focused on the concept of wilderness, the grizzly bear and the wolf, and the mismanagement of some of our greatest parks and wilderness areas. We have seen that these wilderness areas are not nearly as well protected as is generally believed.

Perhaps this chapter reveals that I have a certain passion for wilderness areas and for the protection of endangered species. It is my hope that, on a comparative basis, those responsible for park management can learn from the experience of others in the United States and Canada in order to avoid the mistakes of the past.

It is also my hope that Canada will significantly improve its conservation record by taking major steps to preserve wilderness in Waterton, the four Rocky Mountain parks, and Kluane. My final hope is that Canadians have the will to save wilderness before it is too late.

22 / Activist Roundtable: What Have We Learned?

PARTICIPANTS:

The Honourable Pauline Browes, P.C., former federal Secretary of State of the Environment and currently working as an environmental consultant
Adriane Carr, Executive Director and Campaigner, Western Canada Wilderness Committee
Harvey Mead, President, Union Québécoise pour la conservation de la nature
Robert (Bob) Sopuck, Executive Director, Sustainable Development Coordination Unit, Government of Manitoba

MODERATOR:
Pegi Dover, Vice-President, Communications, WWF Canada

PEGI: Is the Endangered Spaces campaign important for Canada?

PAULINE: Even a few years later, the *Endangered Spaces* book remains tremendously relevant. The campaign has been tremendously important in pushing politicians. It has also enhanced public awareness of the loss of wilderness and has underlined the real advantages for future generations.

HARVEY: I agree. Before the campaign, there wasn't an organized constituency. It was good that the primary focus was on the government agencies responsible for it and getting that commitment was a very positive step.

BOB: It is not as important as it once was, because it falls far short of the protection of ecological processes. The program has great difficulty in appreciating the dynamism in both the landscape and the economy. And the program is a little too resistant to change because of that.

PEGI: Would anyone like to respond to Bob?

PAULINE: When this campaign got under way, all the polls were showing that the number-one issue on people's minds was the environment. But that waned very quickly. I think that the recession has had a tremendous effect on this. I also agree that ecological processes are what we really need to look at.

HARVEY: I think the way Bob's putting it gets so big as to be unmanageable. It starts to encompass the whole effort on environment and economy issues.

BOB: The Endangered Spaces program is not helping us with the protection of processes. I am not advocating that it be expanded to deal with that. But, with the publicity and hype, there is a lot of public-sector time spent on the program and we are not getting our environmental bang for the buck.

PEGI: Speaking from the campaign's perspective, I think the campaign has a very targeted goal, and that, in a way, is its beauty. But we have always said that was only a part of getting to sustainability. In addition, we need sustainable use on the rest of the landscape to protect biodiversity. The Endangered Spaces campaign can't do it on its own. Adriane, what is your response to the first question in terms of whether the campaign is an important one for Canada?

ADRIANE: There's a major problem with the campaign. Deciding to establish a network of representative protected areas is like deciding to set aside some museum pieces. To really conserve the natural heritage and biodiversity of Canada, we can't just set aside an area per ecosystem unit, because one area cannot possibly serve to represent a whole ecosystem. And one area, if it is not linked to other areas or is not a large enough size to truly maintain the variety of life, won't work. I think that B.C. is probably the greatest success of the Endangered Spaces campaign and also its greatest failure. A really good example of that is on Vancouver Island, where they've set aside 13 per cent of the representative areas of the landscapes there. But they set aside a preponderance of alpine and sub-alpine regions and a very small proportion of valley-bottom old-growth forests.

HARVEY: The whole point that I would make for the Endangered Spaces campaign is that there has to be a lobby for preservation and, without that, we are weaker.

ADRIANE: The problem is that with the notion of representation comes a level of satisfaction when you've gained one representative area, and that doesn't cut it biologically. The goal ought to be to maintain integrity.

BOB: But I tell you, the program is a politically maximum goal. It is as far as it is going to go. Our framework in Manitoba is, quite definitively, sustainable development. We will not, in order to achieve any goals in the Endangered Spaces program, cause either economic or social hardships to communities.

ADRIANE: I'd like to point out that I recently talked with the author of the 12 per cent target, Jeff McNeely, and he confirmed that there is no confidence in the figure. He said that, in Canada, 12 per cent doesn't really make sense.

PEGI: The 12 per cent was meant only as a baseline in the sense that, if we do the job, it may be at least this much. We are just releasing two key science papers for the campaign next week, where we talk about ecological integrity, which is what I think you are getting at, Adriane. The question is whether a protected area can sustain ecological values over the long term. But, moving on, what do you think will be the cost if the goal of the Endangered Spaces campaign is not met?

HARVEY: We'll lose our museum. I have no problem thinking of these protected areas as museums. What we'll be faced with is human intervention in the entire landscape. I'd rather have museums than put my confidence in the ability of the human species or our governments to manage properly.

BOB: The cost will be quite minimal if the goal isn't met. Everybody is getting the notion of wilderness preservation and biodiversity totally confused. As I said earlier, you can have a preserved wilderness, and biodiversity can degrade. For example, in Grasslands National Park, we found out that, because grazing has been eliminated from the park, biodiversity is declining rapidly.

PEGI: Before Adriane speaks, can I just clarify something. Bob, are you saying that you don't believe protected areas are essential for attaining your goals of sustainable development in Manitoba?

BOB: Again it goes back to the definition of protected areas. Is WWF's goal the conservation of biodiversity or is it the preservation of wilderness? In many cases, they are two different things. So if we are going to have biodiversity conservation, we need, in many, many instances, human intervention, and the program specifically does not allow that. Therefore, in the private land zone of prairie Canada, your chances of achieving the goals of the Endangered Spaces Program are slim to nil.

ADRIANE: I just wanted to very quickly respond to that by saying that I don't think that the confusion is between protected areas and conservation of biodiversity. The confusion is between conservation of biodiversity and the rest of the land base that is not protected, which causes tremendous pressure on the protected areas. So, again, it's the broad land-use issues that need to be addressed.

PAULINE: I think that even in protected areas constant vigilance is required. In terms of the costs of the goal not being met, I want to point out that if we don't get these areas protected, they can be destroyed. It's the continual changes and economic activity that give an urgency to the program.

BOB: I completely reject the notion that the only two choices you have are protection or destruction. That's how the debate is always framed, both in the media and anywhere else, and this is where the politics comes in. Yet, in the southwest corner of Saskatchewan, antelope, deer, and all kinds of native birds are at record numbers. This is in spite of the fact there are ranching communities making a living from livestock in an environmentally sound way. The problem with the Endangered Spaces Program is that it has mistakenly framed the debate as to the choices between destruction or protection, and that there is nothing in between.

ADRIANE: For my part, I am absolutely convinced that unless we choose to set areas aside from any kind of major disturbance, we will lose the natural processes that give rise to the natural biodiversity that has been in those places.

HARVEY: I think that we could find both negative and positive examples of human intervention. I've been concerned about parks for thirty-some years. There are developers who have not been concerned about biodiversity for a lot longer than I've been around. I think our debate is whether or not protected areas are of any value. I guess I hear Bob saying they are not, or next to not. I'm just claiming that we want to save some because we are not confident that sustainable development is going to take place in the rest.

BOB: Okay, what we are arguing about is what wilderness advocates are really arguing against — change. And landscapes change, people change, and economics change. The key is the preservation of ecological processes.

ADRIANE: Bob, what is going on is change. The problem is, we are losing species at a rate of a thousand times faster than any natural process, because of human activity. So, as wilderness advocates, we are trying to stop the unnatural processes which are depleting biodiversity and creating the problems for life on this planet.

PEGI: Can we move on to the next question? I think we are probably not going to get this resolved today. What are the main strengths of the Endangered Spaces campaign in your view?

ADRIANE: What the Endangered Spaces campaign has done is raise public support for wilderness preservation. There are more people in Canada aware of the need to preserve and conserve biodiversity and natural wild areas because of the campaign than there were before.

HARVEY: I think it sets targets. If we don't set targets, you're never going to be able to aim at political intervention or be able to evaluate the result of your activity. One of the important elements of the Endangered Spaces campaign has been setting up plans for the representation of a federal or provincial system for parks.

PAULINE: From my perspective, I think that the idea that there was a plan in place and that politicians could see what needed to be done, was very important. It was a vision that people could see could be accomplished. It was the strength of that vision that really brought the Tri-Council together.

PEGI: Bob, any strengths?

BOB: I agree regarding the targets. Our premier himself made the commitment. The targets were a strength. Because the program was quite well defined, it was somewhat easy to sell to the resource industries.

I know I'm not the boss of the environment but what do you think you're doing? You think you're going to help all those poor animals with only 12% of Canada's land? Come on, put your act together!! Get with it, and not at the year 2000. Get with it at the year 1997!
A Grade 5 Student

ADRIANE: The setting of targets is both a strength and a weakness, so I'll address the strength part of it right now. Industry and governments were constantly asking us, "What would you be satisfied with? It seems you always want more, is there a limit?" So what the B.C. government did was set a limit, and I guess from that point of view, there's a strength in that. It offered people a reassurance around what would be the final decisions on land use. And that brings into the process an acceptance of a certain level of wilderness preservation.

PEGI: Okay. Let's address the weaknesses of the campaign.

PAULINE: I think that the issue became bigger than perhaps anyone expected. I don't think we anticipated the level of cooperation that would be required, particularly in terms of Native peoples. There is a real challenge for us of just how we do this in terms of joint ownership or joint protection. Another problem is that of growing costs. I think South Moresby hit the limit in terms of costs.

HARVEY: I think that clearly the program has underlined the weakness of museums, and I'm willing to live with this. I like visiting museums where I have no alternative, but it is a weakness that you can't even protect the areas unless proper development is going on outside. And at the same time you've got to be working on both.

ADRIANE: The issue of an ecologically sustainable network is really what I think was missed when the term "representative network" became the goal of the campaign. Because of this, it may be that the campaign doesn't achieve its overall goal of the protection of biodiversity.

BOB: And now we're looking at corridors and some other means of trying to improve the situation, even though this will be impossible to implement in many areas.

ADRIANE: Right from the very beginning, when Paul and I first met with Monte and he encouraged us to sign onto the campaign, which we did, we said that we're really worried about the 12 per cent. We felt it was viewed as a maximum and not a minimum. The campaign has built public support and political will and then capped it with that 12 per cent.

HARVEY: I would like to give the point of an Easterner who grew up out west, and say that I'm unable to imagine sustainable development in the redwoods or the Carmanah Valley or in the old-growth forests. I don't think that sustainable development has any meaning in the case of old-growth forests. So, what we are working with in the East is holding on to what we've got.

ADRIANE: This may be picky, but we have a problem with these report cards issued by the campaign each year. When you have a report card based on averaging how a country or jurisdiction is doing by ecological units, you can end up praising overall a government for doing well in one unit when they did dastardly in others. This is the case in B.C. But, a country that was really wise in managing its land would hang on to its very precious ecosystems, like wetlands and temperate forests. It may mean that we need to protect 40 per cent to truly protect biodiversity.

BOB: One of the big weaknesses of the program is inconsistent management. The grading and the definition of what counts as endangered spaces have been inconsistent. In P.E.I., when they submit lands for inclusion in the Endangered Spaces program, they include managed pine plantations, which we would never even consider submitting under the program, given the criteria that your office and my office agreed to. My last point is that the program doesn't acknowledge the people who live on the landscape. And so far, the Endangered Spaces program in the private-land landscape of prairie Canada has been doing a terrible job. I have in front of me a resolution by Manitoba's Union of Municipalities, opposing the inclusion of any more lands in the program. Wilderness advocates have made themselves enemies of the private landowner.

ADRIANE: I don't know of a major environment group that conceives of itself as an enemy of those who are trying to achieve sustainable economic development on the majority of the land base. We are not fashioning the debate as an either/or, as a win/lose in terms of preservation of the land base. It's industry that is fashioning that debate, and I think government, in many cases is promulgating it.

PEGI: Okay, let's move on to the key challenges or obstacles to meeting the Endangered Spaces goal over the next years.

BOB: Right now, rural Canadians are feeling very much under siege, both economically and environmentally. We see in the U.S. the rise of the wise-use movement, and that rural people in Canada are finally starting to get organized. They can buy a stewardship agenda like what Ducks Unlimited is doing under the North American Waterfowl Management Plan. But when it's presented to them as an either/or thing, there is a problem. For example, we have a community around Riding Mountain National Park that is more and more distrustful of park officials, and more and more contemptuous of the environmental community. What is new is that the rural people are starting to organize. Look at Share B.C. and the wise-use movement.

PEGI: I would like to ask Adriane to answer that same question in terms of the challenge and maybe how the Western Canada Wilderness Committee is dealing with rural concerns.

ADRIANE: I probably have a very different opinion of the rural movement. When Share B.C. was first organized, it worked out of a corporate forest-company headquarters. And its funding continues to come from forestry corporations. In terms of tapping into the local level, I think the Endangered Spaces Local Action Fund was a brilliant idea. But, I think that the campaign has lost touch with the grass-roots and needs to get back in touch. The way we win is to make sure that the voice of the people is behind wilderness protection.

PAULINE: I live in Scarborough, but I grew up on a farm on Rice Lake which is about 65 miles [about 100 kilometres] east of Toronto. First, I think that the recession and the economy have been a real challenge, because the government doesn't have any money. Also there are other things that people are putting their minds to instead of the environment. Also, the people of Canada are feeling as if their own empowerment has gone and that they are not in control of their own lives. There needs to be empowerment within the community, and one way to do this is through small, community-based projects.

BOB: But stewardship programs are not allowed to be "counted" under the program.

PEGI: Private stewardship initiatives can, and will, be part of the campaign, but the issue is that of long-term security. And that may be the sticking point.

HARVEY: The fact that there are examples of human intervention improving the ecosystem doesn't deny the fact that that's not the general experience. In Québec, we have 5.5 million hectares reserved in the north, and the mining potential of these lands is large. I hope Bob is not going to try and tell us that mining is a way to improve the ecosystem.

BOB: Mining can be done so that it does not compromise biodiversity.

HARVEY: The challenge in Québec in those northern reserves is going to be to work out an intelligent negotiating strategy with the First Nations. I don't think Endangered Spaces is going to be able to do much about it. The second challenge, in southern Québec, is going to be to find money to buy private lands for the park system and at the same time continue to work in the areas around what might be future parks, to ensure that development is compatible with the maintenance of biodiversity.

PAULINE: On the issue of private stewardship, I wanted to say that we were not able to get through, when I was in government, this tax benefit of donating land for environmental purposes. But it is something we still need to keep working on. [A tax incentive for the donation of private land was included in the federal Budget of February 1995, which was released subsequent to this discussion. — Ed.]

ADRIANE: I was going to raise two issues that are challenges. One of them is the cost of establishing new parks. And to me that comes down, in many cases, to the challenge of corporate control over the land base. In B.C., the government has sewn up the land base in tenure agreements with corporations. And there is an incredible opportunity for the B.C. government to change some of the terms of those agreements to permit the use of the land base for other purposes. The second challenge that I really see the campaign facing is one that was born out of the 12 per cent minimum having turned into the 12 per cent maximum. A good case where it has come up is in the Cariboo Mountains, where WWF was one of the key players in negotiating the Cariboo land-use decision which ended up being a 12 per cent decision that left out some key habitats.

PEGI: I would like to raise an issue that Pauline brought up about people's concerns being on the economy, the recession. Do you see the challenge of political will or public support being a strong one for us; do people still care about this issue?

ADRIANE: Well, our membership and donations are going up.

PAULINE: I think the partnership is important. I think that if we are expecting government to do it all, it's not going to happen. Depending on government to do a lot of this is not realistic.

HARVEY: My sense is that we've succeeded in incorporating the environment into the economic and social sectors. Even the private sector is willing to accept the reduction of subsidies that have led to unsustainable development.

BOB: A good point regarding the program is that we don't need any more money to fulfil the goals of the Endangered Spaces program, especially in our Crown-land zone. Harvey's point that the environment is being considered in economic decisions is absolutely true, and it's one of the things that I've been most gratified about. On the other hand, I have yet to see the environmental community come out on behalf of development in some areas.

HARVEY: That's not our job.

PAULINE: I am not that pessimistic as it relates to environment. I think that there are going to be jobs opening up in environmental industries. But to set up a national park costs taxpayers money.

It is with pleasure that I inform you officially of the decision of the Division of Mission in Canada of the United Church of Canada to endorse the Canadian Wilderness Charter. Please know of our support for your continued efforts in this critically important work.
GERRY HOPKIRK, General Secretary, Division of Mission in Canada, The United Church of Canada

ADRIANE: There are other ways to approach it, too, in that there are costs associated with the current economic developments that we tend to ignore. And we don't do a fair trade-off in terms of the costs and the price-tag associated with protection. For example, in Port Alberni, the forest industry has laid off 1400 people over the last five years, and the unemployment insurance bill is $27 million a year.

PEGI: What you are saying is that those layoffs aren't a result of protected areas but technology changes.

ADRIANE: Exactly. But the point is that there is a tremendous potential for eco-tourism development in the west-coast area. There are 500,000 visitors a year that go to Pacific Rim National Park and they have one wilderness trail to hike on. There's got to be a creative solution at the regional level which allows the protection of that natural ecosystem while deriving economic-development benefits.

PEGI: Let's move on in terms of key strategies for the next five years. What needs to be done if we are to accomplish this goal?

HARVEY: I would hope that the next five years might involve some attempt by WWF to develop monies to purchase private lands. In southern Québec, we need funding to buy these lands.

PAULINE: I think we need to look at heritage parks or small pieces of geography. And I guess maybe it's because I'm in southern Ontario, where there isn't a big swathe of wilderness land that's left. We need to go for the smaller pockets.

PEGI: What motivates you to work on these issues at all?

PAULINE: Well, I guess it's my two wonderful grandchildren, and I feel completely committed that I have to keep going on this.

HARVEY: I'm an unabashed romantic. I've been involved in parks since I was a little kid, and I'm fifty-five, and I'm not giving it up. It's part of what makes me who I am. So my motivation is that I still have a sense of wonder, when I can dive in a reef or I can walk in a forest or hike a mountain range.

BOB: My motivation in dealing with these issues primarily stems from the fact that I own a piece of land myself. And I find myself totally obsessed with finding solutions so that human beings can interact with the environment and maintain diverse ecosystems. I am an unabashed advocate for rural life. I am almost desperate to do whatever we can to preserve that life in all its diversity.

ADRIANE: I guess like Pauline, I think first of my children. I have an eleven-year-old daughter and a seven-year-old son, and I think about their future all the time. I wonder if our planet is going to give them the opportunity that I had when I was growing up. And my memories of my own childhood were walking down a river in the Rocky Mountains, fishing with my dad, going out and swimming in wilderness lakes. I get my sense of self and peace by being in the wild. I feel so privileged as a Canadian that we have the opportunity to get out somewhere beyond humanness into a place that makes me connect to the source of what I think life is all about.

PEGI: Thank you, all.

23 / Live and Let Live

STAN ROWE

Behold the busy beaver, toothy mascot of Team Canada. It logs the land beside lakes and rivers; so do we. It dams streams and creates reservoirs, building comfortable waterfront lodges; so do we. Settled down, home and food assured, beavers produce surplus progeny; so do we. And when they have used up the poplar-and-willow resource in one place, they simply move on and do it all over again. Here apparently is the ideal fur-coated totem for a northern entrepreneurial society.

But look a little deeper and the similarity in habits and customs between symbol and nation fades. Pursuing its instinctive goals, the beaver clan largely lets the wild world be and needs no Endangered Spaces campaign. Not so the human clan, pushed in destructive directions by the promptings of a culture that has severed its ecological roots and chosen not to be-at-one with Nature, with Planet Earth.

The beaver colony, like the human community, plays an active role in shaping its environment — but within limits. Patch clear-cutting of aspen is a common practice, but wholesale devastation of forests over hill and dale is eschewed. Dams and lodges are built of Earth materials to meet vital needs of foraging and home comfort, not to satisfy extravagant wants. The goal is sufficiency in food and shelter, not conspicuous or excessive consumption. But perhaps the most striking difference between societies of *Homo sapiens canadensis* and *Castor canadensis canadensis* is the tolerance exhibited by the beaver towards other users of its home terrain: the dams and ponds and their surrounds. Beavers participate as members of the ecosystems they design and use, without commandeering them and marking them "off limits" to everything else. Mutual tolerance permits all species to co-evolve. This is the way of the world that allowed our own vulnerable ancestors to survive. By contrast, in modern human societies the indiscriminate killing of everything non-human is condoned, a rejection of the primary Law of Nature: "Live and let live."

Now and again this law stirs into consciousness as a deeply felt urge to perpetuate the undomesticated world in all its strange and marvellous diversity by simply letting it be. This powerful source of the preservation ethic is positively expressed as actions taken and, especially, actions curbed to ensure the continuance of wild Nature. The most significant consequence of a successful Endangered Spaces campaign will be general acceptance of the idea that values are inherent in all parts of Earth, quite apart from human purposes, and that the liberation of Earth spaces from human control is good in itself — with the happy side-effect that, biologically and ecologically, it will do us good too.

Given reliable reasons, humans can relearn to be as forbearing as the fur-bearer in attitude and action relative to the rest of the world. Fortunately, a solid ecological rationale for tolerance and the preservation of non-human Nature has developed in the last few decades. But even as it gathers strength, drawing from both science and philosophy, its opposition also grows. In this chapter I examine the new ecological world-view and discuss obstacles in the way of its acceptance, as well as reasons for the disregard and disparagement of the changed way of living it implies.

BARRIERS TO KNOWING WHO WE ARE

Because we are social animals, culture shapes the content of our minds, which in turn determines the way we view reality. Thus the conscious faculty has been likened to a piece of smoked glass that dims ecological understanding of our Earth-relatedness, just as it intercepts the light of instinctive intelligence. Full illumination requires cleansing the windows of perception, opening consciousness to the wild nature that is *outside and around us* while also letting the wild nature that is *in us* shine through. Both are important as Tsung Ping, a fourth century A.D. Chinese landscape painter explained:

> Landscapes have a material existence, and yet reach into a spiritual domain. The wild beauty of their form, the peaks and precipices rising sheer and high, the cloudy forest lying dense and vast, have brought to the wise and virtuous recluses of the past an unending pleasure, a joy which is of the soul and of the soul alone. One approach to the Tao (the Way) is *by inward concentration alone* — another, almost the same, is *through the beauty of mountains and water.* (emphasis added)

Note the two converging paths to enlightenment, the inner psychological and the outer ecological. The British physicist David Bohm was intrigued by the inspiration that comes from "inward concentration" and by the road-blocks that a high-tech culture throws up to deter us from this path. The more we surround ourselves with self-made things and the more we immerse ourselves in technology, the more we enter a world of our own thoughts. Self-domesticated, we live in the virtual reality of our heads — as if watching TV 24 hours a day. During waking hours, the mind's contents are mostly busy ideas that have little to do with instinctive promptings from within or with sensations and rhythms from outside our cultural skins. City living, for example, requires that there be many rules and regulations with rewards and punishments, plus various other inducements to be on time, to meet schedules, to obey orders, to suppress natural feelings, and to cooperate in boring and unpleasant jobs.

Memory, the repository of day-to-day cultural themes, functions like a programmed computer disk that flashes automatic thoughts on the mind-screen when word-buttons are pressed. Like a city "strip" at night, our waking minds are constantly lit up with blazing signs that prevent perception of the moon and stars. Thus clear-minded understanding of ourselves and our fundamental problems is blocked out of consciousness. The harmony that in simpler times existed between reason and emotions is upset. The solution, Bohm suggested, begins with small groups of people supporting one another in a common purpose: to still the clamour of thought/memory so that the subtle subliminal intelligence of every mind can rise healingly to the surface. In effect this is to regain the fresh at-one-with-the-worldness of the child.

Clearing away the mind's fussy clutter, quietly meditating until the mud settles, is an ancient technique rediscovered and practised by many in today's secular society as a means of reducing stress. That it works raises the question of the nature of the healing insights that emerge when the clamorous mind is stilled. Logic points to instinctive recollections of a different way of being engraved in organs, tissues, cells, and genes, to feelings of belonging in a world where our lineage goes back to the beginning of time. Human nature evolved in companionship with Earth–Nature, implying a profound resonance between the two. This suggests the second path to enlightenment broached by Tsung Ping, the outward-looking perspective that sees into "the beauty of mountains and water." Appreciation of the superb world revealed through the senses provides a healthy and necessary balance to the inward gaze. The latter's goal too easily becomes the impossible quest of self-benefit alone — at the risk of forfeiting the world.

Ecology points to the importance of Nature in which all organisms, including humans, are embedded. From this a new philosophical perspective emerges — variously called Ecosophy, Earth wisdom, or Earth spirituality — orienting people to their ecological roots, and encouraging a wide and deep communion turned outward to embrace the whole Earth. When we understand ourselves as parts of Earth, recognizing that the purpose of parts is to assure the integrity and health of the whole, then new possibilities for healing personal, social, and environmental ills are revealed.

Believing is seeing. The way we picture ourselves and understand our external relations to Earth is a direct consequence of the belief-systems or paradigms, the stories and myths, by which our culture is defined. All myths of who we are and where we came from are necessarily anthropomorphic, meaning always formed from human viewpoints, but this does not mean that they have to be anthropocentric, focused exclusively on humanity. In fact, the most coherent and convincing account of genesis so far fabricated is Earth-centred rather than people-centred. In the following sections I examine some of the archaic fables that thwart recognition of our Earth-born status, blocking the instinctive allegiance owed by everyone to the world.

OLD-TIME RELIGION, HIERARCHY, AND PATRIARCHY

Our bodies are made from surface materials of the planet: blood saline like sea water; bones from limestone and phosphate sediments upraised in mountains; flesh from soils, humus, plants, and other animals. One might expect that religions would celebrate this manifest Earth origin.

Instead, by tradition, our Earth-source has been judged a prison of the soul, a regrettable stopover on the route to somewhere else — namely, Heaven. Ours is the legacy of ancient theologians who closed their eyes to the wonders of existence in this beautiful world and instead sought salvation from it.

A belief that the first man and woman broke the harmony of the universe, a theory of original sin and suffering, turned attention away from Earth towards a

Man–God rift and the need to mend it. Add to this the dogma of God as transcendent — outside rather than in the world — and the stage was set for denial that Earth too has its divinity.

Finally, the assignment of special status to people as spiritual beings, with an eternal destiny that placed them above other members of the created world, alienated them further from Nature. Yet surely our fulfilment is not in isolated grandeur, ourselves set above the rest of creation, but rather in intimacy with the Earth community to which we are tied physically and spiritually. True to our ecological roots, we should celebrate the connections between human body/mind and Earth rather than rejecting them as evils that stand in the way of a "more spiritual" and "higher" existence.

Implicit in that old-time religion with its exaltation of spirit-soul over body-Earth, is the idea of grades of importance in a stratified universe, with God at the top and Earth at the bottom. This is "hierarchical thinking," a hierarch, in the original Greek, being the chief priest presiding over priests of lower rank. Our culture is shot through and through with ideas of lower and higher, not only in society, but in the wider world. In the latter, the usual sequence from lowest to highest begins with "environment" — the inorganic parts of Earth: rocks, soils, water, atmosphere — followed by "life" wrongly conceived as only organic things: microorganisms, plants, animals, primates, *Homo sapiens*. Within society the sequence is animal pets, children, women, and Man.

A high degree of inventiveness was needed to justify the position of the human male at the top of the pyramid of excellence. But the patriarchal sages who wrote the book of Genesis were equal to the task. Masters of fiction, they contrived to have Adam created first, with Eve born later out of his body — the female out of the male — a reversal of the usual system of animal propagation. Furthermore, they made Eve the villain who tempted Adam with the fruit of the tree of knowledge, leading to expulsion from the Garden of Eden. The blame for humanity's punishment — the switch from happy fruit-pickers to sorry farmers — is squarely laid at woman's door. By such fables men's domination of society has been justified.

Patriarchy, the very model of hierarchical thinking, is entrenched not only in myth but also in language and custom. Its malign effects include the unjust treatment of women and of Earth, the two perceived as sharing a sensual and sinful physicality that distracts men from pursuit of their more ethereal aspirations.

Members of the male sex elevate in importance what they do best: *things of the mind*. Occasionally men conceive, but only ideas and artifacts, the content and trappings of culture: theologies, ideologies, the laws of science, the imaginative fancies of the arts, the conception and making of contraptions, giving birth to machines. When given the chance, women can do these things too, but additionally they can conceive and bear children, *things of the body* impossible for men. Small wonder that patriarchy elevates things-of-the-mind over things-of-the-body, intellect over feeling, culture over nature. When mind and its rationality are assumed to be superior to the body and its feelings, then praise of the former as "good" requires that the latter be vilified as "bad." Mind-soul is exalted as pure and immortal, reaching towards heaven and spiritual happiness. Body-nature is denigrated as impure and mortal, liable to sins of the appetites, to death, and to physical torture in Hell —

hence, the in-built tendency in present-day patriarchal society to disparage the body with its feelings and emotions, to belittle the carnal female, to ridicule in the male any "feminine" sensibilities, and to disdain Earth-nature as no more than "natural resources," "raw materials," "environment."

Crime statistics leave little doubt that men are more unruly than women. Physical size and testosterone make the male potentially more dangerous than the female, particularly in a society that condones violence. From such facts and the behaviour patterns of selected animals, sociobiology and neo-Darwinism argue that men are by nature dominating, that patriarchal society merely reflects biological reality. Yet non-violent cultures have existed in which the sexes were partnered socially without domination, where biological differences were not judged in terms of superiority and inferiority, where Earth and body were revered as the source of life and bounty.

From all of this the hopeful conclusion can be drawn that cultural beliefs are the villains, fostering patriarchy and the violence that goes with the presumed "right to power." Provided with an ecologically truer myth, humans — female and male — are capable of living in partnership with Earth. Preservation of the non-humanized world is the way to begin.

HUMAN-CENTREDNESS

Escape from salvational theologies, from patriarchy and its particular ideas of hierarchy, is not to escape all mythic dangers. Vanity and excessive pride in being members of *Homo sapiens* and in being "alive" relative to the worthless "dead" stuff of Earth are misconceptions that also cloud the vision of who we really are. Homocentrism, species-centred humanism, takes it for granted that people are so important that all else on Earth must serve or be sacrificed to their needs and wants. This is the fixed idea behind much public policy.

Protecting the "environment" — that is, Nature, the Ecosphere and its terrestrial ecosystems — is usually justified because its deterioration affects the welfare of people, not because of the intrinsic importance of the living globe as a thing-in-itself. Thus the Law Reform Commission recommended that extravagant instances of environmental pollution be made criminal offences, because of their adverse effects on human health! Here is the reason, too, for the sociological component of environmental impact assessments, heavy with economic analyses of risks and cost/benefits. Behind them lies the assumption that environmental impacts merit scrutiny only if somewhere, sometime, they adversely affect *people*. Again and again it needs repeating that preserving and protecting Earth is an end in itself, not a crass attempt to ensure the economic and cultural survival of one species.

Consider the debate about the optimum size of the country's population. Few, if any, doubt that the topic is all about people and their numbers. Immigration asks, "What should the population of Canada be in 2025?" A chorus answers, "thirty million, or perhaps 35 million, or maybe 40 million." Only a few voices for the wilderness suggest perhaps human population should decline to 15, 10, or 5 million, in the interests of also supporting 250,000 black bears, 25,000 grizzlies, 15,000 wolverines, and so on for each of the thousands of companion species who also make this land their home.

Globally, deserts are on the march, forest lands degrading, biodiversity declining, yet burgeoning human numbers that degrade Earth and drive other species to extinction elicit little public outcry. Instead, we hear the soothing suggestion that better distribution of land resources, along with education and the economic betterment of women, will take care of future population problems. Besides, are not humans the ultimate and final creation for which the world was made? Surely there cannot be too many of us!

Stephen J. Gould reminds humanity — gigantic not only in numbers but also in technologic appendages — that in this world "small is beautiful," and indeed essential. Today is not the Age of Man, he says, but the Age of Bacteria, "as it was in the beginning, is now, and ever shall be." Bacteria, not humans, are the backbone of Earth's ecosystems. More than this, research reveals that bacteria are also the building blocks of "higher" organisms. Without them, no people. Our brains, for example, are apparently confederacies of spirochetes — and that should make everyone think!

Nature knows no hierarchy of species-importance, with the big and brainy confirmed as the apex of creation. Therefore, care and appreciation of species other than our own is a step forward. But simply widening the circle of *organic* importance leads to another trap: biocentrism. Enthralled with organisms, from bacteria to chimpanzees, people are prone to accept them as the only important phenomena, crediting organisms rather than Earth with the enigmatic essence called "life."

BIOCENTRISM OR ECOCENTRISM?

The popular journal *Scientific American* recently devoted its pages to a series of articles under the banner "Life in the Universe." Throughout the text the words "life" and "organisms" were used interchangeably as synonyms, which they are not.

"Life" is an immaterial organizing principle whose source can as logically be attributed to the outside as to the inside of organisms. A viable environment is prerequisite to a viable organism. Curiously, none of the authors acknowledged that organisms exhibit "aliveness" only in the context of Earth and Earth's ecosystems. The vitality of the latter is unrecognized.

This is as if, by analogy, everyone agreed that only a tree trunk's cambial layer is "alive," while the bole of bark and wood that envelops and supports the cambium is "dead," or that only the parts inside the chitinous exoskeletons of insects are "alive." Favoured with the outside view of such creatures we perceive them to be totally "alive."

The separation of "living" organisms from their supportive "dead" environments is a fallacy, fostered by the absence, until recently, of an outside world-view. The prejudice is based on reduction: thinking small instead of thinking big, emphasizing parts and ignoring wholes.

Ecology refutes this kind of reductionism. Both organic and inorganic are functional parts of ecosystems, of which the largest one accessible to direct experience is the global Ecosphere. To attribute the organizing principle "life" to Earth — to the Ecosphere and its aquatic and terrestrial ecosystems — makes more sense than attempting to locate it in organisms divorced from their indispensable air, water, and rock-derived sediments.

The "biocentric" view misleads in assuming that organisms are more important than their ecosystems, species more important than Earth. A realistic "ecocentric" perspective places Earth first and species second, ecosystems before their parts, eco-diversity before biodiversity. Endangered Spaces must take precedence over Endangered Species, otherwise the latter will soon be museum pieces (and ourselves Exhibit A).

CELEBRATING EARTH

The time has come to renounce past errors and to celebrate this planet whose creativity and mystery surpass human understanding. Neither organism nor superorganism, the Ecosphere and its ecosystems are SUPRA-organismic: magnificent levels of organization embracing organisms but far more important than they.

Humans have demeaned the Earth in various ways: naming it a "vale of tears" compared to an imagined, other-worldly paradise, equating it disparagingly with the female sex and debasing both. We have designated the Earth to be "our environment" — no more than a God-given storehouse of wealth to be unsustainably developed for the human economy.

Earth is also demeaned in more subtle ways when "life" is denied it and conferred only on organisms. When mental doors are barred against the idea of aliveness everywhere, Earth and its ecosystem spaces lose their worth, and can be treated carelessly. This conceptual denial clearly stands in the way of a healthy human-nature symbiosis, exemplified nationally by a lethargic approach to the protection of networks of representative natural areas.

To return to the diligent beaver, its tolerance of other members of the plant and animal community makes it a fitting emblem of the forbearance philosophy. The symbolism is further enhanced when the beaver is perceived as a part and partner in the pond-and-forest ecosystems that are home to it. The lesson for people is that we, too, should be cooperating components of a world far larger, grander, and more vital than any human enterprise.

Earth and its creative spaces, with all their marvellous contents, should be the primary focus of human veneration, care, and celebration. Wherever they are on Earth, here and now, all people can practise the live-and-let-live philosophy. Preservation of Earth-spaces is one vitally important activity to which everyone, everywhere, can contribute.

Postscript to a Hope

The international accounting firm Price Waterhouse has estimated that a 10 per cent reduction in the annual allowable cut from British Columbia's forests would result in more jobs lost than all those lost so far from the collapse of Canada's East Coast fishery.

If true, this cold statistical statement is pregnant with meaning for the future of Canada's wild places. It reveals how desperately dependent the short-term Canadian economy and people's every-day lives have become on abusing Nature. It also explains why it is going to be very difficult to rescue virtually anything in a wild state over the next few years. How hideously illogical it is to be told that, if we do not continue to overexploit our forests, the economic consequences will be worse than when we overexploited our fish.

It is occurring to an increasing number of people that this kind of thinking has got everything backwards and is a prescription for disaster. Instead, would it not make sense to start asking about the positive consequences of humans living within the carrying capacity of Earth's ecosystems? Should we not be estimating what the toll will be if we *do* continue to overexploit our forests, or how much better things would have been had we *not* wiped out the fishery? Rather than kowtowing to the short-term consequences of discontinuing abuse, shouldn't we be asking what we can do now to get on a more sustainable path which does not rely on running down Nature's capital or sacrificing wilderness?

These are weighty questions which have become mired in abstract arguments over "sustainable development," short-term versus long-term economic benefits, and transition strategies to move us literally from an exploitative, unsustainable stage of civilization to one based on an acceptance of Nature's limits to growth. Central to the debate is controlling human population growth, everywhere. Meanwhile, while we humans ruminate about the Earth-undermining forces we have set afoot, Nature looks on from the sidelines as the principal casualty.

Perhaps we aren't going to solve the problem of sustainability at such a theoretical macro-level, but through very practical specific commitments around which a majority of people can rally. I believe the Endangered Spaces goal is just such a commitment. If we agree that we want to establish a network of protected areas which adequately represent the biodiversity of Canada (and apparently we do), then in order to achieve that goal we are going to have to change our ways profoundly. Put less grandly: "If you really *want* it, folks, there are certain things you have to do to *get* it."

A popular commitment to protecting the beauty and inspirational power of wild Nature could serve as the catalyst for a host of changes needed to ensure the long-term sustainability of human society. In effect, the Endangered Spaces campaign is an invitation to back into sustainability through the door of wilderness. This certainly gives new meaning to Thoreau's oft-quoted phrase, "In Wildness is the preservation of the World."

To illustrate these points using the specific example cited above, and based on research now published by WWF Canada, I am convinced that we cannot establish an adequate network of protected areas in British Columbia without reducing the annual allowable cut by at least 10 per cent, in fact by a lot more, and in many other forested provinces as well. In this case, then, the implications of meeting a bare-minimum commitment to wilderness through the Endangered Spaces goal would bring about far-reaching changes elsewhere in B.C. society and in the provincial economy. I am equally convinced that had we established an adequate network of marine protected areas off Canada's east coast, including areas to protect critical stages in the life-cycle of the northern cod, we would not have reduced that stock to commercial extinction. Here again, the catalytic commitment would have been to maintaining representative samples of ocean ecosystems in a natural state. But the consequences would have extended broadly and positively into the regional economy and day-to-day lives of those inhabiting coastal communities.

To get modern society on to this new path, it is necessary, but not enough, to be dissatisfied with our current course. That dissatisfaction must be linked with the *hope* that things can be better. Otherwise, we are left only with cynicism. Those hopes, in turn, can be expressed through dreams and measurable goals such as those of the Endangered Spaces campaign, which will be achieved only through practical plans such as those outlined in Section Two of this book.

In contemplating the meagre Draba — "the smallest flower that blows" — Aldo Leopold declared it a "postscript to a hope," because the Draba so often goes unnoticed: "He who hopes for spring with upturned eye never sees so small a thing as Draba. He who despairs of spring with downcast eye steps on it unknowing. He who searches for spring with his knees in the mud, finds it, in abundance."

The last chance has come for Canadians to pursue our hopes in practical terms and to get involved by "searching for spring with our knees," as Leopold put it. Like the humble Draba, some wilderness is still out there to be "found in abundance," if we are prepared to do what is necessary to identify and protect it. But we have run out of time. As the legal owners of Canada's endangered spaces, we can exert the care and responsibility associated with that ownership now, or we can continue to treat our natural birthright as a commodity to be sold and eventually lost forever.

Today, on a hike with my son in early spring from our cabin on Loon Lake, I contemplate a small, persistent wintergreen plant with dark green waxen leaves and an

WWF Canada's Endangered Spaces campaign is an ambitious program stretching over ten years to complete a comprehensive system of protected areas throughout the country that will ensure the survival of Canada's rich and diverse biological heritage. The success of the campaign will be to Canada's immediate and lasting advantage, but it will also be making a significant contribution to the maintenance of global biological diversity.
PRINCE PHILIP, 1989

alert red berry, even under the snow. Reflecting on Leopold's Draba, I ask myself what this tiny brave offering of Nature tells us about ponderings on the future of human society. Simply this: if we can extend our concern to such small creatures by saving adequate wild places for them, we might well save ourselves.

Monte Hummel

Appendices

Canadian Wilderness Charter

1. Whereas humankind is but one of millions of species sharing planet Earth and whereas the future of the Earth is severely threatened by the activities of this single species,
2. Whereas our planet has already lost much of its former wilderness character, thereby endangering many species and ecosystems,
3. Whereas Canadians still have the opportunity to complete a network of protected areas representing the biological diversity of our country,
4. Whereas Canada's remaining wild places, be they land or water, merit protection for their inherent value,
5. Whereas the protection of wilderness also meets an intrinsic human need for spiritual rekindling and artistic inspiration,
6. Whereas Canada's once vast wilderness has deeply shaped the national identity and continues to profoundly influence how we view ourselves as Canadians,
7. Whereas Canada's aboriginal peoples hold deep and direct ties to wilderness areas throughout Canada and seek to maintain options for traditional wilderness use,
8. Whereas protected areas can serve a variety of purposes including:
   a) preserving a genetic reservoir of wild plants and animals for future use and appreciation by citizens of Canada and the world,
   b) producing economic benefits from environmentally sensitive tourism,
   c) offering opportunities for research and environmental education,
9. Whereas the opportunity to complete a national network of protected areas must be grasped and acted upon during the next ten years, or be lost,

We agree and urge:
1. That governments, industries, environmental groups and individual Canadians commit themselves to a national effort to establish at least one representative protected area in each of the natural regions of Canada by the year 2000,
2. That the total area thereby protected comprise at least 12 per cent of the lands and waters of Canada as recommended in the World Commission on Environment and Development's report *Our Common Future,*
3. That public and private agencies at international, national, provincial, territorial and local levels rigorously monitor progress toward meeting these goals in Canada and ensure that they are fully achieved, and
4. That federal, provincial and territorial government conservation agencies on behalf of all Canadians develop action plans by 1990 for achieving these goals by the year 2000.

How You Can Help

The authors of *Protecting Canada's Endangered Spaces* hope that it will inspire readers to make their own contribution to completing a representative wilderness network by the year 2000. These contributions can take many forms:

- If you haven't already done so, join the 600,000 individuals who have signed the Canadian Wilderness Charter, showing their support for the Endangered Spaces Campaign goal. Call World Wildlife Fund Canada at 1-800-26-PANDA for a copy of this important document.

- Use the "power of the pen" and write to your member of parliament and your member of the provincial or territorial government. Urge them to push their ministers and governments to complete representative networks of protected areas in your jurisdiction by the year 2000.

- Become active locally and save an endangered space. Join one of the 300 groups which are now part of the Endangered Spaces Campaign coalition. Many of these groups tackle site-specific conservation challenges, and could use your help.

Monte Hummel
President,
WORLD WILDLIFE FUND CANADA
Suite 504, 90 Eglinton Avenue East
Toronto, Ontario
M4P 2Z7

Conservation Organizations

NATIONAL ORGANIZATIONS

Assembly of First Nations
5th Floor, 55 Murray Street
Ottawa, Ontario
K1N 5M3
Phone: 613-241-6789
Fax: 613-241-5808

Canadian Arctic Resources Committee
1 Nicholas Street, Suite 1100
Ottawa, Ontario
K1N 7B7
Phone: 613-241-7379
Fax: 613-241-2244

Canadian Council on Ecological Areas
    Secretariat c/o Lee Warren
Place Vincent Massey
351 St. Joseph Boulevard
Hull, Québec
K1A 0H3
Phone: 819-953-1444
Fax: 819-953-6612

Canadian Environmental Law
    Association
517 College Street, Suite 410
Toronto, Ontario
M6G 4A2
Phone: 416-960-2284
Fax: 416-960-9392

Canadian Nature Federation
1 Nicholas Street, Suite 520
Ottawa, Ontario
K1N 7B7
Phone: 613-562-3447
Fax: 613-562-3371

Canadian Parks and Wilderness
    Society (CPAWS)
401 Richmond Street West, Suite 380
Toronto, Ontario
M5V 3A8
Phone: 416-979-2720
Fax: 416-979-3155

Canadian Wildlife Federation
2740 Queensview Drive
Ottawa, Ontario
K2B 1A2
Phone: 613-721-2286
Fax: 613-721-2902

Greenpeace
185 Spadina Avenue, 6th Floor
Toronto, Ontario
M5T 2C5
Phone: 416-597-8408
Fax: 416-597-8422

Inuit Circumpolar Conference
170 Laurier Street West, Suite 504
Ottawa, Ontario
K1P 5V5
Phone: 613-563-2642
Fax: 613-565-3089

Marine Protected Areas Network
c/o Martin Willison
Biology Department,
Dalhousie University
Halifax, Nova Scotia
B3G 3J4
Phone: 902-494-3514

Nature Conservancy of Canada
110 Eglinton Avenue West, 4th Floor
Toronto, Ontario
M4R 2G5
Phone: 416-932-3202
Fax: 416-932-3208

Probe International
225 Brunswick Avenue
Toronto, Ontario
M5S 2M6
Phone: 416-964-9223
Fax: 416-964-8239

Sierra Club of Canada
1 Nicholas Street, Suite 620
Ottawa, Ontario
K1N 7B7
Phone: 613-241-4611
Fax: 613-241-2292

Wildlife Habitat Canada
7 Hinton Avenue, Suite 200
Ottawa, Ontario
K1Y 4P1
Phone: 613-722-2090
Fax: 613-722-3318

World Wildlife Fund Canada /
Fonds mondial pour la nature
90 Eglinton Avenue East, Suite 504
Toronto, Ontario
M4P 2Z7
Phone: 416-489-8800
Fax: 416-489-3611

BRITISH COLUMBIA

B.C. Spaces for Nature
Box 673
Gibsons, British Columbia
V0N 1V0
Phone: 604-886-8605
Fax: 604-886-3768

B.C. Wild
Box 2241, Main Post Office
Vancouver, British Columbia
V6B 3W2
Phone: 604-669-4802
Fax: 604-669-6833

CPAWS — B.C. Chapter
Box 33918, Station D
Vancouver, British Columbia
V6J 4L7
Phone: 604-685-7445

Sierra Club of Western Canada
1525 Amelia Street
Victoria, British Columbia
Phone: 604-386-5255
Fax: 604-386-4453

Western Canada Wilderness
   Committee
20 Water Street
Vancouver, British Columbia
V6B 1A5
Phone: 604-683-8220
Fax: 604-683-8229

ALBERTA

Alberta Wilderness Association
Box 6398, Station D
Calgary, Alberta
T2P 2E1
Phone: 403-283-2025
Fax: 403-270-2743

Bow Valley Naturalists
Box 1693
Banff, Alberta
T0L 0C0
Phone / Fax: 403-762-4160

CPAWS — Calgary-Banff Chapter
1019 Fourth Avenue S.W.
Calgary, Alberta
T2P 0K8
Phone / Fax: 403-232-6686

CPAWS — Edmonton Chapter
Box 52031, 8210 - 109 Street
Edmonton, Alberta
T6G 2T5
Phone: 403-453-8658
Fax: 403-453-8553

Federation of Alberta Naturalists
Box 1472
Edmonton, Alberta
T5J 2K5
Phone: 403-453-8629
Fax: 403-453-8553

SASKATCHEWAN

CPAWS — Saskatchewan Chapter
Box 914
Saskatoon, Saskatchewan
S7K 3M4
Phone: 306-665-7655
Fax: 306-665-3312

Nature Saskatchewan
P.O. Box 4348
Regina, Saskatchewan
S4P 3W6
Phone: 306-780-9273
Fax: 306-780-9263

Saskatchewan Environmental Society
P.O. Box 1372
Saskatoon, Saskatchewan
S7K 3N9
Phone: 306-665-1915
Fax: 306-665-2128

MANITOBA

CPAWS — Manitoba Chapter
Box 344
Winnipeg, Manitoba
R3C 2H5
Phone / Fax: 204-237-5947

Manitoba Naturalists Society
63 Albert Street, Suite 401
Winnipeg, Manitoba
R3B 1G4
Phone / Fax: 204-943-9029

TREE
25 Rue St. Pierre
Winnipeg, Manitoba
R3V 1J5
Phone: 204-269-7477
Fax: 204-261-0984

ONTARIO

CPAWS — Wildlands League Chapter
401 Richmond Street West, Suite 380
Toronto, Ontario
M5V 3A8
Phone: 416-971-9453
Fax: 416-979-3155

Environment North
704 Holly Crescent
Thunder Bay, Ontario
P7E 2T2
Phone: 807-475-5267
Fax: 807-577-6433

Federation of Ontario Naturalists
355 Lesmill Road
Don Mills, Ontario
M3B 2W8
Phone: 416-444-8419
Fax: 416-444-9866

Northwatch
P.O. Box 282
North Bay, Ontario
P1B 8H2
Phone: 705-497-0373
Fax: 705-476-7060

QUÉBEC

La Fondation pour la sauvegarde
   des espèces menacées
8191 Avenue du Zoo
Charlesbourg, Québec
G1G 4G4
Phone: 418-622-0313

La Fondation Québécoise en
   Environnement
800 boul. de Maisonneuve Est,
   2e étage
Montréal, Québec
H2L 4L8
Phone: 514-849-0028
Fax: 514-849-0028

L'Union québécoise pour la
   conservation de la nature
690 Grande-Allée Est, Bureau 420
Québec, Québec
G1R 2K5
Phone: 418-648-2104
Fax: 418-648-0991

NEW BRUNSWICK

Conservation Council of
   New Brunswick
180 St. John Street
Fredericton, New Brunswick
E3B 4A9
Phone: 506-458-8747
Fax: 506-458-1047

Nature Trust of New Brunswick
c/o Hal Hinds
University of New Brunswick
Biology Department
Fredericton, New Brunswick
E3B 5A3
Phone: 506-453-4583

New Brunswick Federation of
   Naturalists
277 Douglas Avenue
Saint John, New Brunswick
E2K 1E5

New Brunswick Protected Natural
   Areas Coalition
180 St. John Street
Fredericton, New Brunswick
E3B 4A9
Phone: 506-452-9902
Fax: 506-458-1047

PRINCE EDWARD ISLAND

Island Nature Trust
P.O. Box 265
Charlottetown, PEI
C1A 7K4
Phone: 902-892-7513
Fax: 902-628-6331

NOVA SCOTIA

CPAWS — Nova Scotia Chapter
73 Chadwick Street
Dartmouth, Nova Scotia
B2Y 2M2
Phone: 902-466-7168

Ecology Action Centre
1553 Granville Street
Halifax, Nova Scotia
B3J 1W7
Phone: 902-429-2202

Federation of Nova Scotia Naturalists
73 Chadwick Street
Dartmouth, Nova Scotia
B2Y 2M2
Phone: 902-466-7168

NEWFOUNDLAND

Natural History Society of
    Newfoundland and Labrador
P.O. Box 1013
St. John's, Newfoundland
A1C 5M3
Phone: 709-754-3321 (president
    Len Zedel — home);
    709-737-3106 (president Len Zedel
    — work)
Fax: 709-737-8739

Newfoundland and Labrador
    Environmental Association
c/o Stan Tobin
Suite 603, 140 Water Street
St. John's, Newfoundland
A1C 6H6
Phone: 709-722-1740
Fax: 709-726-1813

Newfoundland and Labrador
    Wildlife Federation
P.O. Box 13399, Station A
St. John's, Newfoundland
A1B 4B7
Phone: 709-364-8415

Protected Areas Association of
    Newfoundland and Labrador
Box 1027, Station "C"
St. John's, Newfoundland
A1C 5M5
Phone / Fax: 709-726-2603

Tuckamore Wilderness Club
11 Carty Place
Corner Brook, Newfoundland
A2H 6B5
Phone: 709-639-1770
Fax: 709-639-8125

Wilderness and Ecological
    Reserves Advisory Council
c/o Parks and Natural Areas Division
Department of Tourism and Culture
P.O. Box 8700
St. John's, Newfoundland
A1B 4J6
Phone: 709-729-2421
Fax: 709-729-1100

YUKON

CPAWS — Yukon Chapter
30 Dawson Road
Whitehorse, Yukon Territory
Y1A 5T6
Phone / Fax: 403-668-6321

Yukon Conservation Society
P.O. Box 4163
Whitehorse, Yukon Territory
Y1A 3T3
Phone: 403-668-5678
Fax: 403-668-6637

NORTHWEST TERRITORIES

Ecology North
4807 – 49th Street, Suite 8
Yellowknife, Northwest Territories
X1A 3T5
Phone: 403-873-6019
Fax: 403-873-3654

Regional Coordinators for the Endangered Spaces Campaign

NATIONAL OFFICE

Arlin Hackman
WWF Canada
90 Eglinton Avenue East, Suite 504
Toronto, Ontario M4P 2Z7
Phone: (416) 489-8800
Fax: (416) 489-3611
e-mail: arline@web.apc.org

FEDERAL GOVERNMENT

Kevin McNamee
Canadian Nature Federation
1 Nicholas St., Ste. 520
Ottawa, Ontario K1N 7B7
Phone: (613) 562-3447
Fax: (613) 562-3371
e-mail: mcnamee@web.apc.org

BRITISH COLUMBIA

Ric Careless
B.C. Spaces for Nature
Box 673
Gibsons, British Columbia
V0N 1V0
Phone: (604) 886-8605
Fax: (604) 886-3768
e-mail: bcspaces@web.apc.org

ALBERTA

Dawn Mitchell
600, 250 – 6th Avenue S.W.
Calgary, Alberta
T2P 3H7
Phone: (403) 261-5622
Fax: (403) 266-2453
e-mail: abspaces@web.apc.org

SASKATCHEWAN

Alan G. Appleby
3079 Athol Street
Regina, Saskatchewan
S4S 1Y6
Phone: (306) 586-3863
Fax: (306) 586-3863
e-mail: aappleby@web.apc.org

MANITOBA

Gaile Whelan-Enns
63 Albert St., Suite 411
Winnipeg, Manitoba
R3B 1G4
Phone: (204) 944-9593
Fax: (204) 943-5711
e-mail: gwhelan@web.apc.org

ONTARIO

Tim Gray
The Wildlands League / CPAWS
401 Richmond Street West, Suite 380
Toronto, Ontario
M5V 3A8
Phone: (416) 971-9453
Fax: (416) 979-3155
e-mail: wildland@web.apc.org

QUÉBEC

Nathalie Zinger
Director, Québec Region
World Wildlife Fund Canada
1253 ave McGill College, bureau 446
Montréal, Québec
H3B 2Y5
Phone: (514) 866-7800
Fax: (514) 866-7808
e-mail: zinwwf@web.apc.org

NEW BRUNSWICK

Dr. James Goltz,
    Roberta Clowater
New Brunswick Protected Natural
    Areas Coalition
180 St. John Street
Fredericton, New Brunswick
E3B 4A9
Jim
    Phone: (506) 459-8685 (after 5p.m.)
    Fax: (506) 453-7918
Roberta
    Phone: (506) 452-9902
    Fax: (506) 458-1047

NOVA SCOTIA

Colin Stewart
Federation of Nova Scotia Naturalists
73 Chadwick St.
Dartmouth, Nova Scotia
B2Y 2M2
Phone: (902) 466-7168
e-mail: cs2@web.apc.org

PRINCE EDWARD ISLAND

Diane Griffin
Island Nature Trust
P.O. Box 265
Charlottetown, Prince Edward Island
C1A 7K4
Phone: (902) 892-7513
Fax: (902) 628-6331
e-mail: intrust@web.apc.org

NEWFOUNDLAND

Laura Jackson
Protected Areas Association of
    Newfoundland and Labrador
Box 1027, Station "C"
St. John's, Newfoundland
A1C 5M5
Phone: (709) 726-2603
Fax: (709) 726-2603
e-mail: paa@web.apc.org

YUKON TERRITORY

Juri Peepre
Canadian Parks and Wilderness
    Society (CPAWS) – Yukon
30 Dawson Road
Whitehorse, Yukon Territory
Y1A 5T6
Phone: (403) 668-6321
Fax: (403) 668-6321
e-mail: peepre@web.apc.org

NORTHWEST TERRITORIES

Chris O'Brien
Ecology North
Suite 8, 4807 49th Street
Yellowknife, Northwest Territories
X1A 3T5
Phone: (403) 873-6019
Fax: (403) 873-3654
e-mail: nwtwwf@web.apc.org

Update on Conservation Lands and Waters

MARCH 1995, AREA (KM^2), NUMBER OF RESERVES

	National Parks	National Wildlife Areas/ Migratory Bird Sanctuaries	Prov/Terr Parks	Prov/Terr Wildlife Management Areas	Prov/Terr Wilderness Areas	Ecological and Nature Reserves/Zones	Provisional Park/ Ecological Reserves	Provincial Forest Reserves	Private Reserves	Natural Areas Protection Act Properties	Conservation Reserves	Louisbourg Game Preserve	Wildlife Refuges	Municipal Lands Conservation Authorities
FED GOV	*218,903 / 36	115,034 / 144												
YT	*36,304 / 3		501 / 2			181* / 2							5,918 / 2	
NWT	*107,197 / 4.2	112,868 / 16	2,775 / 51											
BC	*6,299 / 6	54 / 12	*64,853 / 406	276 / 14	*2,651 / 5	*1,587 / 131			*121 / 89					
ALTA	*54,064 / 4.8	146 / 7	1,427 / 65	943 / 12	*1,008 / 3	*271 / 14			1 / 2	378 / 124				
SASK	*4,781 / 2	776 / 23	*10,993 / 34	*1,154 / 24		*8 / 3		*2,720 / 31	*77 / 109				*31 / 24	*173 / 122
MAN	*2,976 / 1	1 / 2	36,061 / 131	31,866 / 72		*574 / 13		21,985 / 15	*51 / 63		+*325 / 3		2,061 / 50	10 / 11
ONT	*2,190 / 5	418 / 20	*52,531 / 176	271 / 23		*3,810 / 352	746 / 17		*30 / 27		*5 / 4			1,334 / 38
QUE	*927 / 3	653 / 41	*4,249 / 17	68,257 / 24		*642 / 50	*1,152 / 23	391 / 14	*123 / 43				4 / 2	421 / 34
NB	*445 / 2	43 / 6	*213 / 10	*132 / 2	67 / 1	*11 / 13			*2 / 5				50 / 6	
NS	*1,351 / 2	66 / 13	*43 / 7	1,417 / 26		*12 / 7			*9 / 14			*52 / 1		
PEI	*26 / 1	1 / 1	*13 / 8	*25 / 8					*4 / 13	*33 / 36				
NFLD	*2,342 / 2	10 / 33	*351 / 76	*619 / 2	*3,965 / 2	*465 / 8	31 / 2							
CAN	**218,902 / 36	**115,036 / 144	174,010 / 983	104,960 / 207	7,655 / 11	7,561 / 593	1,929 / 42	25,096 / 60	253 / 220	411 / 160	330 / 7	52 / 1	8,064 / 84	1,938 / 205

*   Lands that contribute to "total area protected."

**   Totals may differ from the federal government (e.g. national parks) due to rounding.

*** Includes 1612 km^2 of marine waters in BC not factored into "percent of jurisdiction protected" calculation

n/a Not available

Conservation Land Tax Reduction Program	Conservation Easements	Stewardship Agreements	Provincial/Territorial Park Reserves	Reserves for Campground and Recreation Sites	Provincial Recreation Areas	Critical Wildlife Habitat Program Land	Wildlife Land	Habitat Trust/Foundation Land	Special Lands	Other Reserves	Total Area Protected	Percent of Jurisdiction Protected	Footnotes
											218,903 / 36	2.2	
				14,535 / 54					+12,173 / 1	++80 / 1	36,485 / 5	7.5	+ Old Crow Flats special management area ++ Horseshoe Slough habitat protection area
									+*52,925 / 1		160,122 / 5.2	4.7	+ Thelon Game Sanctuary
										+13,332 / 6	***75,475 / 637	7.8	+ Land use decisions/plan for Clayoquot Sound, Vancouver Isl., Cariboo-Chilcotin, Commonwealth Nature Legacy, East/West Kootenays, Kitlope
				1,214 / 173	598 / 236				+420 / 1	++4,597 / 1	55,343 / 21.8	8.4	+ Suffield National Wildlife Reserve ++ Willmore Wilderness
				75 / 123	*347 / 27	13,760 / n/a		225 / 433	+*57 / 23	++554 / n/a	20,341 / 399	3.1	+ Protected Areas under the *Parks Act.* ++ Wildlife Development Fund Lands
		80 / 168				27 / 32	*10,500 / 1	114 / 96	++*21,480 / 4	+++150 / 39	35,906 / 85	5.5	+ Special Conservation Areas ++ Four new provincial parks, 1995 +++ Voluntarily protected ecologically significant areas
809 / 6,000	*13 / 10	248 / 1,887	42 / 1						+6,024 / 1	++1,191 / 56	58,579 / 574	5.5	+ Recreation zones in Algonquin Park ++ Managed forest agreements
			*57,372 / 18		81 / 6	42,236 / 496			685 / 109	*376 / 7	68,841 / 161	4.2	
		5 / 2	*7 / 2	3 / 24	13 / 34	63 / 13	3,174 / 13		+5,883 / 10	++*56 / 9	866 / 43	1.2	+ Land base restrictions on 10 Crown timber licenses ++ Includes international park
			*79 / 3						+*54 / 17	++118 / 220	1,600 / 51	2.9	+ Unconstituted parks contributing to representation ++ Parks/park reserves not contributing to representation
					6 / 24					+*26 / 1	127 / 66	2.2	+ Newly-protected lands adjacent to PEI National Park
			75 / 5							52,494 / 8	7,742 / 90	1.9	
809 / 6,000	13 / 10	333 / 2,057	57,575 / 29	15,827 / 374	1,045 / 327	58,086 / >541	13,674 / 14	339 / 529	99,701 / 167	72,974 / >348	***517,542 / 2175	5.2	

Notes and Selected Bibliography

INTRODUCTION

Hummel, Monte. 1995. *Science that makes a difference.* Proceedings of the Canadian Council on Ecological Areas Conference, Caring for Southern Remnants: Special Species, Special Places; Windsor, Ontario, June 1994.

Hummel, Monte, ed. 1989. *Endangered Spaces: The Future for Canada's Wilderness.* Toronto: Key Porter Books.

Leopold, Aldo. 1949. *A Sand County Almanac.* New York: Oxford University Press.

Noss, Reed. 1995. *Maintaining Ecological Integrity in Representative Reserve Networks.* World Wildlife Fund Canada/World Wildlife Fund United States Discussion Paper, Toronto.

World Commission on Environment and Development. 1987. *Our Common Future.* New York: Oxford University Press.

World Wildlife Fund Canada. 1994. *A Protected Areas Gap Analysis Methodology: Planning for the Conservation of Biodiversity.* Toronto: World Wildlife Fund Canada.

———. 1995. *Endangered Spaces Progress Report Number 5, 1994–95.* Toronto: World Wildlife Fund Canada.

1/ BUILDING THE ARK: THE SCIENCE BEHIND THE SELECTION OF PROTECTED AREAS

Botkin, D.B. 1990. *Discordant Harmonies: A New Ecology for the Twenty-First Century.* New York: Oxford University Press.

Canadian Council on Ecological Areas. 1992. *Framework for Developing a Nation-Wide System of Ecological Areas: Part 1 — A Strategy.* Prepared by the Canadian Council on Ecological Areas Systems Framework Task Force for the St. John's, Newfoundland, Annual Meeting.

Canadian Environmental Advisory Council. 1991. *A Protected Areas Vision for Canada.* Ottawa: Environment Canada.

Diamond, J.M. 1976. Island biogeography and conservation: Strategy and limitations. *Science* 193: 1027–29.

Geomatics International Inc. 1994. CCEA *Studies on Ecoregion Gap Analysis.* Final Draft Report Prepared for CCEA, February.

IUCN. 1993. *Parks For Life: Report of the IVth World Congress on National Parks and Protected Areas.* Gland, Switzerland: IUCN.

Kareiva, P. 1993. No shortcuts in new maps. *Nature* 365: 292–93.

Levin, S.A. 1992. The problem of pattern and scale in ecology. *Ecology* 73(6): 1943–67.

Nelson, R. 1993. Searching for the lost arrow: Physical and spiritual ecology in the hunter's world. In S.R. Kellert and E.O. Wilson, eds., *The Biophilia Hypothesis*, pp. 201–28. Washington, D.C.: Island Press.

Noss, R.F. 1983. A regional landscape approach to maintain diversity. *BioScience* 33: 700–6.

———. 1987. Protecting natural areas in fragmented landscapes. *Natural Areas Journal* 7: 2–13.

———. 1992. The Wildlands Project Land Conservation Strategy. *Wild Earth*: 10–21.

———. 1995. *Maintaining Ecological Integrity in Representative Reserve Networks*. World Wildlife Fund Canada/World Wildlife Fund United States Discussion Paper. Toronto: WWF Canada.

Noss, R.F., and A.Y. Cooperrider. 1994. *Saving Nature's Legacy: Protecting and Restoring Biodiversity*. Washington, D.C.: Island Press.

Peterson, E.B., and N.M. Peterson. 1991. *A first approximation of principles and criteria to make Canada's protected areas systems representative of the nation's ecological diversity*. Canadian Council on Ecological Areas Occasional Papers.

Prendergast, J.R., R.M. Quinn, J.H. Lawton, B.C. Eversham, and D.W. Gibbons. 1993. Rare species, the coincidence of diversity hotspots and conservation strategies. *Nature* 365: 335–37.

Rowe, J.S. 1994. *Biodiversity at the Landscape Level*. Prepared for Measuring Biodiversity of Forest Policy and Management, British Columbia. February 23–25.

Saetersdal, M., J.M. Line, and H.J.B. Birks. 1993. How to maximize biological diversity in nature reserve selection: Vascular plants and breeding birds in deciduous woodlands, western Norway. *Biological Conservation* 66: 131–38.

Scott, J.M., B. Csuti, J.D. Jacobi, and J.E. Estes. 1987. Species richness: A geographic approach to protecting future biological diversity. *BioScience* 37: 782–88.

Scott, J.M., B. Csuti, K. Smith, J.E. Estes, and S. Caicco. 1991. Gap analysis of species richness and vegetation cover: An integrated biodiversity conservation strategy. In K. Khom, ed. *Balancing on the Brink of Extinction: The Endangered Species Act and Lessons for the Future*, pp. 282–97. Washington, D.C.: Island Press.

Scott, J.M., F. Davis, B. Csuti, R. Noss, B. Butterfield, C. Groves, H. Anderson, S. Caicco, F. D'Erchia, T.C.J.R. Edwards, J. Ulliman, and

R.G. Wright. 1993. Gap analysis: A geographical approach to protection of biological diversity. *Wildlife Monographs* 123: 1–41.

Wilson, E.O. 1992. *The Diversity of Life*. Cambridge, Mass.: The Belknap Press of Harvard University Press.

World Wildlife Fund Canada. 1995. *A Protected Areas Gap Analysis Methodology: Planning for the Conservation of Biodiversity*. WWF Canada Discussion Paper.

2/ MARINE PROTECTED AREAS

Agardy, M. Tundi. 1994. Advances in marine conservation: The role of marine protected areas. *Trends in Ecology and Evolution* 9: 267–70.

Ballantine, William J. 1991. *Marine Reserves for New Zealand*. University of Auckland, Leigh Laboratory Bulletin No. 25. October.

Graham, Robert, ed. 1990. *Marine Ecological Areas in Canada*. Canadian Council on Ecological Areas Occasional Paper No. 9.

Kelleher, Graeme, and Richard Kenchington. 1992. *Guidelines for Establishing Marine Protected Areas*. A Marine Conservation and Development Report. Gland, Switzerland: IUCN.

Lien, Jon. 1989. Eau Canada! A New Marine-Parks System. In Monte Hummel, ed., *Endangered Spaces: The Future for Canada's Wilderness*, pp. 107–19. Toronto: Key Porter Books.

Norse, Elliott A., ed. 1993. *Global Marine Biological Diversity: A Strategy for Building Conservation into Decision Making*. Washington, D.C.: Island Press.

Recchia, Cheri, Carole Saint-Laurent, and Arlin Hackman. 1995. World Wildlife Fund's Endangered Spaces Campaign: *Focus on Marine Protected Areas*. Proceedings of a symposium on marine protected areas and sustainable fisheries conducted at the Second International Conference on Science and the Management of Protected Areas, held at Dalhousie

University, Halifax, Nova Scotia, Canada, 16–20 May 1994. Science and Management of Protected Areas Association, Centre for Wildlife and Conservation Biology, Acadia University, Wolfville, Nova Scotia. pp. 220–26. Editors: Nancy L. Shackell and J. H. Martin Willison.

Thorne-Miller, Boyce, and John Catena. 1991. *The Living Ocean: Understanding and Protecting Marine Biodiversity.* Washington, D.C.: Island Press.

Woods Hole Oceanographic Institution. 1993. Marine Protected Areas. *Oceanus* 36/3 (Fall 1993): Whole issue dedicated to marine protected areas.

World Wildlife Fund. 1994. *Save Our Seas.* Gland, Switzerland: WWF-World Wide Fund for Nature.

3/ ABORIGINAL INTERESTS

Aboriginal Rights Coalition. 1992–93. Casting for justice: Saugeen Ojibways seek recognition of fishing rights. *Aboriginal Rights Coalition Bulletin Solidarité Newsletter,* 2/4: 3.

Barsh, Russell Lawrence. 1994. Canada's Aboriginal Peoples: Social Integration or Disintegration. *Canadian Journal of Native Studies* 14/1: 1–46.

Berger, Thomas. 1991. *A Long and Terrible Shadow: White Values, Native Rights in the Americas, 1492–1992.* Vancouver: Douglas and McIntyre.

Berkes, Fikret. 1990. Native subsistence fisheries: A synthesis of harvest studies in Canada. *Arctic* 43/1: 35–42.

Bobiwash, Rodney. 1992. The provision of aboriginal social services in a native urban self government paradigm. In B. Hodgins, S. Heard, and J. Milloy., eds., *Co-Existence: Studies in Ontario–First Nations Relations,* pp. 58–66. Peterborough: Trent University: Frost Centre for Canadian Heritage and Development Studies.

Erasmus, Georges. 1989. A Native Viewpoint. In Monte Hummel, ed., *Endangered Spaces: The Future for Canada's Wilderness,* pp. 92–98. Toronto: Key Porter Books.

Hackman, Arlin. 1992. The Job to Be Done. In Lori Labatt and Bruce Litteljohn, eds., *Islands of Hope: Ontario's Parks and Wilderness,* pp. 276–81. Willowdale, Ont.: Firefly Books.

King, Cecil. 1992. Review of Angus, And the Last Shall Be First. *Compass: A Jesuit Journal* 10/4 (Sept.-Oct.): 42–43.

Livingston, John. 1992. Attitudes to Nature. In Lori Labatt and Bruce Litteljohn, eds., *Islands of Hope: Ontario's Parks and Wilderness,* pp. 237–40. Willowdale, Ont.: Firefly Books.

Lytwyn, Victor P. 1990. Ojibwa and Ottawa fisheries around Manitoulin Island: Historical and geographical perspectives on aboriginal and treaty fishing rights. *Native Studies Review* 6/1: 1–30.

Marule, Marie Smallface. 1978. The Canadian government's termination policy: From 1969 to the present day. In A.L. Getty and D. Smith, eds., *One Century Later: Western Canadian Reserve Indians Since Treaty 7.* Vancouver: University of British Columbia Press. pp 103–16.

Morris, Alexander. 1880. *The Treaties of Canada with the Indians of Manitoba, the Northwest Territories and Keewatin.* Toronto: Willing and Williamson.

Paz, Octavio. 1990. The Power of Ancient Mexican Art. *New York Review of Books* 37/19: 18–21.

Price, Richard, and Shirleen Smith. 1993–94. Treaty 8 and traditional livelihoods: Historical and contemporary perspectives. *Native Studies Review* 9/1: 51–91.

Reid, Ron. 1992. Ontario Parks. In Lori Labatt and Bruce Litteljohn, eds., *Islands of Hope: Ontario's Parks and Wilderness,* pp. 45–46. Willowdale, Ont.: Firefly Books.

Saunders, Aubrey. 1963. *Algonquin Story.* Toronto: Ontario Department of Lands and Forests.

Scott, Colin. 1989. Knowledge construction among Cree hunters: Metaphors and literal understanding. *Journal de la Société des Américanistes* 15: 193–208.

Smith, Donald B. 1987. *Sacred Feathers: The Reverend Peter Jones (Kahkewaquonaby) and the Mississauga Indians*. Toronto: University of Toronto Press.

Snyder, Gary. 1990. *The Practice of the Wild*. San Francisco: North Point Press.

Tough, Frank. 1984. The establishment of a commercial fishing industry and the demise of Native fisheries in northern Manitoba. *Canadian Journal of Native Studies* 4/2: 303–19.

Usher, P.J. 1987. Indigenous management systems and the conservation of wildlife in the Canadian North. *Alternatives* 14/1: 3–9.

Usher, P.J., F. Tough, and R. Galois. 1992. Reclaiming the land: Aboriginal title, treaty rights and land claims in Canada. *Applied Geography* 12: 109–32.

Utley, Robert M. 1973. *Frontier Regulars: The United States Army and the Indian, 1866–1891*. New York: Macmillan.

Van West, John J. 1990. Ojibwa fisheries, commercial fisheries development and fisheries administration, 1873–1915: An examination of conflicting interest and the collapse of the Sturgeon fisheries of the Lake of the Woods. *Native Studies Review* 6/1: 31–65.

Wells, Michael, and Katrina Brandon. 1992. *People and Parks: Linking Protected Area Management with Local Communities*. Washington, D.C.: The World Bank, World Wildlife Fund, U.S. Agency for International Development.

World Wildlife Fund. 1986. *Whales Beneath the Ice: Final Report, Conclusions and Recommendations Regarding the Future of Canada's Arctic Whales*. Toronto: WWF Canada.

4/ BUSINESS, ECONOMICS, AND THE WISE-USE MOVEMENT

Helvarg, David. 1994. *The War Against the Greens*. San Francisco: Sierra Club Books.

Hummel, Monte, ed. 1989. *Endangered Spaces: The Future for Canada's Wilderness*. Toronto: Key Porter Books.

White, Adam. 1993. *The Economic Benefits of Conserving Canada's Endangered Spaces*. Toronto, A World Wildlife Fund Canada Discussion Paper.

5/ WORKING WITH GOVERNMENT

Fisher, Roger, and William Ury. 1983. *Getting to Yes: Negotiating Agreement without Giving In*. New York: Penguin Books.

IUCN. 1993. *Parks for Life: Report of the IVth World Congress on National Parks and Protected Areas*. Gland, Switzerland: IUCN.

Lee, Kai N. 1994. *Compass and Gyroscope: Integrating Science and Politics for the Environment*. Washington, D.C.: Island Press.

Rourke, Francis E. 1984. *Bureaucracy, Politics and Public Policy*. Toronto: Little, Brown.

Snow, Donald, ed. 1992. *Voices from the Environmental Movement: Perspectives for a New Era*. Washington, D.C.: Island Press.

6/ USING THE LAW TO PROTECT WILD PLACES

Canadian Environmental Assessment Act, S.C. 1992, c.37 and S.C. 1994, c.46.

Canadian Parks and Wilderness Society v. Minister of Environment, Superintendent of Wood Buffalo National Park et al. Fed. Ct., June 1992.

Canadian Parks and Wilderness Society v. Superintendent of Banff National Park et al (1993) 63 F.T.R. 241 (Fed. Ct.), affirmed (1994) Fed. Ct. App. A-587-94.

Canadian Wildlife Federation v. Canada Minister of Environment (1990) 2 W.W.R. 69 (F.C.A.).

Elgie, S.A.G. 1993. Environmental Groups and the Courts: 1970–1992. In B. Thomson, et al., eds. *Environmental Law and Business in Canada*. Aurora: Canada Law Book.

Energy Resources Conservation Board. 1994. *Amoco Whaleback Ridge Area* Decision D 94-8, September.

Environmental Assessment and Review Process Guidelines Order SOR/84-467 June 22, 1984.

Finlay v. Canada (Minister of Finance) (1986) 33 D.L.R. (4th) 321 (S.C.C.).

Friends of the Oldman River Society v. Canada (Minister of Transport) (1992) 88 D.L.R. (4th) 1 (S.C.C.).

Grand Council of the Crees (of Quebec) v. Canada (National Energy Board), 1994 1 S.C.R. 159.

Green v. The Queen in Right of the Province of Ontario (1972) 34 D.L.R. (3d) 20.

National Parks Act R.S.C. c.N-13.

National Park et al. (1993) 63 F.T.R. 241 (Fed. Ct.), affirmed (1994) Fed. Ct. App. A-587-94.

National Parks Act R.S.C. c.N-13.

National Park Service Organic Act 16 U.S.L. 1(1988).

Natural Resources Conservation Board, Decision Report Application #9103 Three Sisters Golf Resorts Inc. (Canmore), November 1992.

Natural Resources Conservation Board, Decision Report Application #9102 Vacation Alberta Corporation (West Castle Valley), December 1993 and Order in Council (Alberta) 746/94.

Obiter Dicta, November 8, 1976 (publication Osgoode Hall Law School), source of Estey quote.

Reese v. Alberta (1992) 85 Alta. L.R.(2d) 153 and 5 Alta L.R. (3d) 40.

Report of the Environmental Legislation Review Panel (Alberta), January 11, 1991.

Sierra Club v. Morton 405 US 727 (US S.Ct.).

Sunshine Village Corporation v. Superintendent Banff National Park et al. (1994) Fed. Ct. T.D.T-137-94.

Wilderness Society v. Tyrell 701 F. Supp. 1473 at 1492 (Cal. D.C. 1988): *Friends of the Earth v. Brznegar* 518F 2d. 322 (9th Cir. 1975) for waiver of undertaking in an injunction application.

7/ BRITISH COLUMBIA

Allan, John. 1994. *Completing the Protected Area System on Vancouver Island*. Report of the Chair, Protected Areas Boundary Advisory Team, British Columbia.

———. 1995. *The Cariboo-Chilcotin Land Use Plan — 90-Day Implementation Process Final Report*. Victoria: Government of British Columbia.

Canadian Parks and Wilderness Society. 1992. *BC Wildlands — Thompson Okanagan Region*. Information brochure.

———. 1993. *BC Wildlands — Southeast British Columbia Region*. Information brochure.

———. 1994. *BC Wildlands — Central Interior Region*. Information brochure.

———. 1995. *BC Wildlands — Southwestern British Columbia Region*. Information brochure.

Friends of Clayoquot Sound. 1994. *Rainforest Action Handbook*.

Government of British Columbia. 1995a. *The East Kootenay Land-Use Plan*. Information brochure. Victoria: Queen's Printer.

———. 1995b. *The West Kootenay–Boundary Land-Use Plan*. Information brochure. Victoria: Queen's Printer.

Owen, Stephen. 1994a. *Cariboo-Chilcotin Land Use Plan*. Commission on Resources and Environment, British Columbia. 233 pp.

———. 1994b. *East Kootenay Land Use Plan*. Commission on Resources and Environment, British Columbia.

———. 1994c. *West Kootenay Land Use Plan*. Commission on

Resources and Environment, British Columbia.

Parks Canada, Department of Canadian Heritage. 1994. The Churn Creek proposed protected area — A submission to the B.C. Commission on Resources and Environment. Unpublished report.

Province of British Columbia, Ministry of Environment, Lands and Parks. 1995. *New Provincial Parks & Protected Areas in British Columbia.* Information brochure. Victoria: Queen's Printer.

Province of British Columbia. 1993. *A Protected Areas Strategy for British Columbia, Best P.A.S. Report — Identification, Evaluation and Ranking of Areas within the Kootenay Region that meet the Protected Areas Strategy Goals and Criteria.*

The Sierra Club of Western Canada. 1993. *Ancient Forests at Risk, Final Report of the Vancouver Island Mapping Project.*

8/ ALBERTA
Alberta Energy Resources Conservation Board. 1994. *Application for an Exploratory Well Amoco Canada Petroleum Company Limited Whaleback Ridge Area Decision D 94-8.*

Alberta Wilderness Association. 1993. *Wild Alberta . . . Our Last Best Hopes: A Listing of Alberta's Endangered Wilderness.* Draft.

Barnett, Vicki. 1994. Mission urgent environmentalists fighting to preserve Alberta's disappearing wilderness. *Calgary Herald*, October 18.

Calgary Herald. 1995. Both Sides Win: Editorial. January 20.

Canadian Parks and Wilderness Society. 1993. Alberta's endangered spaces. *Borealis*, 12.

Government of Alberta. 1992. *Special Places 2000: Alberta's Natural Heritage. Completing Alberta's Endangered Spaces Network.* Draft, November 20.

———. 1993. *Special Places 2000: Alberta's Natural Heritage. Report of the Advisory Committee.* November 15.

Pachal, Dianne. 1991. *Wilderness: An Alberta Conservation Strategy.* Background Paper. October.

World Wildlife Fund Canada and The Dunvegan Group Ltd. 1994. *Special Places 2000 Opinion Poll.* June 17.

9/ SASKATCHEWAN
Cranna, Marilee D., and J.S. Rowe. 1974. *Natural Areas in Saskatchewan: International Biological Programme — Conservation Terrestrial Summation Report.* National Research Council, Ottawa.

Federation of Saskatchewan Indian Nations. 1992. *Treaty Land Entitlement Framework Agreement.* Regina: Federation of Saskatchewan Indian Nations.

Hummel, Monte, ed. 1989. *Endangered Spaces: The Future for Canada's Wilderness.* Toronto: Key Porter Books.

Jonker, Peter, ed. 1992. *Saskatchewan Endangered Spaces: An Introduction.* Saskatoon: University of Saskatchewan, Extension Division.

Lawton, Laura, and Angela Hickie. 1993. *Protected Areas in Saskatchewan: A Statistical Report.* Regina: Saskatchewan Environment and Resource Management.

Saskatchewan Department of Parks and Renewable Resources. 1990. *Provincial Parks System Plan.* Regina: Department of Parks and Renewable Resources.

World Wildlife Fund. 1990. *Endangered Spaces Progress Report Number 1.* Toronto: WWF Canada.

10/ MANITOBA
An Action Plan for a Network of Special Places for Manitoba. 1994. Winnipeg: Sustainable Development Coordination Unit, Executive Council, Province of Manitoba.

Candidate Sites for the Endangered Spaces Campaign. 1994. Winnipeg: Sustainable Development Coordination Unit, Executive Council,

Province of Manitoba.

Watkins, William, Dean Berezanski, Elaine Murkin, and Cathy Hummelt. 1994. *Describing Manitoba's Natural Regions and Determining Landscape Units.* Winnipeg: Parks and Natural Areas Branch, Manitoba Department of Natural Resources.

What you told us, Vol. 2: *Natural Lands and Special Places: Policy Areas 1–5.* 1994. Winnipeg: Manitoba Round Table on Environment and Economy.

11/ ONTARIO

Erdoes, Richard, and Alfonso Ortiz, eds. 1984. *American Indian Myths and Legends.* New York: Pantheon Books.

Forest Industry Action Group. 1993. *Hard Choices — Bright Prospects: A Report and Recommendations from Labour, Industry and Government to the Ontario Ministry of Natural Resources.* Toronto: Ministry of Natural Resources.

Hummel, Monte, ed. 1989. *Endangered Spaces: The Future for Canada's Wilderness.* Toronto: Key Porter Books.

Hummel, Monte. 1991. Whither Wilderness in Canada? *Wild Earth*, 1/4 (Winter 1991/92): 12–15.

Killan, Gerald. 1993. *Protected Places: A History of Ontario's Provincial Parks System.* Toronto: Dundurn Press.

Labatt, Lori, and Bruce Litteljohn, eds. 1992. *Islands of Hope: Ontario's Parks and Wilderness.* Willowdale, Ont.: Firefly Books.

Provincial Parks and Natural Heritage Policy Branch. 1992. *A Natural Heritage Areas Strategy for Ontario: Responding to the Endangered Spaces Challenge* (Draft for Discussion). Toronto: Ministry of Natural Resources.

12/ QUÉBEC

Bourages, Jean-Luc, and Nathalie Zinger. 1993. La conservation des paysages naturels au Québec: mythe ou realité? *TRAMES* 9: 66–71.

Mead, Harvey. 1989. Quebec's Natural Heritage. In Monte Hummel, ed., *Endangered Spaces: The Future for Canada's Wilderness*, pp. 152–64. Toronto: Key Porter Books.

Ministère de l'Environnement et de la Faune. 1995. *Les activités reliées à la faune au Québec—profil des participans et impact economique en 1992.* Québec: MEF.

Ministère du Loisir, de la Chasse et de la Pêche. 1992. *La nature en héritage, un plan d'action sur les parcs.* Québec: MLCP.

World Wildlife Fund. 1990 to 1995. *Endangered Spaces Progress Reports (nos. 1 to 5).* Toronto: WWF.

Zinger, Nathalie. 1995. *Espaces protégés au Québec — une ressource menacées. Teoros* 14/1: 28–30.

13/ NEW BRUNSWICK

Clowater, Roberta. 1994. Toward a Protected Natural Areas System for New Brunswick — An ENGO Position Paper. New Brunswick Protected Natural Areas Coalition. Unpublished report.

Daniel Arbour & Associés, Lavalin. 1990. *Provincial Parks and Heritage Sites Master Plan — Final Report.* Fredericton: New Brunswick Department of Tourism, Recreation and Heritage.

Dearden, Philip, and Rick Rollins, eds. 1993. *Parks and Protected Areas in Canada — Planning and Management*, Henderson Book Series #22. Don Mills, Ont.: Oxford University Press.

Dionne, Leo A., Dorothy M. Farmer, and C. Mary Young, eds. 1988. *Critical Natural Areas in New Brunswick.* New Horizons Critical Natural Areas Committee, Fredericton.

Government of New Brunswick. 1992. Protected Areas Policy.

Wein, R.W., ed. 1975. *Ecological Reserves in New Brunswick.* Fredericton: University of New Brunswick.

Personal Communications with: David Coon, Roland Chiasson, Dr. Michael Dillon, Harold Hinds, Peter

Pearce, and especially my Endangered Spaces partner in coordination, Dr. James Goltz.

16/ NEWFOUNDLAND AND LABRADOR

Meades, Susan. 1991. *The Natural Regions of Newfoundland & Labrador.* Protected Areas Association of Newfoundland and Labrador.

Rivers, Patricia. 1995. *A Protected Natural Areas Strategy for Newfoundland and Labrador.* Protected Areas Association of Newfoundland and Labrador.

18/ YUKON

Campbell, B. 1994. *Economic Analysis of Protected Areas: Methods and Yukon Economic Impact Analysis.* CPAWS–Yukon Research Paper #2.

Peepre, J., and B. Jickling, eds. 1994. *Northern Protected Areas and Wilderness.* Whitehorse: CPAWS–Yukon and Yukon College.

Umbrella Final Agreement between The Government of Canada, The Council for Yukon Indians, and The Government of the Yukon. 1993.

Yukon Department of Renewable Resources. 1990. *Yukon Conservation Strategy: For Our Common Future.*

———. 1991. Parks and Outdoor Recreation Policy. Parks, Resources and Regional Planning Branch.

19/ FEDERAL GOVERNMENT

Anon. 1957. *Wisdom's Heritage: The National Parks of Canada.* Ottawa: Department of Northern Affairs and Natural Resources.

Auditor General of Canada. 1989. *Report of the Auditor General of Canada to the House of Commons.* Ottawa: Supply and Services of Canada.

Environment Canada, Parks. 1987. *Our Parks — Vision for the 21st Century.* Report of the Minister of Environment's Task Force on Park Establishment. Waterloo: University of Waterloo.

Liberal Party of Canada. 1993.

Creating Opportunity: The Liberal Plan for Canada. Ottawa: Liberal Party of Canada.

McNamee, Kevin. 1993. From wild places to endangered spaces: A history of Canada's national parks. In Phil Dearden and Rick Rollins, eds., *Parks and Protected Areas in Canada.* Toronto: Oxford University Press.

———. 1994. *The National Parks of Canada.* Toronto: Key Porter Books.

Parks Canada. 1995. *State of the Parks — 1994 Report.* Ottawa: Supply and Services Canada.

21/ PLAYING GOD IN ENDANGERED SPACES: PERSPECTIVES OF A DONOR

Carson, Rachel L. 1962. *Silent Spring.* Boston: Houghton Mifflin.

Chase, Alston. 1987. *Playing God in Yellowstone: The Destruction of America's First National Park.* Orlando, Fla.: Harcourt Brace Jovanovich.

Craighead, Frank C., Jr. 1979. *Track of the Grizzly.* San Francisco: Sierra Club Books.

Dearden, Philip, and Rick Rollins, eds. 1993. *Parks and Protected Areas in Canada: Planning and Management.* Toronto: Oxford University Press.

Herrero, Stephen. 1985. *Bear Attacks: Their Causes and Avoidance.* Edmonton: Hurtig Publishers.

Hummel, Monte, ed. 1989. *Endangered Spaces: The Future for Canada's Wilderness.* Toronto: Key Porter Books.

Labatt, Lori, and Bruce Litteljohn. 1992. *Islands of Hope: Ontario's Parks and Wilderness.* Willowdale, Ont.: Firefly Books Ltd.

McNamee, Thomas. 1982. *The Grizzly Bear.* New York: McGraw-Hill Paperback, 1986.

———. 1994. *The National Parks of Canada.* Toronto: Key Porter Books.

Mowat, Farley. 1984. *Sea of Slaughter.* Toronto: McClelland and Stewart.

Seymour, Kevin, ed. 1993. *Algonquin Park at One Hundred: A Question of Survival*. Toronto: The Wildlands League.

Wilderness Now: A Statement of Principles and Policies of the Algonquin Wildlands League. 1972. Toronto: Algonquin Wildlands League.

Important Papers and Personal Communication. Barichello, Norman. 1994. Predicted impacts of the Aishihik Wolf Kill on the ecological integrity of the Kluane National Park Reserve. Draft in Prep. for Canadian Parks Service.

Glick, Dennis, et al. 1991. *An Environmental Profile of the Greater Yellowstone Ecosystem*. Bozeman: Greater Yellowstone Coalition.

Herrero, Stephen. 1995. *The Canadian National Parks and Grizzly Bear Ecosystems: The Need For Interagency Management*. In press.

Herrero, Stephen. 1995. Pers. comm.

Kluane: National Park Reserve Management Plan Summary. 1990. Ottawa: Environment Canada.

Kluane Region Tourism Development Plan. 1989. Whitehorse: DPA Group Inc. For Yukon Tourism.

Mattson, David J. 1993. *An Estimation of the Effects of the Proposed Sunshine Ski Area Expansion on Grizzly Bears in Banff National Park*.

———. 1995. Pers. comm.

Paquet, Paul. 1994. Large carnivore conservation in the Rocky Mountains. Draft in prep. for WWF.

———. 1995. Pers. comm.

Servheen, Chris. U.S. Fish and Wildlife Service. 1995. Pers. comm.

Theberge, John B. 1994. Why fear the wolf? It's time to end the myths and stop our senseless war on the wolf. *Equinox*, February, pp. 42–51.

The Greater Kluane Land Use Plan Recommendations. 1990. Whitehorse: Yukon Land-Use Planning Office.

The Yukon Wolf Conservation and Management Plan. 1992. Whitehorse: Yukon Wolf Management Planning Team, Yukon Renewable Resources.

Van Tighem, Kevin. 1990. Waterton, Crown of the Continent. *Borealis*, May-July. Edmonton: CPAWS.

23/ LIVE AND LET LIVE

Berry, Thomas. 1990. *The Dream of the Earth*. San Francisco: Sierra Club Books.

Bohm, David, and Mark Edwards. 1991. *Changing Consciousness*. San Francisco: HarperCollins.

Eisler, Riane. 1987/1988. *The Chalice and the Blade*. San Francisco: HarperCollins.

Evernden, Neil. 1992. *The Social Creation of Nature*. Baltimore and London: The Johns Hopkins University Press.

Gould, Stephen J. 1994. The evolution of life on earth. *Scientific American* 271/4.

Gray, Elizabeth Dodson. 1979/1981. *Green Paradise Lost*. Wellesley, Mass.: Roundtable Press.

Livingston, John. 1994. *Rogue Primate*. Toronto: Key Porter Books.

Quinn, Daniel. 1993. *Ishmael*. New York: Bantam Books.

Roszak, Theodore. 1992. *The Voice of the Earth*. New York, London, and Toronto: A Touchstone Book, Simon & Schuster.

Rowe, Stan. 1992. Biological fallacy: life equals organisms. Viewpoint. *BioScience* 42/6: 394.

Tsung Ping, 4th century A.D. Chinese landscape painter, quoted in Tom Bender. *Environmental Design Primer*. New York: Schocken Books, 1976, p. 145.

POSTSCRIPT TO A HOPE

Leopold, Aldo. 1949. *A Sand County Almanac*. New York: Oxford University Press.

Price Waterhouse. June 1994. *The Forest Industry in British Columbiain 1993*. Vancouver.

Author Biographies

Alan G. Appleby is the Saskatchewan Coordinator of the Endangered Spaces campaign and the principal of Alan G. Appleby Consulting Services, operating out of Regina. He has worked in environmental consulting, and for the governments of Ontario and Saskatchewan. Over a seventeen-year career with the Government of Saskatchewan, he was Director of Resource Lands, Director of Parks, and Assistant Deputy Minister of Renewable Resource Programs.

John Broadhead, who lives on Haida Gwaii (The Queen Charlotte Islands), works as a graphic designer and writer, and serves as a director for B.C. Wild, the Sierra Club of B.C., and the Gowgaia Institute. He received the Canadian Nature Federation's Douglas Pimlott Award in 1987 and the Governor General's Conservation Award in 1988 for his efforts to protect the Gwaii Haanas area, formerly called South Moresby.

Ric Careless is B.C.'s Endangered Spaces director, Executive Director of B.C. Spaces for Nature, and a director of B.C. Wild. He led the campaign to protect the one-million-hectare Tatshenshini, which was declared a provincial park by the B.C. government in 1993 and a World Heritage Site in 1994. In 1994, Ric received British Columbia's 1994 Environmental Achievement Award and was also awarded the Order of British Columbia. In 1991 he was named "Environmentalist of the Year" by *Equinox* magazine, and in 1993 he was recognized by the conservation organization American Rivers, as Outstanding River Conservationist of 1993.

Roberta Clowater, a native of Fredericton, has a Bachelor's degree in biology from the University of New Brunswick and a Master's degree in park planning from the University of Waterloo. She is an environmental consultant, with a particular interest in park and land-use planning and environmental advocacy. Roberta is the New Brunswick coordinator for the Endangered Spaces campaign, Secretary-Treasurer of the New Brunswick Protected Natural Areas Coalition, and a volunteer with the Conservation Council of New Brunswick.

Glen W. Davis is a "semi-retired" Toronto businessman. Since 1985, he has provided financial support for a number of conservation projects, generally through WWF Canada as part of its Endangered Spaces program. He has also supported projects of the Canadian Parks and Wilderness Society and the Sierra Club of Canada. As an "ecotourist," Glen has travelled extensively in the western United States and Canada.

Jerry Valen DeMarco is a board member of both the Wildlands League in Ontario and the Canadian Parks and Wilderness Society. He served as acting executive director of the Wildlands League in early 1995. He holds degrees in geography (Windsor), environmental studies (York), and law (Toronto).

Pegi Dover, who holds a Master's in journalism from Northwestern University, has worked on communications issues with WWF Canada for ten years. As part of her work with WWF, she helps to organize the public-awareness activities of the Endangered Spaces campaign. A key component of this effort is the annual release of the Endangered Spaces Progress Report.

Stewart Elgie is a lawyer with the Sierra Legal Defense Fund, a public-interest environmental law organization which he founded in Canada in 1990. He also works part-time as an assistant professor of law at the University of British Columbia. Stew has been counsel on a number of significant lawsuits to protect Canada's parks and wild places. He received his LL.M. from Harvard Law School in 1987, and worked from 1988 to 1990 as a lawyer with the Sierra Club Legal Defense Fund in Alaska where he was involved in cases to protect Alaska's wilderness.

Tim Gray is Executive Director of the Wildlands League, a chapter of the Canadian Parks and Wilderness Society. The League has fought long and successfully to protect Ontario's Quetico, Killarney, and Algonquin provincial parks. Tim has acted as co-chair of the Forests for Tomorrow Coalition in the Provincial Timber Class Environmental Assessment hearing and served as a member of the Ontario Cabinet-appointed Old Growth Forest Policy Advisory Committee. He is also the Ontario Coordinator of the Endangered Spaces campaign.

Diane Griffin is Deputy Minister of the Prince Edward Island Nature Trust and a former member of the National Round Table on the Environment and the Economy. She is WWF Canada's Marine Protected Areas Coordinator for Atlantic Canada. Diane, who graduated from Acadia University in 1973 with an M.Sc. in biology, is a former Natural Areas Coordinator for the province of Alberta.

Arlin Hackman, as Director of the Endangered Spaces campaign, has been responsible for the overall design and operation of the campaign since its launch in 1989. He has held policy-research and advocacy positions with a wide variety of environmental organizations over twenty years, participating in many decisions on protected-areas and land-use issues. Between 1978 and 1983, he led the successful campaign to establish 155 new provincial parks in Ontario, the first comprehensive expansion of a protected-areas system in Canada.

Monte Hummel, President of WWF Canada since 1978, is the founder of a number of environmental groups (including Pollution Probe and the Canadian Coalition on Acid Rain); a frequent public speaker; the author of four books, many book chapters, and more than 100 journal and popular articles, and an experienced northern wilderness guide. He holds two Master's degrees, one in philosophy, the other in forestry. Monte lives with his wife, Sherry Pettigrew, in the country north of Toronto.

Tony Iacobelli is the principal researcher conducting protected-area gap analysis for the Endangered Spaces campaign. He has written for scientific publications on the topics of plant ecology and forest microclimatology, and has participated in studies of forest decline and island biogeography. Tony's consulting company, Clover

Environmental Consultants, specializes in landscape ecology, conservation biology, ecological land classification, biophysical mapping, and GIS spatial analysis.

Laura Jackson is Executive Director of the Protected Areas Association of Newfoundland and Labrador (PAA), and the Newfoundland Coordinator of the Endangered Spaces campaign. Before moving to St. John's in 1990, Laura spent sixteen years in central and coastal Labrador working for the Memorial University Extension Service. She is a member of the province's Wilderness and Ecological Reserves Advisory Council and the board of trustees of the Canadian Parks and Wilderness Society.

Kevin Kavanagh is Manager of Research and Special Projects for the Endangered Spaces campaign. He has worked extensively in the field of forest ecology, participated in vegetation classification work with the Nature Conservancy of Canada, is a former president of the Wildlands League in Ontario, and currently serves on the board of the Canadian Council on Ecological Areas.

Harvey Locke is a partner in the MacKimmie Matthews law firm in Calgary, and the volunteer president of the Canadian Parks and Wilderness Society. He has a great passion for national and provincial parks, and is an avid photographer. Harvey was legal counsel for a variety of environmental coalitions in the Alberta Whaleback, Three Sisters, and West Castle cases. He is also a director of the Wildlands Project, headquartered in Tuscon, Arizona.

Kevin McNamee is the Wildlands Campaign Director for the Canadian Nature Federation, and the federal coordinator for the Endangered Spaces campaign. He worked on campaigns to establish the Ellesmere Island, Gwaii Haanas, and Grasslands national parks; to protect the Tatshenshini watershed as a provincial wilderness park; and to strengthen the conservation provisions of the National Parks Act. A former executive director of the Canadian Parks and Wilderness Society and lecturer at Trent University, he has written extensively on wilderness issues and is the author of *The National Parks of Canada*.

Dawn Mitchell is Regional Director, Alberta, for WWF's Endangered Spaces campaign. She has a master's degree in political science from the University of Calgary and fifteen years' experience in the oil and gas industry. Prior to joining the Endangered Spaces team in 1994, Dawn was Corporate Communications Manager for Husky Oil. She is the past Industry Chair of the Alberta Ecotrust Foundation.

Jim Morrison is an ethnohistorian and heritage consultant with extensive experience in aboriginal claims research and policy. Among his many clients over the past twenty years have been Grand Council, Treaty Number 9 (now Nishnawbe-Aski Nation) in Ontario; the Gitksan-Wetsu'we'ten Tribal Council in B.C.; and the Moose River/James Bay Coalition. A resident of Haileybury in northeastern Ontario, Jim was an executive member of the Lady Evelyn Wilderness Alliance, which lobbied in the early 1980s for the creation of the Lady Evelyn-Smoothwater Wilderness Park.

Since 1992, he has been chair of the Temagami-area Wendaban Stewardship Authority.

Reed Noss is editor of the scientific journal *Conservation Biology*, an international consultant in conservation, Science Director of The Wildlands Project, a research scientist at the University of Idaho, and a research associate at Stanford University, and is on the Fisheries and Wildlife faculty at Oregon State University. He lives with his wife, three children, two dogs, and a cat in the foothills of the Oregon Coast Range outside Corvallis.

Chris O'Brien lives in Yellowknife, N.W.T. Besides his work with WWF, he keeps himself busy writing and working on a range of other environmental issues. He is one of the directors of Ecology North, an N.W.T. environmental organization. Each summer, Chris spends lengthy periods of time out on the land with his wife, Brenda McNair, doing biological field work or just camping.

Dianne Pachal, a wilderness enthusiast and activist, has worked for wilderness with Alberta's major conservation groups for the past sixteen years and is presently the Conservation Director for the Alberta Wilderness Association. Since moving with her family from Manitoba to Alberta at the age of ten, she has explored much of Alberta, including many of its wild places on foot or horseback.

Juri Peepre is Chair of the Canadian Parks and Wilderness Society — Yukon Chapter, and is the Yukon Coordinator of the Endangered Spaces campaign. He is active with the Yukon Wildlands Project and works full-time on protected-area issues.

Cheri Recchia is Manager of Marine Protected Areas for the Endangered Spaces campaign. She has spent most of her life around water, from childhood summers on the shores of Georgian Bay to undergraduate research on marine mammals and seabirds in the Bay of Fundy, to graduate studies on whales and dolphins in the Beaufort Sea, the Gulf of Maine, the Gulf of Mexico, and the Mediterranean. Cheri obtained her Ph.D. in biological oceanography from Woods Hole Oceanographic Institution and Massachusetts Institute of Technology in 1994.

Stan Rowe was born in southern Alberta. He worked for nineteen years as a research forester with the Canadian Forestry Service, and in 1967 joined the Department of Plant Ecology at the University of Saskatchewan. In 1990, five years after retirement, he moved to New Denver, B.C., where he continues to pursue his interests in forest ecology and environmental ethics. His best-known books are *Forest Regions of Canada* and *Home Place: Essays on Ecology*.

Colin Stewart is a biologist with a long-standing interest in conservation, particularly through protected areas. His background includes involvement with many non-government organizations, including recreation (cross-country skiing) as well as natural history (Halifax Field Naturalists) and conservation (Canadian Parks and Wilderness Society, Nova Scotia Nature Trust). He currently works on the Endangered Spaces campaign through the Federation of Nova Scotia Naturalists.

Bill Wareham currently works for the B.C. Endangered Spaces campaign. He is involved with land-use planning and protected-area campaigns throughout the province. Bill serves as president of B.C. Wild, a coalition of environmental organizations working towards completion of the protected-areas system and improved forest management in B.C. He also chairs the B.C. Environmental Network Parks and Wilderness Caucus. An avid naturalist and outdoor adventurer, Bill lives with his wife, Karen, in Gibsons.

Gaile Whelan-Enns is the Manitoba Coordinator of the Endangered Spaces campaign, a role she has occupied since 1993. She brings the skills of a communications specialist to the position, including research, writing/editing, and public and media relations. Her professional history includes managing community organizations, advocacy campaigns, and communications strategies. Conservation lobbying and communications have been her passion since the beginning of the Endangered Spaces campaign.

Adam Zimmerman was born in Toronto. After graduating with a B.A. and a C.A., he joined Noranda Mines in 1958. For the next thirty-four years his responsibilities enlarged from being assistant comptroller to president and director of Noranda and chairman/C.E.O. of its forests products subsidiary. For much of this time, his work involved responding to the environmental imperative and establishing the systems whereby the company could manage its increasing environmental responsibility — an area in which Noranda has become an acknowledged world leader.

Nathalie Zinger, the Québec Coordinator of the Endangered Spaces campaign, has worked on the campaign since joining WWF in 1990. For the past fifteen years, she has been actively involved with a number of conservation organizations. In addition to an M.Sc. in landscape planning, obtained at L'Université de Montréal, she holds a B.Sc. in Agriculture (Wildlife Resources) from MacDonald College and a diploma from the McGill University Centre for Northern Studies and Research. Her field experience includes projects in wilderness protection, marine conservation, and advocacy.

Illustrations

Index